THE WAR
of
JENKINS' EAR

The Forgotten Struggle for North and South America:
1739–1742

ROBERT GAUDI

PEGASUS BOOKS
NEW YORK LONDON

THE WAR OF JENKINS' EAR

Pegasus Books, Ltd.
148 West 37th Street, 13th Floor
New York, NY 10018

First Pegasus Books cloth edition November 2021

Interior design by Sheryl P. Kober

ISBN: 978-1-64313-819-0

10 9 8 7 6 5 4 3 2 1

Printed in the United States of America
Distributed by Simon & Schuster
www.pegasusbooks.com

For D.H.W. in gratitude for his many kindnesses.

And for my children, with love.

Historians are dependent on their sources. Had I more time and ability, I should have made this book a novel, for there are so many things the sources do not tell. There are heroisms unrecorded, great moments of beauty and courage that have left no trace, unknowable human experiences that would teach wisdom and understanding . . . The historian can never construct a record of events. All he can do is construct a record of records.

—J.H. POWELL, *BRING OUT YOUR DEAD*, 1949

Our Merchants and ears a strange bother have made,
with Losses sustained in their ships and their trade;
But now they may laugh and quite banish their fears,
Nor mourn for lost Liberty, riches and ears.

—ENGLISH STREET BALLAD, C. 1739.
(Written upon declaration of war against Spain.)

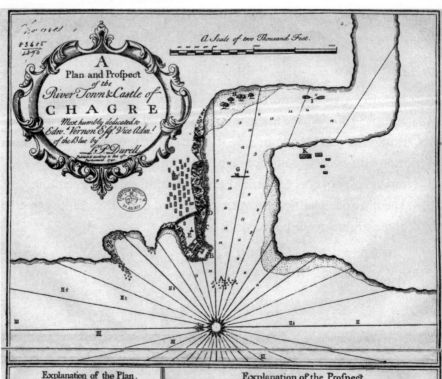

A
Plan and Prospect
of the
River Town & Castle of
CHAGRE
Most humbly dedicated to
Edw.ʳ Vernon Esq.ʳ Vice Adm.ˡ
of the Blue by
P. Durell

A Scale of two Thousand Feet.

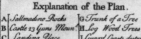

Explanation of the Plan.		
A	Sallmadino Rocks	G Trunk of a Tree
B	Castle 23 Guns Mount.ᵈ	H Log Wood Trees
C	Landing Place	I Guard Coasts destroy'd
D	Guard House	K Custom House
E	Draw Bridge	Italick fig. dypth in feet
F	Parade	Roman fig. depth in fath.

Explanation of the Prospect.		
A	Strafford Adm.ˡ Vernon	G Cumberland Fire Ship
B	Princess Louisa	H Terrible Bomb
C	Falmouth	I Eleanor Fire Ship
D	Norwich	K Prize Brig
E	Alderney Bomb	L Pompey Tender
F	Success Fire Ship	M Goodly Tender

N Prize Sloop
It being Shots a good dist.
from Shore We were obliged
to engage at a Mile distance
Lat. of Chagre 9.º 20. N.

A Prospect of the CASTLE and TOWN of CHAGRE

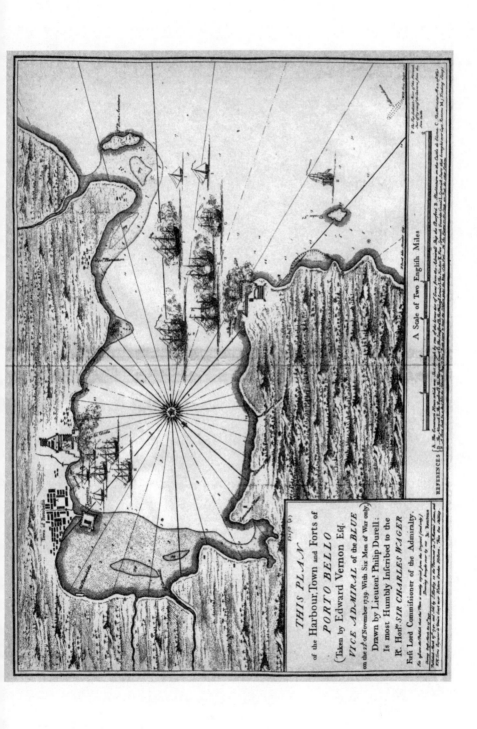

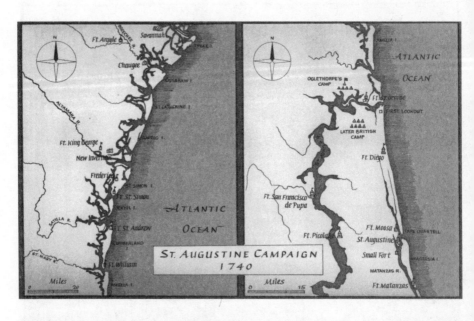

ST. AUGUSTINE CAMPAIGN 1740

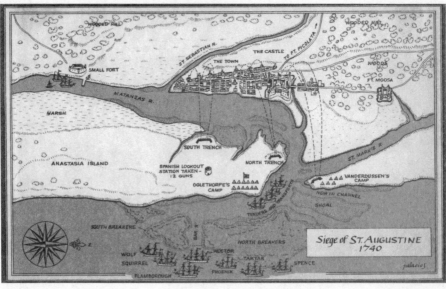

Siege of ST. AUGUSTINE 1740

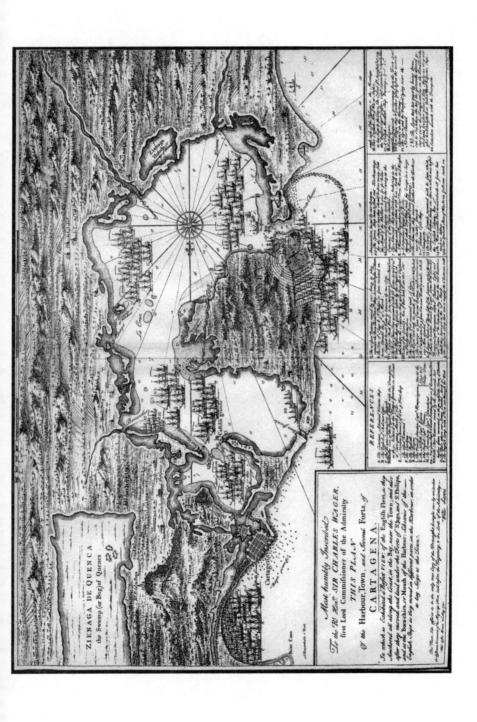

CONTENTS

At the Georgetown Flea

1.

The medal gleamed in the dealer's glass case. A tarnished disc, perhaps brass, about the size of an old half-dollar coin, resting incongruously beside pocket watches, silver cigarette cases, and an array of collectible spoons. Sun baked the asphalt; a hot wind blew from the direction of Wisconsin Avenue. A sweaty, heat-struck crowd shuffled between the booths. A few women carried sunbrellas; one man wore a sort of French Foreign Legion hat, the neck kerchief fluttering. This made a kind of sense; Washington, DC, in August is as hot as the Sahara, only with humidity.

The medal was crudely done, cartoonish even, and in dealer-speak had "some age on it," maybe a couple of hundred years.

The dealer, a large, shaggy man wearing a Hawaiian shirt stepped over, eager for a sale.

"That's a commemorative piece," he said. "British. Got some age on it."

"That's what I was thinking," I said. "But what does it commemorate?"

"Here—"

Without being asked, he opened the case, placed the medal on a velvet pad and handed me a magnifying glass.

The medal was encased in a clear plastic sleeve. It depicted an eighteenth-century gentleman, periwigged and wearing a tricorn hat, accepting a sword from a kneeling man dressed like a clown. In the kneeler's other hand a conical fez-like hat; above his head the words DON BLASS, with the "N" backward. Over his shoulder, a sailing ship that looked like it had been rendered by a child. Through the magnifying glass, I could just make out the inscription around the circumference, worn to a sheen by the years but not illegible: THE PRIDE OF SPAIN HUMBLED BY ADM. VERNON. The obverse showed the battlements of a fortified port city defended by cannon and watched over by a church with a tall spire. Four men-of-war stood at anchor in the wavy lines meant to indicate the waters of a bay beneath the city walls. Another inscription here read VERNON CONQUERED CATAGENA with the date APRIL I 1741.

All this rang a very faint bell. I am a writer of historical narrative, but my era of specialization begins about a hundred years after the date on the medal and ends with the surrender of von Lettow-Vorbeck in the jungles of East Africa in 1919, the subject of my last book.

"What's your price on this?" I said at last.

"Six hundred," the dealer said. "It's a rare piece."

I dropped the medal to the velvet pad as if my fingers had just been burned.

"A little rich for my blood," I said.

"Look it up online," the dealer countered. "Search 'Admiral Vernon Medals,' check out the prices. Trust me, they're a thing."

I stepped away, but something stopped me. I hesitated. "Do you mind?" Then I pulled out my phone and snapped a few pictures of the medal, both front and back.

The dealer said he'd be here at the flea market in the same spot every Sunday for the rest of the month and that he had a little room to negotiate on the price. I'd do some research and get back to him, I said—but I didn't. I went to Nags Head to the beach the next weekend and the weekend after that it rained the tropical torrents we get here in late summer and the Georgetown Flea Market was reduced to a few sodden booths, their awnings dripping in the rain, and the dealer with the medal wasn't one of them.

2.

Months passed. I forgot about the odd little medal, about Admiral Vernon and the kneeling Don Blass. Then, one afternoon, going through the photos on my phone, deleting selfies and shots of the delicious pho at Rice Paper and the crab Benedict brunch at BlackSalt, I came across the photos of the medal and settled myself at my computer and searched "Admiral Vernon Medals" and sat back, astonished at what I found:

There wasn't just one Admiral Vernon medal but at least a thousand different varieties, so many that they constituted an entire subcategory in the field of numismatics. Scholarly tomes had been written on the subject going back to 1835, with Leander McCormick-Goodhart's authoritative study taking up a whole issue of *Stack's Numismatic Review* in 1945. McCormick-Goodhart, perhaps the most ambitious collector of these medals had amassed over ten thousand examples of nearly a thousand different types before his death in 1965. The most recent addition to what I suppose must be called "Admiral Vernon Medal Studies" came out less than a decade ago: *Medallic Portraits of Admiral Vernon*, cowritten by a pair of dedicated numismatists, John Adams and Fernando Chao, and published by Kolbe and Fanning Numismatic Books of Gahanna, Ohio. A first edition hardcover is available from Amazon for the exalted price of $149.85, shipping not included.

Meanwhile, several online coin auction sites featured a bountiful array of Admiral Vernon medals for sale, of several different kinds and qualities. Some of the medals were finely wrought, others looked like kindergarten blobs, but they all showed Vernon in various poses and in various places, some at Cartagena with the kneeling Don Blass, some at Chagres or Porto Bello—both located in present-day Panama. Several showed Vernon alone, looking stalwart, the pommel of his sword placed in such a way and at such an angle as to resemble a rather impressive erection. By far the most popular type depicted the Admiral standing in front of a town identified as PORTOBELLO WHICH HE TOOK WITH SIX SHIPS ONLY. A few of the rare ones showed Vernon as part of a triumvirate, like the famous statue of the Byzantine Tetrarchs built into the wall of the Basilica San Marco in Venice—Vernon's companions here identified as Ogle and Wentworth, whoever they were.

Medals depicting Vernon at Cartagena with the kneeling Don Blass—a few exactly like the one at the Georgetown Flea Market—were relatively plentiful, with examples ranging in price, depending on condition, from around $275 to $1,800. The Georgetown dealer's price of $600 seemed a little high for the condition of his medal, which looked like it might be rated somewhere between "F" for Fair and G for "Good" by the trade. In addition to the coin auction sites, the medals were available on eBay and Etsy—the latter offering them alongside beaded purses and hand-knitted kitty socks, used Doc Martens and other Etsy-friendly merchandise. The cheapest medal I found, on Seattle Craigslist, had lost the bottom third and most of the remaining details sometime during the last two hundred and seventy-odd years and could be purchased for a mere $29.

Suddenly, Admiral Vernon medals seemed as common as pennies in a penny jar. Could you find them down at the local Walmart? The sheer ubiquity of so many eighteenth-century medals honoring a British admiral I'd never heard of seemed to posit the existence of a parallel historical universe in which an outsized naval hero conquered his way through strange foreign cities where he was forever presented with the sword of a hapless harlequin named Don Blass. Were these real historical figures? Or the mythic figments of some long-gone medal-makers' imagination, a pot-metal British version of the Baron von Munchausen saga?

I decided to find out.

3.

Days in libraries turned into weeks, months, a year, and resulted in the modest volume you now hold in your hands. I learned many things during this period—among them that Admiral Vernon and the kneeling Don Blass did exist, along with Ogle and Wentworth, though not exactly as portrayed. "Don Blass" for example (a Spanish Basque Admiral, real name Blas de Lezo y Olavarrieta) never knelt to anyone, and not just because he had a wooden leg. And I learned that these four men and many others (including the great British novelist Tobias Smollett and a certain Captain Lawrence Washington, beloved half-brother of the better known George) were players in a forgotten conflict of vast proportions: a war in which an armada of transport vessels carried more than twenty-thousand British soldiers and sailors across the Atlantic to the West Indies to fight Spain as another squadron sailed around Cape Horn and into the Pacific all the way to the coast of China and on around the globe for the same purpose—arguably the first true "world war" known to history.

One of the most respected historians of the period, Harold W. V. Temperley, considers this forgotten war of such great import to subsequent events that the year it started, 1739, is to him "a turning point of history." Also, as Temperley says, the war prefigures modern conflicts as "perhaps, the first of English wars in which the trade interest absolutely predominated, in which war was waged solely for balance of trade rather than for balance of power."

Another historian, none other than the famous Thomas Carlyle, gave the war the funny name by which it is now generally known: the War of Jenkins' Ear. Though, for the record, he called it the War *for* Jenkins's Ear, a ridiculous moniker anyway, bequeathed to subsequent generations of historians and scholars offhandedly, in tiny type, in one of the many footnotes to his multivolume *History of Friedrich II of Prussia, Called Frederick the Great*, written more than a hundred years after the events in question. As Carlyle says:

> This War, which posterity scoffs at as the *War for Jenkins's Ear*, was, if we examine it, a quite indispensable one . . . a most necessary War, though of a most stupid appearance. A war into which King and Parliament, knowing better, had been forced by public rage, there being no other method left in the case.

Carlyle got his funny name for the war full of disease, disaster, and fatal miscalculation ("begun, carried on, ended as if by a people in a state of somnambulism!") from an infamous incident involving—yes—a severed ear, and a mariner named Jenkins, whom we'll meet in the ensuing pages. But the war itself, a contest between the British and Spanish empires in the Americas which lasted roughly four years and resulted in the deaths of thousands, wasn't funny at all.

The Admiral Vernon Medallions

Sir Robert Walpole

ONE

The Incident

1.

On the morning of April 9, 1731, the British trading brig *Rebecca*, under the command of a tough, choleric Welshman by the name of Robert Jenkins, found herself becalmed in the dangerous waters off the Cuban coast, near Havana. She was London bound, out of Jamaica, carrying a load of sugar for the teas and cakes of England. From dawn, for hours, no wind stirred the *Rebecca*'s square-rigged sails; her spankers and booms hung slack in the hot, bright air as the sun rose.

April makes decent sailing weather in the Caribbean, hot and dry, comfortably removed from hurricane season, though occasionally afflicted with periods of deadly calm. The perilousness of the *Rebecca*'s situation in the Florida Straits that morning came not

1

from wind or wave or underwater obstruction, but from far more sinister man-made dangers: a long series of uncomfortable treaties between successive British monarchs (Queen Anne, George I and II) and Felipe V of Spain, fixing the spoils of war and the parameters of trade between the two countries.

These included the 1713 Treaty of Utrecht which brought the devastating War of Spanish Succession to an unsatisfactory conclusion; subsidiary treaties of December 14, 1715 and May 26, 1716, attempting to clarify certain vague clauses in the Treaty of Utrecht regarding British trading rights with Spanish colonies; the Treaty of London of 1718, establishing the Quadruple Alliance of Great Britain, France, the Holy Roman Empire, and the Dutch Republic against Spain; the Treaty of the Hague of February, 1720, which ended the misbegotten war resulting from that alliance; the Treaty of Madrid of June 1721 and the 1729 Treaty of Seville, officially ending the brief Anglo-Spanish War of the preceding two years.

All this diplomatic paperwork, engineered by royal negotiators in Madrid, London, and elsewhere had in the end created an impossible situation for Jenkins and his crew. According to "refinements" stipulated in the Treaty of Seville, any British merchant ship sailing near Spanish possessions in the West Indies might be stopped and searched for contraband trade goods or the proceeds from such, by the Spanish *guarda costa* (coast guard) at any time. Says historian Philip Woodfine:

> Once a ship had put in close to Spanish colonial coasts, it came under suspicion of being an illegal trader to settlements there, and became liable to investigation by the *guarda costas* who were commissioned to search and, where necessary, to seize vessels carrying contraband cargo. Ship and crew in such cases were conveyed to a nearby colonial port, where an enquiry, and often seizure, followed. It was enough

2

to have aboard the smallest quantity of Spanish Colonial produce, or the Spanish coin of 8 Reales, the "pieces of eight," which were the common currency of the whole Caribbean.

This much abused right of search-and-seizure had been negotiated and renegotiated between Spain and Great Britain as a part of the *Asiento de Negros*. This infamous contract, a monopoly granted by Spain to Britain in the Treaty of Utrecht, allowed the latter exclusive right to trade a fixed number of African slaves each year and a limited amount of manufactured goods to Spanish colonies in the Americas. On paper, the devil's bargain worked for both parties; in practice, the only way to turn a profit at *Asiento* trade was to turn smuggler.

The *guarda costa*'s fleet of fast, armed sloops had been commissioned by the Spanish government to interdict the smuggling everyone knew would inevitably arise—a mission that brought its own inevitable consequences. *Guarda costa* captains too often brutalized British crews and their captains and took whatever they wanted, including the ships in question, and occasionally the crews to use as convict labor, legal evidence of smuggling be damned. They generally acted, Temperley says, "as pirates toward the Englishmen, while posing as official vessels, very much the same way a clever thief robs a law-abiding citizen by impersonating a tax collector."

2.

Now, Captain Robert Jenkins watched with growing apprehension from the *Rebecca*'s taffrail as an oared sloop approached from the direction of the Cuban coast, a low green line about ten miles to the starboard. The vessel drew closer; Jenkins recognized it for a *guarda costa*, and his heart filled with dread. He had good reason for this uneasiness: scores of British ships had been taken in these waters, their cargoes ransacked and looted, their crews roughly handled, their captains tortured. Jenkins would have been generally familiar with the litany of recent outrages cited by merchant traders in England and later brought to the attention of the king in a series of increasingly aggrieved petitions. Here is a list of just a few of the claims:

The British galleys *Betty* and *Anne* seized, taken to Spanish ports and sold at auction, their crews imprisoned in filthy, vermin infested cells; the brig *Robert* taken, her captain, an Englishman named Storey King tortured for three days (*guarda costa* bravos had, among other cruelties, fixed lighted matches between Captain King's fingers and crushed his thumbs with gun-screws); the crew of the sloop *Runslet* taken, its crew abused with gun-screws in a similar manner, gun-screws apparently a popular form of torture on the Spanish Main that year; a captain named Thomas Weir, "maimed in both arms and confined to his berth" reportedly murdered by Spanish officials, along with eight of his men. And, most gruesomely, a Dutch captain's hand had been chopped off, the severed appendage boiled then fed to him one finger at a time. The Dutchman finished by eating the whole hand as *guarda costa* ruffians no doubt loomed about snickering, cutlasses drawn. One hesitates to imagine what he thought of this ghastly meal.

A few years later, in the anxious months leading up to war in 1739, King George II would send an irate memorandum to His Most Catholic Majesty, Felipe V of Spain, citing fifty-two British ships attacked and seized, with damages claimed in the hundreds of thousands of pounds—a mere fraction, British merchants asserted, of actual damages.

The most detailed account of what happened next to Captain Jenkins and the *Rebecca*, comes from an American source, Benjamin Franklin's *Pennsylvania Gazette* in the issue of October 7, 1731, six months after the incident. The wealth of detail offered by Franklin suggests he spoke to an eyewitness, perhaps one of the seamen aboard Jenkins's ship that fateful morning. A brief description of Jenkins's ordeal in the *Gentleman's Magazine* of June 1731, the captain's own deposition, and tidbits gleaned from correspondence between Thomas Pelham-Holles, the Duke of Newcastle, Secretary of State for the Southern Department and Benjamin Keene, British ambassador to the Spanish court, add descriptive flourishes—a bit of dialogue, a few conflicting details—to the dramatic scene Franklin presents.

3.

The *guarda costa* sloop, called either *La Isabela* or the *San Antonio*, depending on the source, drew closer across the glassy sea, her sixteen sweeps striking the water, rhythmic, inevitable. Presently, she came within hailing distance, but the sloop's captain eschewed the hailing-horn and began the conversation with three cannon shots across *Rebecca's* bow. He then identified himself as Juan de León Fandiño, a notorious *guarda costa* privateer (or misidentified himself as the pseudonymous Juan Francisco, according to Franklin's account). Whatever his name and whatever the name of his ship (let's call him Fandiño of *La Isabela*, the generally accepted identity of both captain and vessel), he called for a delegation to bring the *Rebecca's* sailing orders and cargo manifest to him for inspection.

Jenkins lowered the ship's boat and sent his first mate bearing only *Rebecca's* clearances from the Governor of Jamaica, expecting "this document would give sufficient satisfaction, it being a Time of profound Peace with Spain." But Fandiño was not convinced by the clearances. He seized the hapless mate as a hostage and returned the boat bearing a dozen armed men. He then lowered his own boat and followed with another dozen. Once aboard, no courtesies were exchanged. Instead, Fandiño and his contingent of "swarthies," later described as "negroes, mulattoes, and Indians," set about ransacking the ship.

"They broke open all the Hatches, Lockers and Chests," looking for smuggled Spanish raw materials, generally "Logwood, Hides or Tallow, the Product of the Spanish settlements in America," or quantities of Spanish money generated from the illegal sale of British manufactured goods to Spanish colonists. Jenkins initially welcomed the search of his ship. He understood that per treaty agreement, the *guarda costa* as "the King of Spain's Officers . . . might do their duty, for there was nothing on board but which was the Growth and Produce of Jamaica," a chief British colony in the West Indies.

Fandiño's men spent the next two hours at their destructive task as Jenkins and his crew stood by helplessly. At last, finding nothing, Fandiño, in a rage, resorted to the terror tactics for which the *guarda costa* had become infamous in the West Indies. First, he lashed Jenkins to the foremast and forced the Welshman to watch as *guarda costa* ruffians brutally beat the *Rebecca*'s mulatto cabin boy in an effort to extract the location of any money hidden aboard. Perhaps it might be found in a secret compartment somewhere in the hold of the ship, as was often the case. But the cabin boy, knowing nothing, revealed nothing, and collapsed under the beating.

Though later commentators insist that Jenkins must have been a smuggler because everyone else was a smuggler in those days on the Spanish Main, no evidence has ever been found to support this claim. In fact, the known details of Jenkins's career supports the opposite conclusion: he seems to have been an honest merchant captain, trusted by his employers and bearing nothing more than a load of Jamaican sugar for the London exchange.

Fandiño, however, remained certain the *Rebecca* concealed hidden treasure; his efforts to find it grew increasingly frenzied. He tied the bleeding, insensate cabin boy around Jenkins's legs as dead weight, tightened a noose around the Welshman's neck and tossed the other end of the rope over a spar. Jenkins, unlashed from the mast, was then "hoisted up the Foreyard, but the boy, being light, slipt through . . . to the Captain's great ease." Fandiño ordered Jenkins hoisted into the yards two more times, each time "to the point of Strangulation." Each time he demanded Jenkins reveal the whereabouts of his treasure; each time the pugnacious Welshman asserted "that they might torture him to Death, but he could not make any other Answer."

Fandiño then threatened to burn the *Rebecca* to the waterline along with the crew, who as English Protestants were all "obstinate Hereticks," and thus good candidates for a Spanish Inquisition-style auto-da-fé. But even under threat of immolation, Jenkins still couldn't reveal the whereabouts of a treasure he didn't possess. Fandiño, mistaking innocence for stubbornness, left Jenkins gasping on the deck and conferred with his second-in-command, a man Franklin's account identifies as Lieutenant Dorce. Perhaps some fresh torture might be devised?

Dorce, "who had just put the rope around [Jenkins's] neck," then searched the Welshman's pocket, stealing a small amount of personal money he found there and also the silver buckles off Jenkins's shoes. At a gesture from Fandiño, his men then hung Jenkins again, this time leaving him dangling in the foreyards "until he was quite strangled." At the last possible moment, however, Fandiño ordered his men to release the rope. Jenkins dropped abruptly and with such force he bounced down the forward hatch, crashing onto the ship's casks of fresh water stored below.

From here, they dragged a bruised and bleeding but still alive Jenkins by the rope around his neck back up through the hatch. For a long time, he lay motionless on the hot deck, beside the broken form of his cabin boy. The long day waned. The sun, now high overhead, dropped in the west over the blue water and the distant coast of New Spain. How much longer could Fandiño and his men tarry aboard the *Rebecca*, dealing with these ridiculous Englishmen? Maybe there was no treasure aboard this ship after all. Fandiño decided to give it one last try. He ordered Jenkins bound to the mast again and taking up a cutlass and pistol charged at him screaming "Confess or die!"

But the unfortunate Jenkins could not confess. The ship's money included only what they had taken from his pockets and a small bag of coins—found in his cabin—reserved for operating expenses, consisting of "four Guineas, one Pistole and four Double Doubloons." A reasonable sum, but not enough to justify the seizure and ransacking of a British ship and the torture of its captain and crew. The *Gentleman's Magazine* picks up the narrative from here:

Fandiño, beside himself, "took hold of [Jenkins's] left ear and with his cutlass slit it down, and another of the Spaniards [Lieutenant Dorce?] took hold of it and tore it off, but gave him the Piece of his ear again and made threats against the King, saying 'the same will happen to him [King George II] if caught doing the same [i.e., smuggling].'" A statement rendered all the more absurd as Fandiño hadn't been able to find any smuggled merchandise aboard the *Rebecca*. (An image out of classical mythology suggests itself here: Jenkins bound to the mast like Odysseus approaching the rock of the Sirens—but head bowed, blood pouring down the side of his face, the most consequential severed ear in history lying on the bloody deck at his feet.)

Determined to commit a final barbaric act, Fandiño—according to Franklin's account—decided to scalp the much-insulted Jenkins; finding the Welshman's head too closely shaved, he gave up on this idea as impracticable. With daylight fading, and the general appetite for torture nearly sated, Fandiño's men contented themselves with beating the mate and boatswain "unmercifully." They then stripped the *Rebecca* of everything portable, including bedding and the clothes of the crew, leaving them standing naked on the deck. From Captain Jenkins they additionally took a "Watch of Gold, Cloathes, Linnens & etc. on a moderate valuation of 112 pounds, sterling." They also took a "tortoise shell box" and some old silverware.

Finally, Fandiño himself confiscated the *Rebecca*'s navigational equipment (maps, sextant, compass) and her store of candles—contraband, Fandiño asserted, made from Spanish tallow. More than an act of theft, a deadly act of sabotage designed to leave the *Rebecca* wallowing in darkness on unknown seas.

Later, in a letter of protest to the Spanish governor of Cuba, British Rear Admiral James Stewart, ranking naval officer at the Jamaica Station, cited the theft of the *Rebecca*'s navigational equipment as one of the most serious aspects of Fandiño's crime, as it indicated his intention had been "that she should perish in her passage [across the Atlantic]."

At last, Fandiño and his ruffians returned to *La Isabela* and sailed off. Jenkins' terrified and naked crew then quickly unbound their captain, brought him back to consciousness with rum and water and bandaged his bloody stump of ear. Immediately realizing the *Rebecca*'s predicament, a revived Jenkins set a course for the closest port, Havana, where he hoped to meet with another British ship from whom he "might procure sufficient necessities to enable him to proceed on his voyage"—and perhaps lodge an official complaint regarding the savage treatment he had received at the hands of the *guarda costas*. But Fandiño and *La Isabela* lurked just over the horizon. Coming alongside the British vessel once again, Fandiño called a warning to the mutilated Jenkins: make for open waters or this time he really would set the ship on fire!

So, "rather than have a second visit from them," Franklin reports, "captain and crew of the *Rebecca* recommended themselves to the Mercy of the Seas."

Crossing the Atlantic proved difficult. The crew made rudimentary garments out of sailcloth and sacking. Without candles, they burned oil and butter in the binnacle to steer by; without compass and sextant, Jenkins navigated by the stars and "by his nose," which is to say he used the excellent seamanship which would save his life and the lives of other crews time and again throughout his long career on the world's oceans. At last, after two months and "many Hardships and Perils," on June, 11, 1731, the *Rebecca* crossed the bar into the River Thames.

4.

Not long after Jenkins's return, his severed ear "preserved in a bottle," he personally presented an account of his suffering and the sufferings of his crew to King George II. Perhaps his Majesty might arrange for compensation for Jenkins's lost ear from the King of Spain. This audience, arranged by Secretary of State Newcastle at the behest of a group of London merchants, set off a brief diplomatic flurry. Furious letters flew back and forth between the Spanish and English courts; British Ambassador Benjamin Keene made a formal protest to the Spanish king; members of Parliament in opposition to the pacific policies of First Minister Robert Walpole agitated for a more vigorous attitude toward the Spaniards in the Caribbean. Rear Admiral Stewart again "specifically mentioned the case to the Spanish governor of Cuba as part of a series of complaints for which he demanded satisfaction."

Then, nothing happened.

The Jenkins matter was dropped and things went on as before. Anything, Walpole and his ministry believed, was preferable to war with Spain, which he guessed would be far more costly to commerce than a handful of ransacked ships and abused sailors. So the outrages of the *guarda costa* upon British trading vessels in the West Indies continued as British merchants—particularly the South Sea Company—hungry for profit, ramped-up their smuggling activities under the cover of the *Asiento de Negros*. Captain Robert Jenkins' ordeal, after "exciting some little attention" in the press of the day, all but faded from the national consciousness.

Years would pass before the British people heard of him again.

Emperor Charles II of Spain

TWO

Deep Background

FROM THE BEWITCHED KING TO THE SOUTH SEA BUBBLE,
1665–1720

1.

The War of Jenkins' Ear—or Carlyle's "War for Jenkins's Ear" or, to the Spanish, *la Guerra del Asiento*, or the "Anglo-Spanish War of 1739," so-called by modern historians, who like to suck the juice out of everything—perhaps became inevitable the day Felipe IV of Spain died. The Spanish king breathed his last on October 15, 1665, eyes fixed on the same miracle-working crucifix that had comforted his ancestors since the death of the great Holy Roman Emperor Charles V more than a hundred years earlier.

Though Felipe suffered from a variety of serious ailments—probably exacerbated by syphilis acquired from a lifetime's indulgence in the brothels of Madrid—it was thought at court that his demise had been the result of sorcery. In fact, evidence of a black magic assassination attempt had been uncovered: the bag supposed to contain holy relics always worn around the king's neck had been found to contain instead a miniature portrait of himself stuck with pins, a tiny book of evil spells, hair, teeth, and other Satanic odds and ends. The horrified priest who had discovered the contents of the bag quickly burned it on the altar of the chapel of Our Lady of Atocha—alas, too late. This exorcism could not save the king whose death had already been predicted by the appearance of a comet in the sky above Madrid in December 1664. Nor could it extinguish the darker fate brought on by generations of close inbreeding that now descended like a curtain on Spain's Hapsburg dynasty.

Dying, Felipe left his tragically deformed and perhaps imbecilic son, Carlos II, called *el Hechizado*, "the Bewitched," in possession of a globe-spanning empire. The new king's vast inheritance included half of Europe, the Spanish West Indies, the Philippines, Florida, that portion of South America not encompassed by Brazil, half of North America, and a few scattered cities on the North African coast. But along with all this excellent real estate came a nightmarish array of in-bred genetic infirmities. Carlos II's father and mother, for example, had been uncle and niece—a pattern repeated several times in preceding generations, going back to a schizophrenic ancestress named Joanna the Mad, every Hapsburg's crazy great-great-great-great grandmother. Carlos's degree of consanguinity, expressed by geneticists in the following terms: $F_{,}(O.50)^3 \times(1)+(0.5)^3\times(1)=0.25$ added up to one of the highest possible inbreeding coefficients, an equation worthy of Satan himself.

Poor Carlos! Despite the presence of Spain's holiest relics at his birth (the three thorns from Christ's Crown of Thorns, a piece of the True Cross, a scrap of the Virgin Mary's mantle, the sacred walking stick of Santiago, and his miraculous belt) he failed to thrive. His sad eyes stare out at us accusingly across the centuries from dozens of royal portraits, though all the artifice of the court painters couldn't conceal the monstrosity they portray: His enormous misshapen head, terminating in the famous jutting "Hapsburg jaw," so misaligned that his teeth failed to meet, made it impossible to chew food (wet nurses fed him on breast milk through most of his childhood), while a huge tongue inhibited the ability to speak. His spindly legs barely supported the weight of his upper body. Thus unbalanced, Carlos was prone to falling, a tendency not improved by periodic epileptic fits.

When exhibited to the world in the first royal audience following the death of his father, Carlos at age six was unable to walk on his own. His nurses held him up by strings attached to his limbs, like a marionette.

"The King of Spain supported himself on his feet propped against the knees of his Menina who held him by the strings of his dress," wrote the French ambassador, M. de Bellefonds. "He covered his head with an English-style bonnet, which he had not the energy to raise. . . . He seems extremely weak, with pale cheeks and a very open mouth, a symptom, according to the unanimous opinion of his doctors, of some gastric upset . . . [they] do not fortell a long life, and this seems to be taken for granted in all calculations here."

Premature loss of teeth and hair, chronic dizziness, and suppurating ulcers—leaking what Carlos's doctors called "a laudable pus"—posit an additional diagnosis of syphilis inherited from his father. As does his frequent hallucinations and the long bouts of melancholy during which he held strange midnight conversations with the exhumed corpses of his royal predecessors. Ignorant of world affairs, barely able to read or write, his only playmates a surreal collection of dwarves, clowns, and continually lactating nurses,

Carlos had been deliberately undereducated by his powerful mother, Mariana of Austria, who sought to rule the kingdom on her own. Still, foreign ambassadors visiting the Spanish court found him lucid and reasonably intelligent, if under the thumb of his domineering mother and her favorites.

But Carlos's early death, constantly predicted, eagerly awaited by some, never came to pass. For thirty-five years after the puppet show of his first audience, he stubbornly refused to die. In his obstinacy, in his reverence for the Spanish Crown which he hoped to pass undiminished to another generation, and most of all in the enormity of his suffering, he might be accounted among the noblest of the Spanish Hapsburgs, second only to Charles V himself, Holy Roman Emperor and illustrious founder of the dynasty.

Unfortunately for Hapsburg dynastic survival, Carlos's most severe deficiency lay in the sexual realm. Married twice to women from aristocratic families of exemplary fertility, he failed to provide the required heir. Urologists now suspect that his habit of premature ejaculation had its causes in a "posterios hypospadias"—he passed urine and ejaculate through an opening half way down the penile shaft—or that he may have been intersex, with ambiguous genitalia.

2.

The greatest challenge of Carlos's fraught reign awaited him in his last weeks of life. Leaving no heir, he was forced to choose the next king of Spain, the inheritor of her European provinces and endless overseas empire. Two leading candidates emerged: a cousin, the Archduke Charles of the Austrian branch of the Hapsburgs, and Carlos's grandnephew, Philippe, Duc d'Anjou of the French House of Bourbon, grandson of Louis XIV, the glittering *Roi Soleil* of France.

Carlos wavered. Royal lawyers drew up two wills, the first favoring Archduke Charles, the second Philippe—which one would he sign? Europe held its breath. Most worried that Bourbon control of both France and Spain would ruin the carefully orchestrated balance of power that had kept Europe in a relative state of peace since the ruinous Thirty Years' War that had ended in 1648. Such a union, they said, would "level the Pyrenees," the spiky mountain range separating the two kingdoms, and create a massive superpower that might dominate the world.

Factions of the Spanish court and half of Europe lined up behind one candidate or the other: Austria, half of Spain (including Catalonia and Aragon), Portugal, the Dutch Republic, and certain German principalities of the Holy Roman Empire all backed the Archduke Charles. England (seven years before the Act of Union transformed her into Great Britain) also backed Archduke Charles. The rest of Spain, Louis XIV's France, Catholic Bavaria, and other ducal odds and ends backed Philippe.

On his deathbed, Carlos writhed in an agony of pain and indecision. His second wife, Maria Anna of Neuberg, nursed him tenderly through his final torments, feeding him "milk of pearls" (pearls crushed in wine or vinegar), standing by anxiously as the doctors put "cantharides" (the aphrodisiac Spanish Fly, which in a poultice does double duty as a blistering agent) on his feet, dead pigeons on his brow to cure his headaches, and laid the entrails of freshly slaughtered lambs on his stomach to keep him warm. Pulled this way and that, swayed by courtiers who favored the Archduke, now by those who favored the French candidate, Carlos finally stood on his own two feet, figuratively speaking: he signed the will naming Philippe d'Anjou as his heir—though, to become Felipe V of Spain, the latter would have to renounce any claims to the Crown of France.

Carlos fell back exhausted. He had just completed the hardest work of his life. He lingered in terrible pain for another week.

"Many people tell me," he gasped, "that I am bewitched, and I well believe it, such are the things I experience and suffer."

At last, on All Souls Day in 1700, he died, a "quintessence of weakness" but one upon which "men and women of strong will and fierce ambitions broke as against a granite rock."

The autopsy, performed by the court physician, probably exaggerates the extent of Carlos's deformities—but barely: "His corpse did not contain a single drop of blood," noted the autopsy report, "three large stones resided in his kidneys," also "his heart was the size of a peppercorn; his lungs corroded, his intestines rotten and gangrenous. He had a single testicle, black as coal, and his head was full of water." It is that solitary testicle, shriveled as a raisin, dangling over history like a curse, that in the end haunts the imagination.

The general opinion in Madrid, wrote the Austrian ambassador "is that the death is due to witchcraft."

3.

Whatever the cause of Carlos II's death, the last of the Spanish Hapsburgs had gone to meet the ancestors with whom he had so often conversed as they lay decomposing in their coffins. He had made his decision. But would the silver mines of Peru, the gold of the Incas, the orderly cities of the Spanish Netherlands, the rose-red castles of Aragon, the fat provinces of Italy, the galleons full of treasure, the numerous rivers and impenetrable forests of the New World, the plantations with their thousands of African and Indian slaves—would all of it go to a Frenchman without a fight because Carlos the Bewitched had scrawled his name on a bit of parchment?

A titanic struggle ensued over the resolution of this troubled bequest: the War of Spanish Succession. Its protracted sieges and bloody battles whose names, though fading, still echo down the centuries (Blenheim and Oudenarde, Ramilles and Denain and Malplaquet); its epic marches and countermarches and grand strategies; the famous soldiers on both sides, the incomparable John Churchill, Duke of Marlborough, great-great-great-grandfather of Winston; the brave, diminutive Prince Eugene of Savoy; the magnificent French Marshals, Villars and Vendome and Bouffleurs—all this is best reserved for another volume.

Suffice to say that at Malplaquet, on September 11, 1709, over a period of seven hours 30,000 men died. It was the bloodiest battle of the eighteenth century—indeed, one of the bloodiest in history to that point—with a single-day butcher's bill unequaled until World War I's Maxim guns and gas attacks. British soldiers fighting over the same ground in 1914 reportedly discovered skeletons lying beside rusted muskets in sunken earthworks crossing the Wood of Sars, scraps of red cloth stuck to the bones, all from the 1709 clash. (The battlefield in Northern France remains remarkably unchanged today—the same bleak fields, the same woods and thickets. There are one or two crumbling monuments; grass has grown over the graves of the dead. In the nearby village of Taisnieres, in a café on the *place*, you can drink a *Cognac fine a l'eau* not far from the spot where the cavalry of the *Maison du Roi*, led by Boufflers himself, charging six times, drove Prince Eugene's Allied cavalry back through the battered redoubts.)

The slaughter at Malplaquet sickened a Europe poised on the threshold of the Age of Enlightenment, but it did not end the war. Shortly after the battle, Britain rejected a peace treaty offered by Louis XIV granting all the Allies major demands. The French king even acceded to Charles of Austria's elevation to the Spanish throne—cutting out his own grandson—against the advice of Marshal Villars, who saw the Allied victory over the French at Malplaquet as pyrrhic. "The enemy cannot afford many such victories," he told his royal master. But Marlborough wanted to crush

France. Nothing less than the total destruction of Louis's showy regime would answer his ambitions.

The blood of Malplaquet soaked slowly into the ground.

4.

Six years later, with the great Marlborough deposed and discredited by his political enemies, England at last made a separate peace with France and Spain. She thus broke a promise to her allies to fight on; the Dutch in disgust closed the gates of their fortresses to retreating, exhausted English troops who had thrown down their arms.

The terms of the peace looked like this: Charles of Austria formally renounced his claims to the Spanish throne; Spain retained her overseas empire but relinquished her provinces in Northern Europe, including the Spanish Netherlands (present day Belgium), Luxembourg, and her provinces in Italy (Milan, Naples, Sicily), but kept her French Bourbon king who renounced his right to inherit the French throne. Gibraltar and Menorca went to England; Sicily to Savoy; Sardinia to Austria. European maps had to be redrawn; territory and allegiances shifted. As Carlos the Bewitched had intended, Philippe, Duc d'Anjou would now be acknowledged by all as His Most Catholic Majesty Felipe V of Spain. He began a long, weird reign during which he would exhibit his own share of Hapsburg madness, inherited through the maternal line.

And yet, England's armies under Marlborough had been largely victorious. She would be compensated for her success on the battlefield. She was now in a good position to acquire through negotiation long-sought trading rights with Spain's South American colonies as one of the spoils of war. These trading rights embodied in the notorious *Asiento de Negros*—the exclusive contract to supply African slaves to Spain's South American colonies—had been held by France for the previous dozen years.

5.

The history of the *Asiento de Negros* begins in 1517 when Holy Roman Emperor Charles V (also Carlos I, King of Spain) granted the original slaving contract to a court favorite, a Flemish noble-man, Laurent de Gouvenot. Not wishing to sully his hands with commerce of any kind, particularly not with the dirty business of slaving, Gouvenot immediately sold his contract to a cabal of Geno-ese merchants based in Seville for 25,000 ducats.

The Portuguese had dominated the nascent trade in African slaves for the hundred years or so preceding the first *Asiento*. Bartolomeu Dias, the Portuguese mariner, rounded the Cape of Good Hope in 1418, the first European to do so. Where he went, Portuguese slavers would follow. African slaves worked sugar plan-tations on the Portuguese island of Madeira as early as 1460; the Portuguese built the first European slave fort off the coast of what is now Ghana in 1481. Most have forgotten that the Portuguese were the original European explorers of West Africa, the original European colonizers, the original European slave traders.

In the early years of Spain's empire in the New World, colo-nists made use of an easily accessible labor source—the indigenous inhabitants of the Americas—whose abuse the Dominican Friar Bartolomé de las Casas decried in his famous, controversial tract *A Brief Account of the Destruction of the Indies*. After twenty-five years of harsh Spanish rule, a brief generation, the indigenous popu-lation of New Spain had nearly collapsed. Wars, torture, insurrec-tion, but mostly disease, had swept away untold thousands. Ravished from pristine forests by brutal conquerors, uprooted from a state of primeval freedom, the native people preferred to die rather than work the silver mines and bean fields for their Spanish oppressors. Thus, the importation of enslaved Africans became necessary for the survival of Spain's colonial enterprise.

But few Spaniards cared to pursue the lamentable trade. Nor were the resources available in Spain (the ships and men, the expert knowledge of African coasts) so they farmed it out to others via the *Asiento*. The original 1517 contract offered a monopoly of the slave trade for eight years, with a maximum of 4,800 slaves sold per year to Spain's colonies, divided between male and female, young and old for a price not exceeding 45 ducats per slave. An additional complication divided each slave into fractions of a slave called *piezas de Indias*—literally "Indian Pieces"—units of trade that graded each slave like a slab of supermarket beef graded today by the USDA.

"When a slave ship arrived in a Spanish-American port, the royal officers examined the negroes for disease and measured them as so many units of *piezas de Indias* in order to compute the duties due to the King of Spain," writes John G. Sperling, one of the foremost experts on the *Asiento*. "Negroes in perfect health were counted as follows: from 5 to 10 years they equaled ½ of a *pieza*, from 10 to 15 they equaled ⅔, from 15 to 30 they equaled 1, and above thirty they equaled ¾. Smallness, deformity or sickness altered the measurements."

(This idea—that a single enslaved African might be divided into fractions of himself—had a discomfiting afterlife. Surely its echo can be seen in the Three-Fifths Compromise at the US Constitutional Convention of 1787, in which delegates agreed, for the purposes of census taking, to count slaves as ⅗ of a human being.)

From Gouvenant and the Genoese, the *Asiento de Negros* quickly passed back to the Portuguese and through many other hands, though, like a hot potato, none held it very long: A succession of Portuguese merchants through the sixteenth century gave way to the Dutch in the seventeenth. Despite their blindingly white lace and Calvinistic probity, the Dutch made enthusiastic slavers. In the end, sharp business practices and Dutch-Spanish hostilities brought them down. Then, in 1702, the French, in the guise of a state-owned enterprise called *la Compagnie de Guinée*, received the *Asiento* as a reward for backing their own candidate, the Archduke Charles, for the Spanish throne in 1700.

It had taken the War of Spanish Succession to reverse this bequest.

6.

In Bristol they called him the "Sunday Gentleman." A failed hosiery salesman, cat farmer, tile maker, importer of Spanish wines—also an inexhaustible pamphleteer, political journalist, novelist, and all-around literary genius—named Daniel Defoe. But geniuses generally make terrible businessmen. In those days, debt was a criminal offense; debtors' prison loomed for the insolvent. Often on the run from the collapse of one-or-another moneymaking scheme, some plausible, some ridiculous, Defoe fled London for Bristol in March 1692. (All this happened about fifteen years before he sat down to write a book called *Robinson Crusoe*. Only the Bible has been translated into more languages.)

In Bristol, Defoe hid from the authorities, firing off letters to London friends begging loans; to creditors, craving indulgence; to his disappointed wife, explaining himself: Admittedly, the cat-farming hadn't gone well. These weren't ordinary cats, but civets, valued for scent glands indispensable to the making of strong perfumes in a stinky age. Picture cages full of angry felines awaiting their fate at the hands of the gland extractors and the difficulties of such an undertaking becomes clear. Also, he had sold the cats to two different investors simultaneously while defrauding his mother-in-law of 400 pounds. Even after the lapse of three centuries, you can almost hear the writer equivocating: he'd had no choice, he was very sorry, but he needed the money and had to unload the cats.

Like most writers, Defoe had a taste for showy clothes: lace cuffs, velvet coats, silver-buckled shoes; not to mention the extravagant wigs of the era, rising above his steep forehead like a cumulonimbus full of heat lightning. He emerged from his secret Bristol lair every Sunday in his best duds to stroll the town since custom forbade the arrest of debtors on Sundays—hence the "Sunday Gentleman."

A decade and many schemes later, authorities caught up with the dandyish Defoe at last. Government wanted posters offering fifty pounds for information leading to his arrest described him as

the author of slanderous and seditious Publications . . . a middle-sized, spare man, about 40 years old, of a brown Complexion . . . wears a Wig, a hooked Nose, a sharp chin, grey Eyes, and a large mould near his Mouth. Was born in London and was for many years a hose factor . . . a Seditious man of a disordered mind and a person of bad name, reputation and Conversation.

An acquaintance betrayed him to the authorities; since the days of Judas there's always been some rat around willing to perform this function for cash. Convicted of "Seditious Libel," the writer received a heavy sentence at the hands of a notorious hanging judge with the sinister name of Salathiel Lovell: first, three days in the pillory at Stoke-Newington, a stone's throw from the Defoe family home (this location deliberately chosen for its humiliation value), then a heavy fine and incarceration in the dreadful Newgate Prison until that fine might be paid in full. For a man of Defoe's epic insolvency, this amounted to a life sentence. And yet he feared the pillory most of all. Men had died on the pillory, head and hands locked in the iron stocks, pissing themselves, exposed to the weather and the abuse of sadistic crowds, pelted with rotten vegetables, stones, excrement.

Defoe, tougher than he looked, survived the pillory, and was eventually freed from Newgate's "stench and nastiness" by a political enemy, a prominent Tory politician, Robert Harley, later Earl of Oxford. Let's consider for a moment the political landscape in England of Defoe's day. English parliamentary politics of the eighteenth century allowed for only two parties, Tory and Whig. The former generally aristocratic, conservative, isolationist, on the side of a strong monarchy; the latter generally middle-class, business oriented, and comparatively progressive, in favor of more liberty for more people as long as those liberties coincided with the making of money. The nation swayed back and forth between these two poles. The Whig vs. Tory political struggle—marked by assassination attempts, power grabs, and deadly rivalries—at times played out like a Jacobean revenge play, but no more corrosive to the public good than the bitter party politics of our own era.

Even by eighteenth-century standards, Robert Harley was an alcoholic. Heavy drinking affected his behavior and speech; he was often drunkenly inarticulate in the presence of the reigning monarch, Queen Anne. When Harley did manage to get the words out, it was not easy to understand what he meant, complained the poet Alexander Pope.

"That lord," Pope asserted, "spoke with serpentine convulsions and talked of business in so confused a manner that you did not know what he was all about; and everything was in the epic way, for he always began in the middle." Harley "flustered himself daily with claret," added the historian Macauley, though this drinking habit, "was hardly considered a fault by his contemporaries." It was a hard-drinking age.

Claret-flustered or not, Harley possessed a clear political vision. He knew England would most probably soon acquire the *Asiento de Negros* from Spain as spoils of war, and that the nation would have to create a vehicle to administer this acquisition. And he needed Defoe's genius to help him devise a scheme that would harness the *Asiento*'s potential for profit-making and enrich both himself and the nation in the process. The writer had long been fascinated by the South American continent—specifically that part bordering the "South Seas," by which he meant Chile's lengthy Pacific coast and the coast of Peru, an area that would later become the fictional setting for his masterpiece *Robinson Crusoe*. Defoe thought the "South Sea Coast" of South America ripe for exploitation, the perfect arena for British investment and colonization. As Defoe wrote in *An Essay on the South-Sea Trade* in 1709:

Great Quantities of Silver which the French squadrons, and Private Merchant Ships, have brought Home from the South-Seas have been spoken of . . . frequently accompanied with Reflections, and a general Regret, that these happy Advantages should pass by us. That the English nation, who are so much better qualified in every Way, both by their Manufactures to Trade with, Islands to Trade From, and Naval Strength to manage and protect that Trade, should so long lie still and leave unattempted a Trade, which in the Enemies Hand, is so fatal to us, and which in our Hands might be so fatal to them.

He further recommended "the Planting of our own People in those Rich Climates, where, by laying a Foundation of Trade which was never yet ingaged in, Our Subjects might come to be enrich'd." And so on for several thousand words.

England's acquisition of the *Asiento* would dovetail nicely with Defoe's South American fantasies and Robert Harley's political schemes.

Meanwhile, created Chancellor of the Exchequer in 1710, Harley faced an insurmountable national debt brought on by the War of Spanish Succession, nearing its tenth year. The nation's "floating," that is, short-term debt, largely caused by the war, now stood at nearly ten million pounds and threatened economic stability.

"This 'unfunded' debt in the form of tallies, interest arrears, and other claims on government spending" explains forensic economist and historian Richard Dale, "would be rolled over if it could not be refinanced longer term. By 1711, interest arrears had built up and . . . was being traded in the secondary market at deep discounts averaging around 32%." National insolvency, a black mountain covered with ice, grew ever higher, looming over everyone's shoulder.

Harley wanted a single scheme to solve several key matters, all intertwined; one that might: (1) lessen the government's dangerous level of indebtedness, (2) secure a profitable peace with France and Spain, and (3) reduce the financial power of Harley's Whig political enemies.

For inspiration, he turned to his creature, Defoe. The writer soon dreamed up a concept of characteristic genius, eventually known as the "South Sea Scheme," which Harley just as characteristically presented as entirely his own—despite Defoe's contributions and the involvement of a trio of shady "stock jobbers" (speculators), Elias Tuner, Jacob Sawbridge, and George Caswall.

These men hoped for immense profits from the Defoe/Harley scheme which advocated the creation by act of Parliament of a public-private joint-stock corporation to be called the "South Sea Company." This company would eventually derive—it was assumed—vast profits from the *Asiento* trade. It would also privatize the vast national debt by "persuading [the government's] creditors to accept shares in the South Sea Company as payment. The Government would be relieved of an enormous burden . . . and would only need to find the money to pay the interest."

7.

On September 8, 1711, after a season of heavy politicking and a couple of assassination attempts against his life, Harley at last pushed the South Sea Company through Parliament, with himself as its first governor. This trading firm, derisively dubbed "Harley's Masterpiece" by the skeptical Whig opposition, would become the commercial vehicle to administer the *Asiento*, should it land in England's lap—which everyone counted on. From the beginning, the South Sea Company took shape as an unholy public-private partnership, ripe for exploitation by unscrupulous politicians and financiers, with shares traded in the coffee houses of "Exchange Alley," London's eighteenth-century version of Wall Street.

A corrupt speculator named John Blunt drafted the company charter, taking the Bank of England as a model. Blunt however added certain stipulations that made stock manipulation and corruption inevitable. Following Harley's tenure as governor, "control of the Company would pass to a small group of directors," explains Sperling—a fraction of the Company's unwieldy thirty-three member board, who would be "given the unique power to act in anything committed to them as fully as the entire Court of Directors might lawfully do. This seemingly innocuous provision was designed . . . to enable them to take over power once the politicians had left the scene."

The governorship eventually became a figurehead position and later passed to the ruling monarch, King George I. Any criticism of the Company's financial dealings thus became tantamount to treason.

The South Sea Company quickly established its headquarters in an impressive new building at the corner of Threadneedle Street and Bishopsgate in London. It was granted a coat of arms by the College of Heralds, described in heraldry speak as "Azure, a globe wheron are represented the Straits of Magellan and Cape Horn all proper and in sinister chief point two herrings haurient in saltire argent crowned or, in a canton the united arms of Great Britain." Translation: two crossed fishes wearing crowns dangling over a map of the ass end of the world. They took as their motto "From Cádiz to the Dawn," a reference to the Spanish port city of Cádiz, from which Spain's treasure galleons traditionally set out for the West Indies.

To go along with this fanciful logo, the South Sea Act granted the Company an equally fanciful monopoly on trade with "the kingdoms, lands etc of America, on the east side from the river Aranoca [Orinocco], to the most southern part of the Terra del Fuego, on the west side therof, from the said most southern part through the South Seas to the most northern part of America, and into, unto and from all countries in the same limits reputed to belong to the Crown of Spain, or which shall be hereafter discovered." Additionally, the Company would receive "an annual payment from the Exchequer of £568,279, to be secured on specific customs revenues . . . representing 6 percent return on £9.5 million of outstanding short-term government debt." This to be converted by its holders into South Sea Company stock:

> "The Company would acquire claims to the same value against the government," in what Richard Dale calls "a large-scale debt-equity swap. . . . In less than ten years the South Sea Company was to become a corporate monster with a market capitalization of over £200 million, although like the modern dot.com equivalent, its trading operations remained minimal and mostly loss-making."

Two years later, the South Sea Company, to this point something of an empty vessel, received the bitter liquor for which it had been designed: according to the Treaty of Madrid, signed on

March 26, 1713, as part of the general Utrecht agreement, Great Britain at last officially became the twenty-fifth recipient of the *Asiento de Negros* slave trading contract in just under two hundred years. It was a dream of cornucopia, an inexhaustible source of gold bullion, silver ingots, and emeralds in exchange for African slaves and British manufactured goods. But this dream came with responsibilities. The contract to be administered by the South Sea Company, boiled down, looked like this:

1. English "Asientists" were required to transport the traditional 4,800 *piezas de Indias* annually to Spanish America each year for thirty years—a *pieza* being here defined as an African slave between the ages of fifteen and thirty, at least fifty-eight inches tall, with no physical defects.
2. Payment for both African slaves and trade goods could be received in money, gold, silver bullion, or "fruits of the country," that is, via barter.
3. African slaves could be carried by English vessels to all Spanish-American ports.
4. English Asientists had the right to send each year a single *navio de permiso*—permission ship—containing 500 tons of trade goods to the fairs at Cartagena, Porto Bello, or Vera Cruz. The King of Spain was to receive 28¾ percent of the profits from this venture.
5. Factories, comprising warehouses, slave pens, offices, and living quarters, staffed by four to six Englishmen could be established to carry out the *Asiento* trade, but they could not be fortified.

Sperling concludes:

This contract was drawn up on the assumption that Spain's colonial system accorded with Spanish colonial theory, and that the *Asiento* company would adhere to the terms of the agreement. "Unfortunately, the agreement was incapable of working smoothly. No amount of explanation or clarification of the terms of the contract, nor bribing of Spanish officials could mask the incompatibility between the Company and the Spanish colonial system.

By the end of 1713, the Company was ready to engage in the new transatlantic "negro trade" to the Spanish colonies. They had set up factories in Porto Bello, Cartagena, Vera Cruz, Havana, Caracas, and Buenos Aires and transported 1,540 African slaves before the fall of 1714.

More slave ships followed; most of their human cargo was purchased from British Royal African Company's castles along the Guinea Coast, and from private traders at the slave "refreshment stations" at Jamaica or Barbados. But the Spanish objected to slaves who had spent more than a few days in English colonies, regarding them as possibly "tainted with Protestantism," and dangerous to the Catholic faith. What they wanted were *bozales*, slaves brought directly from Africa—and thus generally considered adherents of a primitive animism and ripe for conversion. For their part, Jamaican slave dealers regarded the latter as potentially diseased (infected with yellow fever, malaria, and other tropical maladies) and imposed an illegal tax on each slave, over and above the duties already required by both the Spanish and British crown.

"The many disabilities under which the slave trade labored inclined the South Sea directors to consider various plans—to contract with other traders to supply the negroes, or to allow trade by license," Sperling explains. "This would lead one fairly naturally to the conclusion that *the slave trade was not profitable* . . . the tendency of the Spanish officials to reduce their value by registering them as *pieza de India* rather than by head, loss of negroes through sickness and finally the competition from interlopers made it a losing game."

Here we are confronted with one of the great ironies of a history, already replete with too many: That the "legal" slave trade, though possessed of a certain dark glamour, was not profitable. And the annual permission ship couldn't legally carry enough trade cargo to cover the loss. Still, the South Sea Company tried to make it work. Four trade ships sent between 1714 and 1718 netted the Company £105,250—no great amount for a trading concern that had been founded on vast golden dreams, but roughly 75 percent of legal profits made over a twenty-five-year period. This left only the "illegal" smuggling of British manufactured goods in slave ships as a reliable source of profit.

Thus, the shadow of corruption falls early across the already shadowy business of the South Sea Company. No doubt the entire system of Anglo-Spanish trade as organized under the *Asiento* would have been renegotiated, more in England's favor—as South Sea grumblers soon demanded. But another Anglo-Spanish war ended both legal and illegal commerce abruptly with a few well-placed cannon shots off Cape Passaro, Sicily, in August 1718.

8.

We now return to Spain, groaning beneath the haphazard administration of her first Bourbon king, Felipe V. Hagridden, melancholic, prone to fits of antic madness alternating with episodes of catatonic lethargy, he had inherited more than his share of Hapsburg afflictions—a worthy successor to his "bewitched" great-uncle, Carlos II. And, like Carlos, he was tenacious: for forty-six years, longer than any other Spanish monarch, Felipe held the throne like a captain clinging to the bridge of a sinking ship.

The Hapsburgs and their cousins, the Bourbons, alternated from one generation to the next between extreme libidinousness—Felipe IV, Carlos's father, had produced at least thirty known bastards—and a kind of sex-phobia, symbolized by Carlos II's uncertain genitalia. Felipe V seemed to combine both impulses in one person: though a devout and morbidly superstitious Catholic, horrified by the thought of adultery, his carnal appetites rose to the level of a sex addiction—which could only be slaked in the flesh of his wife. Married at seventeen to the thirteen-year-old Maria Luisa of Savoy, Felipe became, as one biographer put it, "a passionate slave to lovemaking." Exhausted by her husband's constant physical demands, Maria Luisa produced four children before succumbing to tuberculosis a few years later.

Felipe, "persuaded only with difficulty to forsake his wife's bed the night before she died," acted with apparent indifference afterward, eschewing her funeral for the usual day's hunting. He watched from a distance, astride his horse, as Maria Luisa's catafalque wound its way toward the Escorial Palace, that gloomy pile wherein lies entombed Spain's royal dead. Then he wheeled about without a word and hoofed it back into the woods. Of course, no one can say what grief filled his secret heart that day. But the great eighteenth-century French diarist Saint-Simon reacted with his usual acerbity when told of this incident:

"Princes, are they human?" he asked.

Perhaps not.

Denied the pleasures of the marriage bed by the early death of his wife, and refusing to accept the consolations of a mistress, Felipe suffered from cold sweats, headaches, and nightmares every bit as terrifying as those which had afflicted Carlos II. Soon, he fell into a fit of melancholy and refused to get up in the morning. Clearly, a suitable bride had to be found before the king's sexless condition drove him completely mad. Several candidates emerged and were rejected: a Bavarian princess—too ugly; a Portuguese princess—a known harridan; another Savoyarde—too capricious; a French duchess—too French. (The mood in the Spanish court, forever flip-flopping, had recently turned against France, Spain's erstwhile ally.)

An acceptable candidate finally emerged: twenty-two-year-old Elizabeth Farnese, Princess of Parma. This small but strategic principality, then as now known for its pungent cheeses and other culinary delicacies, lay sandwiched between Tuscany and the Papal States. Elizabeth, the step-daughter and niece of the current duke (her mother had married her deceased husband's brother) had been proposed by Parma's ambassador to Spain, a talented and completely unscrupulous priest-diplomat named Giulio Alberoni. Some said Alberoni suggested this match sotto voce at Maria Luisa's funeral; most considered him too wily for such an ill-timed breach of etiquette—though they otherwise described him as an unprincipled adventurer who would stop at nothing to advance Parma's interests, as long as those interests coincided with his own.

Born in the tiny village of Fiorenzuola d'Arda, the son of an impoverished gardener and a seamstress, as a youth Alberoni had earned a few pennies ringing the bells at the Duomo in Piacanza, the nearest large town. There, he'd been singled out for his vivid personality and precocious intelligence by the pastor and educated at parish expense. Entering Parma's diplomatic corps, he quickly rose in the service of his country. Saint-Simon, fond of scandalous tales, relates the following anecdote: During the War of Spanish Succession, the Duke of Parma sent Alberoni as special envoy to the notoriously rude French soldier, the Duc de Vendome. Alberoni resisted outrage when Vendome, in a typical display of contempt for all priests, defecated and wiped his ass in Alberoni's presence. Alberoni's predecessor, the Bishop of Parma had previously stalked out at this crude, oft-repeated display, resigning his position in a huff. The adroit Alberoni instead knelt and kissed the Duc's poopy posterior, exclaiming "*O culo di angelo!*" This quite literal brownnosing amused the Duc and made Alberoni's name in European diplomatic circles.

Before long, the ex-bellringer found himself hobnobbing with field marshals and kings as Parma's ambassador to Spain. His rapid rise can't be accounted for by natural intelligence alone, or a nicely timed talent for flattery. Alberoni was also an excellent chef, famous for his complicated and delicious pasta dishes. Now he made good use of what has been called his "sausage and pasta diplomacy"—mated with a low-down, Mafiaesque cunning—to seduce allies and enemies alike into supporting the Parmegian candidate for the Queen of Spain. Alberoni's "voluminous correspondence . . . is an incredible catalogue of detailed orders for hams, cheeses, olives and truffles," one biographer wrote. "Delays, or the shipment of less than choice items, brought reproaches that carefully planned friendships at court were at stake."

The statesman-priest-chef Alberoni learned an important lesson in his years as Parma's ambassador: that a well-prepared *Coppa del Cardinale*—the savory pork dish named after him—served with a side of *Agnolini Parma*, a nice green salad, and a decent Lambrusco could work diplomatic miracles.

9.

On September 16, 1714, Felipe V and Elizabeth Farnese, Princess of Parma—henceforth known as Isabela, Queen Consort of Spain—wed by proxy in Parma's cathedral. On Christmas Day, after a refresher ceremony performed by the Patriarch of the Indies, Felipe and his new queen consummated their union in the village of Guadalajara, Spain. In those days, Spanish royal weddings were often celebrated in such out-of-the-way impoverished hamlets, as tradition exempted residents from taxation for a year: marriage in a large city might have bankrupted the state treasury.

Felipe emerged from the bridal chamber the next morning, wobble-legged and satiated, delighted with his lusty, young Italian wife. It was more than love this time, he told a courtier, he was now her "slave for life." Indeed, Isabela soon established herself as the dominant power in Spain. Though she later ran to fat and walked with a limp, one imagines her, in this period as lush and infinitely desirable—looking a little like the earthy Italian actress Claudia Cardinale at twenty-four years old, in Visconti's classic film *Il gattopardo*—that masterful, melancholy evocation of an aristocracy in decline. Initial reports, engineered by Alberoni, had falsely described her as demure and biddable; the opposite was in fact the case: strong-willed and acid-tongued, Isabela soon earned the sobriquet bestowed by British diplomats at Madrid. To them, she was the "Spanish Termagant."

There had been earlier warnings of Isabela's strident personality. She had refused to accept Felipe's marriage proposal until covered with the jewels of her choice—among these a heart shaped necklace composed of 130 perfect pearls, a rosary of massive coral beads and an emerald ring weighing 74 carats. The Spanish "Plate Fleet" of 1715, already loaded down with three years' worth of silver and gold, lingered at Havana weeks into hurricane season, waiting for Isabela's jewels to arrive from far-flung corners of the empire. On July 31, a murderous storm caught them outward bound in the Florida Straits. Scattered by hundred-mile-per hour winds, eleven of the twelve heavily laden galleons foundered on reefs or capsized; 1500 sailors perished.

Two hundred and fifty years later, legendary treasure hunter Kip Wagner located the first wreck site off what is now Vero Beach, Florida—perhaps the *Nuestra Señora de Nieves*, Our Lady of the

Snows. Eventually, he dredged up millions in silver cobs and gold ingots. The Queen's jewels, however, are still buried somewhere in the reefy shallows off Florida's "Treasure Coast."

10.

The weak-willed, sex-addicted Felipe soon relinquished the running of the kingdom to his wife, retiring to bed for increasingly long stretches. His Hapsburgian tendency toward depression gradually metamorphosed into a kind of hysterical anxiety; this now alternated with the catatonia he'd already displayed. He came to rely on Isabela in all matters and couldn't be away from her for more than thirty minutes without suffering a nervous collapse. He moved into the Queen's apartments where both slept in the same bed—an outlandish habit that scandalized the court.

"[Felipe] loves his wife above all things, leaves all affairs to her and never interferes with anything," commented a contemporary observer. "He is very pious and believes he should be damned if he committed any matrimonial infidelity. But for his devotion, he would be a libertine, for he is addicted to women, and for this reason he is so fond of his wife . . . and because he is very easily led, the Queen won't lose sight of him."

The ubiquitous Saint-Simon, on a visit to Spain, writes of being received by the king and queen "in a bed of four and a half feet at most, of crimson damask with four bed posts." The king, dressed in a sleeping cap and his wife's dirty nightgown, lay propped on pillows beside her while she embroidered. State papers lay scattered about, the Queen's yarn balled atop trade agreements and diplomatic correspondence.

Physical charms aside, Isabela came encumbered with a heavy piece of political baggage—carried on her behalf by Alberoni: the recovery of those Spanish territories in Italy stripped and handed off to Austria and Savoy by the Treaty of Utrecht. The children of Felipe's first marriage to Maria Luisa would rule Spain by hereditary right, with Isabela's own children—eventually six in number—reduced to secondary roles. For them, the Spanish throne itself would be forever out of reach.

Isabela's ambitious nature found this certainty unacceptable. Her own father, Odoardo, Duke of Parma and her father/uncle, Francesco, also Duke of Parma, had died with no legitimate offspring; her second uncle the current Duke also seemed unlikely to reproduce before his demise. This would naturally leave her first son Carlos, Infante of Spain as the inheritor of the Duchy. Seized with a kind of desperation, she became obsessed with the idea of obtaining an Italian kingdom for her second son. Urged on by Alberoni, she schemed to reclaim the former Spanish provinces of Sardinia and Sicily, both torn from the "seamless garment" of Spanish possessions by the Allies. Over these "Lost Provinces" her current and future offspring might rule as independent monarchs.

Felipe, deep in a bout of lethargic melancholia and completely dominated by his wife's ambitions, acquiesced to the grand strategy concocted by the pair of aggressive Parmegianos. Alberoni, an energetic logistician as well as a master chef, managed to assemble an invasion force consisting of several hundred vessels bearing 33,000 troops, 8,000 horses, hundreds of cannon and other armaments, under the command of the Marquis of Lede. On June 17, 1717, this armada, said to be the largest in Spanish history, sailed for points unknown—acknowledged by everyone to be the Sicilian coast.

The perilousness inherent in the enterprise now drove the fragile Felipe into one of his increasingly bizarre manic fits. Nightly, during the first few hours of restless sleep, he tore at his cheeks with his fingernails, waking to a pillow soaked in blood. Unknown bodily secretions produced a weird phosphorescent effect: his pajamas and sheets were suffused with an eerie glow that no amount of vigorous laundering could wash away. More than once he flung himself from his bloody, neon bedding, seized a sword and ran around the palace screaming "Murder, murder!" at the top of his lungs—until subdued by specially appointed guards.

Meanwhile, Spanish troops occupied both Sardinia and Sicily unopposed. Suddenly it seemed that a reinvigorated Spanish empire loomed—or its consequence, a new bloody pan-European war.

11.

On August 11, 1718, in the choppy wine-dark seas off Cape Passaro, Sicily, the Spanish and British fleets encountered each other in a naval battle that can only be called decisive. Buoyed by the spirit of optimism emanating in ripples from the new Queen, Alberoni— now promoted Spain's First Minister—had already sent a letter warning the British to prepare for a humiliating defeat. Such letters are, in hindsight, perhaps better not sent.

Admiral Sir George Byng, commander of the British fleet, was one of those supremely confident professional military men who appear again and again throughout Britain's vigorous eighteenth century. The son of a bankrupt country squire, he had been, as he put it "raised in the King's service," entering the navy as a "King's Letter Boy"—that is, on a sort of naval scholarship—at the age of fourteen. Over the following decades, rising through the ranks, he fought pirates off the Malabar Coast, served in North Africa, the West Indies, the Baltic, and with distinction during the War of Spanish Succession. Under the command of the euphoniously named Admiral Sir Clowdesley Shovell, he participated in the defeat of the French fleet at Vigo Bay in 1702. For his services thwarting a Spanish-backed attempt to place the Stuart pretender James on the throne of Great

Britain, he was knighted and given "a diamond ring of great value" by King George I, who succeeded Queen Anne in 1714.

Now, at Cape Passaro, the Spanish, confident of victory, fired the first shots—or so the British later claimed. And in the engagement that followed, they put the lie to Spanish ambitions: "Sir, We have taken and destroyed all the Spanish ships and vessels which were upon the coast," read a typically terse dispatch from Captain George Walton, one of Byng's sub-commanders. These few words concealed a multitude of seaborne horrors: witheringly accurate British cannon fire; nearly six thousand Spanish sailors and marines killed, captured, or drowned; dozens of Spanish warships set on fire and sunk or, in a few cases, deliberately run aground by their despairing captains.

The conflict known as the War of the Quadruple Alliance had begun. It wouldn't last long, but does presage some of the geopolitics that lead to the War of Jenkins' Ear. Here's the war in brief outline: Spanish and Allied forces—this time France, Great Britain, the Netherlands, and Austria united against Spain—engaged at sea and on battlefields in both the old world and the new. Britain and France invaded Spain. Isabela, wearing a dashing blue and silver uniform custom made in Paris and sporting two large pistols, put herself at the head of a Spanish regiment at the front. Meanwhile, Spain invaded Scotland in support of the Jacobite rising only to be defeated at the Battle of Glen Shiel in 1719; the French captured Pensacola, Florida, preempting a planned Spanish invasion of South Carolina. In all these arenas Spanish arms met with failure—but none so devastating as the initial defeat at Cape Passaro, where the British Navy showed itself to be the most potent military force in the world. In other words, Alberoni and Queen Isabela's grand strategies were utterly thwarted for the moment.

"Human schemes unaided by Divine Providence are of little use," Alberoni shrugs wistfully in his *Memoires*. "The plans I devised—had but one of them been successful—would have been enough to upset the enemy's designs."

He died many years later in Piacenza at age eighty-eight, a cardinal of the Catholic Church, vastly wealthy, the honored founder of a seminary for poor boys which still bears his names. Admired for his audacity and clever stratagems by Voltaire and Frederick the Great, among others, Alberoni remains an exemplar of the adage that a scoundrel who lives long enough becomes respectable, or, in his case, an elder statesmen.

As with many eighteenth-century conflicts, when the War of the Quadruple Alliance ended in 1720 and the cannons fell silent, not much had changed. Only the South Sea Company had suffered any really serious losses—and these to the bottom line. Their profits depended on peaceful trade with Spain. Just a few years before, they had established their factories in the Spanish-American colonies at great expense. After the Battle of Cape Passaro, these factories were seized by Spain, along with all Company goods and all ships flying the Union Jack in Spanish harbors. Up to that point, the Company had made a good faith effort to turn a profit from the "legitimate" slave trade and the infrequent permission ships bearing the allowable tonnage of trade goods to Spanish-America.

The war finished what historians, fond of such labels, define as the "first period" of the *Asiento*, 1715–1718. Losses for the South Sea Company would grow to the hundreds of thousands of pounds by the time peace returned with the Treaty of the Hague in 1720. According to its terms, Felipe V and Queen Isabela, expansionist dreams defeated, withdrew Spanish troops from both Sardinia and Sicily—later swapped by Austria and Savoy—and abandoned for the time being any claims to her former possessions on Italian peninsula; Felipe dismissed Alberoni from his service—a prerequisite demanded by the victors who feared the cardinal's political acumen—and reaffirmed Spain's pledge to abandon any claims on the French throne, as already specified in the Treaty of Utrecht; French and British armies withdrew from Northern Spain; Pensacola was returned a smoking ruin to Spain by the French.

For Spain and her allies, the European balance of power had moved only slightly, like a glacier sliding inch by inch to the sea. For the South Sea Company—as shall be seen—the shift was seismic.

12.

Sometime in late 1719, the directors of the South Sea Company looked across the English Channel to France and their hearts filled with both envy and alarm: a roguish Scottish speculator, gambler, duelist, and financial maverick named John Law had formed, in conjunction with the French government, a trading company similar to the South Sea. Its goal was to both alleviate the national debt and develop France's newly acquired territory in Louisiana.

In August 1717, acting on authority granted him by Philippe d'Orleans, the pleasure-loving Regent of France, Law organized the Mississippi Company, another public-private partnership along the lines of England's South Sea Company, and like that speculative entity, based on a chimera: against the immeasurable riches sure to accrue to France from the as yet unfounded Louisiana colony, Law issued stock at 500 livres per share. He hoped to raise a million livres on the initial offering, all of which would be spent at his discretion on the establishment of a permanent French settlement in the Mississippi Valley. This settlement would repay the Mississippi Company's stockholders by becoming a prosperous colony and thus drive up share prices. The French nation immediately went speculation mad, never mind that *la Louisiane* remained a swampy, hurricane-prone, inhospitable place full of mosquitoes and Indian tribes reluctant to accept the benefits of French civilization. The value of Law's Mississippi stock rose a thousand percent in a period of months; the world's first true financial bubble was born. Law had meanwhile taken complete control of the French economy.

"You must henceforth consider Law as the First Minister," wrote Lord Stair, the British ambassador in Paris, "whose daily discourse is, that he will raise France to a greater height than ever she was, upon the ruin of England." If Law and the French could make so much money by selling stock which supposedly derived its value from as yet unrealized profits sourced in the wilderness of Louisiana, why couldn't the South Sea company make the same kind of money off their own less-than-lucrative trade with the Spanish colonies—which surely, someday soon *must* turn a profit?

"It must have been clear to the directors," Sperling comments, "that financial manipulations were less problematic, less trouble and more profitable than the *Asiento* trade. It is small wonder that they concentrated on these activities when their trade was closed down by war in 1718."

The shady stockjobbers involved with the foundation of Harley's South Sea Company decided to follow Law's example and expand the business of the Company into a purely financial arena. The original speculators—Blunt, Sawbridge, Caswall, and Turner—now expanded their cabal to include the Company treasurer, Robert Knight, and government figures like James Craggs, the postmaster general, and his son James Craggs the Younger, of the Foreign Office. But Blunt's greatest coup was convincing John Aislabie, the new chancellor of the Exchequer to join their scheme. "When one considers the career and characters of Blunt, Sawbridge, and Caswell," Sperling asserts, "the union with Aislabie and Craggs meant the project was in really dangerous hands."

Nor, in all likelihood, would their manipulations be restrained by Parliament. The Tory ruling party had been swept out of power with the death of the previous monarch, Queen Anne. Harley had been forced into retirement after a stay in the Tower upon the accession of the Whig-supported German king from Hanover—George I. The next few decades would belong to the Whigs and their able minister, Robert Walpole. A massive figure both physically and politically, brash, rude, and powerful, Walpole weighed by some estimates, more than twenty stone, which is to say more than three hundred pounds. He was also—so his enemies charged—personally corrupt.

The apotheosis of the stockjobbers had now arrived. Hardly a voice was raised against the wave of ruinous speculation that would soon inundate England.

13.

"It was while Law's plan was at its greatest height of popularity, while people were crowding in thousands to the Rue Quincampoix and ruining themselves with frantic eagerness, that the South Sea directors laid before Parliament their famous plan for paying off the national debt."

So begins Charles Mackay's account of the financial disaster that became known as the South Sea Bubble, in his seminal volume *Extraordinary Popular Delusions and the Madness of Crowds*, one of the first studies of crowd behavior and mass hysteria, published in 1841. (Among skeptical essays on fortune tellers, magnetizers, witch hunters, alchemists, and other quacks, Mackay pauses to examine the emergence and spread of urban slang, which he sees as "one of the popular follies of great cities." One expression, "What a shocking bad hat!" made the rounds of London society circa 1820 before fading out a decade or so later. Like many other slangy refrains, its original meaning—that the person at whom it was aimed wore a really awful hat—expanded over time. Eventually the phrase came to be used as a general exclamation of surprise or derision in any number of circumstances. In the opinion of this writer, it begs for a revival!)

Mackay, however, reserves his greatest scorn for the perpetrators and victims of the South Sea Bubble, which burst over England in 1720, as he put it, "when knavery gathered a rich harvest from cupidity . . . and both suffered when the day of reckoning came."

John Blunt, who "had been following Law's activities with particular interest" emerges as the chief culprit of the debacle. Blunt possessed all of Law's slipperiness, with none of that Scotsman's charm or brilliance. A Baptist, fond of quoting Scripture and urging others to live the virtuous life he failed to live himself, he came from artisan stock: his father had been a shoemaker in Rochester. Blunt began his professional life as a public letter writer in London's Birkin Lane, where he wrote letters for the illiterate for a few shillings and performed minor legal services. Extremely thrifty, he managed to save enough from his penny-ante business to set himself up as a moneylender, for which activity he charged usurious rates. This blatant loansharking enabled Blunt to build up enough of a fortune to indulge his primary passion—the creation of joint stock companies, that is corporations of like-minded investors who hoped to profit off a variety of business or improvement schemes.

Blunt's two major enterprises in pre–South Sea days (a linen cloth manufacturer and a wacky sort of aqueduct on wheels intended to provide fresh water to London) ended in losses for all stockholders involved except one, Blunt himself. He had escaped with a small fortune from both failed enterprises, and with these failures had somehow established a reputation as a businessman of great ability.

A contemporary portrait of Blunt shows a vigorous man, of forty or so, dressed in a conservatively styled but expensive looking coat, his silver-curled periwig artfully arranged. But it is his expression—confident, smug—that strikes the viewer.

"Burly and overbearing, glib, ingenious and determined to get on," writes one biographer, Blunt was "well fitted to make his way in the business jungle. . . . In the techniques of his profession, he was unequaled, and his coarse character contained just the trace of titanism which was to carry him for a moment or two to the summit of politics and finance." Or, in the words of another: "Blunt was a short, plump, unscrupulous little man who loved the feel and manipulation of money." Both these descriptions fail to include the fierce confidence caught by the portraitist; an attitude without which any eighteenth-century "Projector" (speculator) could not prosper.

Blunt's confidence at last earned him a place among the directors of the South Sea Company, which in turn led to an upwardly mobile match with the daughter of a former governor of Bengal. His new wife, an awkward woman named Susannah Cradock, had already outlived two husbands. Uncomfortable at the levees and parties her husband's financial prominence would soon necessitate, she eagerly sought the background as he rose through glittering layers of society to a baronetcy.

14.

In direct emulation of Law's Mississippi scheme then at the height of its maniacal popularity in France, Blunt proposed that the South Sea Company absorb the entire national debt of Great Britain, which amounted to £51,300,000. This sum mostly consisted of "terminable annuities," money lent to the state by private citizens in return for which they would receive a fixed yearly income for life. Blunt explained matters thusly to the astonished South Sea board: The South Sea Company would receive interest at 5 percent for ten years on money they loaned to cover the debt, which would thereafter be reduced to 4 percent. The government could only benefit from this arrangement, Blunt asserted, as the Company would additionally pay £3,500,000 outright for the privilege of lifting the debt off the nation's shoulders. But what would the Company get out of the arrangement? the directors asked.

"The advantages hoped for by the Company were much greater though not equally obvious," answers the editors of the *Britannica*'s venerable 11th Edition.

> The aim of the Directors was to persuade the annuitants of the state to exchange their annuities for South Sea stock. The stock would be issued at a high premium and thus a large amount of annuities would be purchased and extinguished by the issue of a comparatively small amount of stock.

The scheme as perfected by Blunt was poorly understood by the Whig ministers who for the moment held the reins of government: the "Two Earls" Lords Sunderland and Stanhope. The aloof Sunderland, an unfortunate choice for First Lord of the Treasury, disdained all financial matters as beneath his dignity. He had already passed on most of his duties to the decidedly unaristocratic John Aislabie, who had been a merchant associated with the Baltic trade (herring, timber, salt, and other unexciting commodities) and whom he had made chancellor of the Exchequer based on an ability to sell quantities of smoked fish to the English public.

Aislabie at first didn't quite grasp Blunt's purpose when the speculator presented his new South Sea scheme at a private meeting in January 1720. Aislabie was, asserts a historian of the Bubble, "a sly . . . basically stupid Yorkshireman." But after Blunt slowly explained the details, Aislabie, "startled" by its magnitude, suggested a smart adjustment: the Company would only subsume that portion of government debt owed to private investors, bringing the amount covered down to about £30,000,000. Adjustment made, Aislabie, satisfied, offered his critical support.

Par value of South Sea Company stock now stood at £100 per share. Should Parliament agree to the debt conversion Blunt's plan stipulated, it must also agree to allow for the creation of an equal amount of new stock, which the Company could then sell to the annuitants and other members of the general public. Word of Blunt's plan leaked out across the coffee houses of Exchange Alley and South Sea Stock quickly rose to £128. It was a nice bump but not substantial enough for Blunt's purposes. Financial historian and journalist Virginia Cowles explains it best:

> Blunt saw a chance for millions of pounds of profit, not only for the Company, but for private individuals as well . . . if Parliament agreed to the taking over of the national debt it would authorize the Company to strike £100 of new stock for every £100 of debt converted. . . . But suppose that the market price rose to £300. If an individual holding £1,200 of Government securities wanted to convert them to South Sea stock, the Company would be allowed to issue 12 new shares at £100 each. But it would only have to give the creditor four of those shares if the market price was £300. It would then have 8 surplus shares for sale, which would bring it a profit of £2,400.

The success of this scheme depended on the continual inflation of South Sea stock in a limitless bull market—and Parliament's approval.

Blunt had meanwhile received regular news from France regarding Law's publicity campaigns to artificially boost the value of

Mississippi stock—troupes of friendly dancing Indians imported from America; the forced public marriages of convicts and prostitutes to be transported for the peopling of Louisiana; extravagantly illustrated real estate brochures extolling the virtues of bayou living. Similar shenanigans, he believed, wouldn't work in England, the English being naturally less credulous and more obstinate than the French. Blunt now decided on a simple, straight-forward Anglo-Saxon tactic: bribery. And he dreamed up a bold, dastardly plan to bribe with cash or stock every member of Parliament who might be bribable. This included, as it turned out, most of that august body and the king's ministers. (One notable exception was Lord Stanhope, notorious for his incorruptibility in a corruptible age. Stanhope had recently turned down a substantial payment of £40,000 offered by the French minister Dubois for signing a treaty he was going to sign anyway. Dubois found himself utterly baffled by the earl's integrity, and even though he'd secured Stanhope's signature for free, regarded his diplomatic mission a failure.)

At Aislabie's suggestion, Blunt kicked off his bribery campaign with Mr. James Craggs, a man of humble origins, called the Elder, to distinguish himself from his son, James Craggs the Younger. Blunt's first interview with Craggs Sr. proved instantly successful. He easily recruited the postmaster, thus adding two to his conspiracy to bribe Parliament, for the son would always follow the father's lead. Moving in aristocratic circles not open to his father, however, Craggs the Younger brought valuable insight unavailable to the older men: the king's German mistresses must also be bribed, he insisted, their cooperation essential to securing the cooperation of the king, himself. He suggested £10,000 each in South Sea stock as a comfortable amount.

The mistresses—Madame Schulenburg, later Duchess of Kendall and Baroness van Kielmansegge—were dubbed the "Maypole" and the "Elephant" respectively by a contemptuous English public and often heckled when they took their carriages through the streets of London. As their unflattering nicknames infer, one was tall and gangly, the other obese, neither attractive: "The lower orders expect the King to have mistresses," observed a wag, "but not ugly ones." Ugly or not, because they had hold of the king's ear and other parts of his anatomy, they possessed a kind of power beyond that wielded by mere cabinet ministers.

Gifts of stock offered and received (including smaller contributions to Madame Kielmansegge's nieces), it now only remained to get on with the bribing of Parliament itself.

15.

Blunt and Craggs divided the nation's legislative body between them and went to work. More than a hundred MPs secretly accepted the indemnities offered; the king himself, already made honorary governor of the Company had previously received a substantial sum for his patronage. Now, under the influence of his mistresses, he gave his tacit approval as a new South Sea Bill, authorizing the conversion of government debt, rumbled through Parliament. In November 1719, the king had given a speech to the assembled members regarding the debt issue, pointing toward his acquiescence. Because the Hanoverian monarch could not speak English, it had been read out by a herald.

"We must desire you to turn your thoughts to all proper means of lessening the debts of the nation . . ." the herald began, a speech both written and delivered by others as the king sat by, bored.

At last, on January 22, 1720, Chancellor Aislabie proposed the South Sea Company's scheme to convert £30,000,000 into stock to a legislature that had been thoroughly bribed to overlook any deficiencies in the idea. Having said his piece, Aislabie sat down to silence.

"Our great men lookt as if thunderstruck, and one of them in particular turned as pale as my cravate," observed Thomas Broderick, MP, present on that day. The House of Commons had apparently been thrown into a kind of existential shock. After a quarter of an hour's muttering, according to Broderick, a heated debate ensued, pitting Tory against Whig, with much gesticulating and raised voices. It was all for show; the bribes had done their work: in the end, the House of Commons passed the South Sea Act by 172 votes to 55 on March 23, 1720.

The House of Lords, which received the Act for debate on April 7, gave it a far cooler welcome. Lord North, observed that it was "calculated for the enriching of a few and the impoverishment of a great many; and not only made for, but countenanced and authorized the fraudulent and pernicious practice of stockjobbing, which produced irreparable mischief in diverting the genius of the people from trade and industry." The rakish, unstable Philip, Duke of Wharton, from experience an expert in moral turpitude (he had recently seduced Walpole's teenage sister) called the South Sea Company "dangerous bait, which might decoy many unwary people to their ruin and allure them by a false prospect of gain to part with what they had got by their labour and industry to purchase imaginary riches."

Such were the objection of aristocrats—though none strenuous enough to delay passage. Votes had been bought, even in the upper house, even among the most illustrious and oldest names in England. Yes, Walpole had stood against the bill in the House, but with fingers crossed behind his back: he was a personal friend of the king's mistress, Madame Schulenberg, who had herself been among the first bribed. And Walpole, himself—never above an emolument—had been greased with under-the-table gifts of South Sea Stock.

Few would remember the objections of the lords, which in retrospect ring out like a prophecy, as the South Sea Bubble rose, glittering, iridescent, over the crowded coffeehouses of Exchange Alley, over the murky, refuse-strewn Thames.

16.

In England in March 1720, everyone, even those who should have known better remained dazzled by the prospects of Law's unearned millions. This even though the Mississippi Bubble had already burst, sending the French nation into financial ruin and Law into exile. Almost everyone involved with the South Sea scheme failed to see the coming apocalypse, the reflection of their fate in the Mississippi Company's dizzying sudden decline. Even Craggs the Younger, who had been informed of the particulars of the Mississippi disaster by Lord Stair, refused to believe such a thing could happen in England. The South Sea Act had just been bought and paid for and passed. The nation held its breath. And the great swindle began.

Though the government had stipulated that the Company might manufacture only one share of stock per every £100 of privatized debt, Blunt offered twenty thousand "unconverted" shares on April 20, 1720. This offering, technically illegal, went unchallenged by Parliament and generally unexamined in the London press. Everyone wanted a piece of South Sea action and the stock sold out in a single afternoon. Blunt somehow managed to oversell by two-and-a-half thousand shares, claiming that the tumult at South Sea House, where the shares were offered, had prevented the Company's two recording clerks, set up at opposite ends of the main gallery, from communicating with each other. But the same "accidental" overselling occurred at the next stock offering, also illegal, with an additional five thousand shares oversubscribed. Again, no one complained; no legal actions were contemplated.

The buying and selling of stock quickly became a national mania. In just a few weeks England's first stock market boom had taken hold and instantly began to exhibit Mississippi-style excesses.

"Sensible men beheld the extraordinary infatuation of the people with sorrow and alarm," Mackay writes. "England presented a singular spectacle. The public mind was in a state of unwholesome fermentation. Men were no longer satisfied with the slow but sure profits of a cautious industry. The hope of boundless wealth for the morrow made them heedless and extravagant." Though there were still "some both in and out of Parliament who foresaw clearly the ruin that was impending. Mr. Walpole did not cease his gloomy forebodings."

However, these forebodings did not prevent Walpole and others from continuing to invest heavily in South Sea stock. Even ladies raced to join the stockjobbing game—unheard of before the boom, when the coffeehouses had been off-limits to anyone wearing a petticoat. Exchange Alley had lately come to resemble a fashionable brothel, frequented by ladies of quality but also by actresses and whores, as described by a waggish newspaper poet of the day:

> *Our greatest ladies hither come*
> *And ply in chariots daily;*
> *Oft pawn their jewels for a sum*
> *To venture in the Alley.*
> *Young harlots too from Drury Lane*
> *Approach the Change in coaches*
> *To fool away the gold they gain*
> *By their impure debauches.*

Stockjobbing fever soon spread from aristocrats and *demimondaines* to just about everyone else, as catchable as smallpox or gin-induced alcoholism, two other scourges of eighteenth-century London. Warned an editorialist of the popular *Weekly Journal* on March 26, 1720:

'Tis said that abundance of our country gentlemen and rich farmers are upon the roads from several parts of the Kingdom, all expecting no less than to ride down again every man in his coach and six; but if a friend's advice is worth anything, let them take care, for though there are some prizes, they may find many more blanks, and they may happen to lose all that in an hour in Exchange Alley, which the industry and care of their ancestors has been scraping together for some ages.

In an era addicted to gambling, when the gentry wagered and lost thousands nightly at London's gaming tables, the buying and selling of stock had become just another addiction. According to the law, joint stock companies required royal permission in the form of a charter to open their doors to trade. Now, as April warmed to May, dozens of new companies, modeling themselves on the South Sea, offered their stock to speculators, without the requisite charter. These "Bubble Companies," touted a variety of moneymaking ventures, a few legitimate, most laughable, some bizarre, all illegal. Selected from a list of eighty-six such companies provided by Mackay, we have the following:

For importing a large number of jackasses from Spain to improve the breed of British Mules.

For building ships against pirates.

For insuring all masters and mistresses against the losses they may sustain by servants.

For a wheel of perpetual motion. Capital one million.

For an immediate expeditious and cleanly manner of emptying necessary houses throughout England at a cost of L2,000,000.

For insuring marriage against divorce.

For trading in hair.

For effectively settling the islands of Blanco and Sal Tartagus.

For improving malt liquors. Capital, four millions.

For insuring horses.

For the transmutation of quicksilver (mercury) into a malleable fine metal.

Though, arguably, some fine investment opportunities might be found on the partial list above—who wouldn't for example, want to insure marriage against divorce or purchase top-quality human hair?—most ventured into the territory of fraud: a London printer offered stock in a company "for carrying on an undertaking of Great Advantage but no one knows what it is." He sold a thousand shares of this phantom company for two pounds each on the first day. That night he wisely packed up and decamped for the Continent.

These and similar enterprises inspired another London printer to devise a pack of satirical Bubble Playing Cards, each card depicting an absurd company not so different from the real thing: one card touted the manufacture of "Puckle's Machine Gun," which could discharge both round and square cannonballs—the former designed to destroy Christians, the latter Turks; another "for an engine to move the South Sea House to Moorgate"; yet another "for the melting down of sawdust chips and casting them into clean deal boards, without cracks or knots."

A full set of these cards still exists in the British Museum; copies may be had in the museum shop. Play them at your own risk.

17.

The bubble inflated daily through the spring and summer of 1720. With the South Sea Company leading the way: share price rose to £400 by early May, then to £550 by the end of the month. June saw a rise to £890; in July it touched £1000. Still, the avaricious Blunt who had lately become—after the manner of Law in Paris—one of the most sought-after figures in London society, resented the illegal Bubble Companies. He believed they siphoned investors' money that would otherwise go to the South Sea. In March, he had persuaded Parliament to open an investigation into them. Results became known on June 11: the illegal Bubble Companies would be suppressed—though investors couldn't quite believe this would happen. Wasn't everyone happily making money?

The weather in London in July grew miserably hot. No one paid any attention to the rioting that had broken out in France. Sweating in his expensive velvets, Blunt took his wife and family on vacation to the spa at Tunbridge Wells. Publicly he exuded his usual confidence in the limitless potential of South Sea stock; privately he gave the bubble till November, around Guy Fawkes Day. The prudent should "withdraw" by then.

Like a soldier who knows he will be killed in the next battle and whose sad presentiment comes true, the directors of the Company also felt it coming. Members of the Company's "inner circle" agreed with Blunt; meanwhile the national debt of England, supposedly converted by the Company's stock, hadn't been converted at all. As Law had printed increasingly worthless paper money to cover the French debt, the Company had manufactured more stock and offered credit to those who wished to purchase more—against the value of the stock to be purchased. Thousands jumped at this opportunity. It was a financial Ouroboros, a paper snake eating its own tail. Blunt made fifty thousand more shares available at £1000 per share, bumping share price another £50—though everyone had expected a larger boost from the extravagant offering. Suddenly, even the smallest investor could hear the bubble creaking as it slid imperceptibly earthward.

Blunt had left London for Tunbridge Wells a wealthy man, admired by all and no longer a commoner—the king, mightily pleased by his profit of £86,000 had knighted him before departing for Hanover. The pinprick that exploded the bubble came inadvertently from Blunt himself: in mid-August, Parliament at last took action against the multitude of Bubble Companies declared illegal in June at Blunt's insistence and shut them down. Those investors who had bought shares in these companies lost everything they had invested. Now, many set about selling South Sea shares to cover their losses, which immediately launched a frenzy of panic selling.

"Various are the conjectures why the South Sea directors have suffered the cloud to break so early," wrote MP Thomas Broderick, who would eventually demand a parliamentary investigation into the affair. "I made no doubt but they would do so when they found it to their advantage. They have stretched credit so far beyond what it would bear, that specie proves insufficient to support it. Their most considerable men have drawn out, securing themselves by the losses of the deluded, thoughtless numbers, whose understandings have been overruled by avarice and the hope of making mountains out of molehills. The consternation is inexpressible—rage beyond description, and the case altogether so desperate, that I do not see any plan or scheme so much as thought of for averting the blow."

On August 17, South Sea share price stood at £1000; a month later share price had fallen to £190. Financial disaster had come to England. The resulting crash, easily as dire as the New York Stock

Market Crash of 1929 or the US Housing Bubble Crisis of 2008, obtained the same results: mass bankruptcies, social unrest, suicides.

Craggs the Elder took an overdose of opium in the Tower, where he'd been imprisoned pending investigation for bribery and financial irregularities—though this desperate act perhaps had more to do with the death of his beloved son from smallpox a few weeks earlier. Blunt and the other directors who had cynically given the bubble till November had clearly miscalculated. He now returned to London from Tunbridge Wells in haste, at the urgent request of the South Sea board. Stepping out of his new carriage into the unusually bitter heat of August, he protested sourly that "he did not know but it might have cost him his life to have left off drinking the waters so abruptly; and that he had rather given £10,000 than to have come up to town."

In the end, it would cost him—and England—much, much more than ten thousand pounds.

18.

When the dust had settled, those ruined by the South Sea Bubble cried out for revenge. Parliment divided itself in two general factions. The first, led by Walpole proposed a government bailout of the South Sea Company, of which the king was governor and his mistresses major shareholders. The second fumed and vented, calling the South Sea directors "plunderers of the nation" and "parricides of their country." These advocated jail time and even execution for the perpetrators. The astute Walpole, aware that many in Parliament had benefited from South Sea speculations, including himself, sought a middle course: in this, he acted—so said the pamphleteers—as a "skreen" between the guilty and the justice they deserved, earning himself the unenviable title of "Skreenmaster General." The guilty they inferred, hid themselves behind his massive bulk.

Walpole nevertheless steered the nation away from revolution and riot and managed to preserve the status quo. The government and king must be maintained despite all the bankruptcies and fraud. A percentage of South Sea Company debts would be paid from the nation's general fund, while major perpetrators would be punished though the confiscation of their estates and fortunes. The directors of the South Sea Company were on the whole harshly treated. Mandates handed down by a parliamentary "secret committee" chaired by Broderick, resulted in their sacking and the collection of over two million pounds in fines. Most of them were left with enough to live on, squeaking out meager allowances, depending on degree of culpability.

Blunt was left with £1000 and ten times that amount of personal disgrace, but escaped a threatened term in prison. He retired to Bath in comfort, living off an allowance provided by his son, one of those few who had made a tidy sum in the Bubble. Edward Gibbon, grandfather of the author of *Decline and Fall of the Roman Empire*, a prominent South Sea board member, was allowed £10,000 out of a personal fortune of over £100,000:

"On these ruins," commented the historian in his memoirs, "with the skill and credit, of which Parliament had not been able to despoil him, my grandfather at a mature age erected the edifice of a new fortune."

In other words, through ingenuity or connections, the rich generally manage to avoid incarceration and stay rich. The same can be said of those reckless speculators behind the US Housing Bubble Crisis of 2008.

Alexander Pope wrote the South Sea Bubble's epitaph:

At length corruption, like a general flood
Did deluge all, and avarice creeping on
Spread like a low-born mist and hid the sun.

Statesmen and patriots plied alike these stocks,
Peeress and butler shared alike the box,
And judges jobbed and bishops bit the town,
And mighty dukes packed cards for half-a-crown—
Britain lay sunk in lucre's sordid charms.

Walpole, who had sold his South Sea stock at the exact right moment, emerged from the disaster with his fortune intact and unexamined, and his political power solidified. He became "First Minister" in April 1722 and is considered by historians as England's first true Prime Minister—a post he held for the next twenty years, a period of Whig ascendancy, increasing prosperity, and no major wars. England was a trading nation and trade was good. Why should the nation not recover robustly from a brief, sharp financial escapade that had ended badly?

The South Sea Company, with the aid of Walpole, escaped dissolution. With new directors and a renewed mission, it resumed its operations under the *Asiento de Negros* for which it had been designed—that is, trading slaves to the Spanish American colonies, augmented by the proceeds of the annual ships. Unfortunately, with this formula, as everyone knew, no money could be made. The slave trade and the meager profits off a single cargo-load of manufactured goods could not long sustain the shareholders' expectations of profits after the bubble burst.

A new era of smuggling—winked at by the government and Company alike—on a scale never before imagined, had begun.

John Blunt (left) South Sea Bubble (right)

THREE

The Road to Jenkins' Ear

FROM THE 13TH SIEGE OF GIBRALTAR TO WALPOLE'S LAMENT,
1727–1739

1.

On January 1, 1727, the Marquis of Pozobueno, Spanish Ambassador to the Court of St. James, delivered a strongly worded diplomatic message to the Duke of Newcastle, Secretary of State for the Southern Department, in London. This particular diplomatic message, however, would prove anything but diplomatic. Its operative clause boiled down to a single impossible Spanish ultimatum, would lead to yet another costly and inconclusive Anglo-Spanish War, this one unimaginatively dubbed the Anglo-Spanish War of 1727–1729. His Catholic Majesty, King Felipe V of Spain demanded the immediate return of Gibraltar, which had been seized by a daring Anglo-Dutch naval operation in 1704, during the War of Spanish Succession. Never mind that Britain's possession of the famous "Rock" had been subsequently confirmed in Article X of the Treaty of Utrecht, signed by King Felipe himself.

The marquis spoke for the king (and for Queen Isabela, Spain's actual ruler, the king just then suffering from one of his manic-depressive episodes). The loss of Gibraltar had been experienced by Their Catholic Majesties as a painful amputation. It was as if a big toe had been lopped off the Mediterranean foot of Spain. In King Felipe's opinion, Britain had effectively nullified Article X by admitting into Gibraltar "the Jews and Moors, contrary to our Holy Religion," which the Article specifically forbade. More, Britain had allowed into Spain "contrabands, which are carried on to the prejudice of his Majesty's revenues." Here, Pozobueno's message identified two powerful motivations for war, close to the heart of every Spaniard: religion and gold.

At the conclusion of the *Reconquista* in 1492, Spain had forcibly expelled its Jewish and Moorish populations from the Iberian Peninsula. The last of them left from Gibraltar for North Africa that notable year. Spain's Holy Soil had long been purified of these twin scourges; she would not now suffer their return under British auspices. And, as usual with the British, smuggling had become the major occupation of her traders in Gibraltar. The years between 1704 and 1727 had seen a glut of British manufactured goods weaseled around the neck of the isthmus into Spain in exchange for gold and raw materials.

Pozobueno's message was in effect a declaration of war. To Spain, Gibraltar and smuggling were the chief causes, but other issues lurked in the background, having to do with the European balance of power so precious to the eighteenth-century strategic mind.

Spain had once again made common cause with Austria, her old Hapsburg ally, this union sealed by the Treaty of Vienna in

1725. In the terms of this treaty lurked Spain's recognition of the controversial "Pragmatic Sanction" which would allow the Austrian Emperor Charles's daughter Maria-Theresa to inherit the throne and the Imperial title. Spain also recognized the new Austrian "Ostend Company" and gave it leave to trade with her American colonies. Britain had fought bitterly for these trading privileges, obtained by the South Sea Company after great difficulty and the blood of Malplaquet. Spain's bequest of them to an upstart Austrian trading concern could not pass without bloodshed.

Also, reportedly, a secret treaty existed, signed by Felipe and Charles, which yoked their kingdoms in an aggressive war against the rest of Europe. Their united armies would seize Alsace, Roussilon, and Navarre from France, and Gibraltar and Menorca from Britain. The secret treaty has never been located. "Secrecy in history" is a problematic thing, lying as it does halfway between fact and conspiracy. Some historians deny, others assert the existence of this shadowy document. But its existence was widely believed at the time by British diplomats and King George himself, and thus has historic merit if only for how belief in its existence motivated these key players. Thus, anxieties regarding a newly revitalized and antagonistic Spain drove King George to sign a counter-agreement, the Treaty of Hanover with France and Prussia.

It seemed the stage had been set for yet another pan-European conflict, with England and Spain on opposite sides of the chess board once again—the third time in twenty years. The lessons of Malplaquet would have to be learned all over again.

2.

For Britain, the new war with Spain would be fought on two fronts: in the West Indies and at Gibraltar. The Rock would soon undergo what is now identified as its 13th Siege. Fighting began on February 22, 1727 with an exchange of cannon-fire between Spanish forces, led by the impetuous Count de Las Torres de Alcorrín at the head of a besieging army of 18,000 men against Gibraltar's garrison of 1,500, later reinforced by sea to 5,500. When the siege began, both the Governor of Gibraltar, Lord Portmere, and the Lieutenant Governor, Colonel Clayton were in England taking the waters, leaving command to Colonel Richard Kane, lieutenant governor of Menorca, then in Gibraltar on temporary assignment.

From the beginning, the 13th Siege was a quixotic undertaking on the part of Spain. Felipe V had been warned by his senior military advisors of the impossibility of taking the nearly impregnable rock without an overwhelming naval force supporting a massive land assault. But the Spanish Navy, destroyed at the Battle of Cape Passaro in 1718, had not yet been rebuilt. The king's advisors, the Marquis de Villadarias and a battle-hardened Flemish military engineer, the Marquis Verboom both offered carefully considered professional advice: A siege of Gibraltar, under the present circumstances, would fail. But the fiery Las Torres insisted that he could in six weeks deliver Spain from this "noxious settlement of foreigners and heretics," and called into question the patriotism and courage of anyone who disagreed with him. As is often the case, bombastic overheated rhetoric prevailed over common sense. Of course, Las Torres was short on details; no doubt soldierly *elan* and God's status as a Spanish Catholic would win the day.

The count mustered an army of thirty infantry battalions and six squadrons of cavalry; his artillery included seventy-two mortars and ninety-two cannons, along with several big siege guns brought from Cádiz. His army, though nominally Spanish, consisted mostly of foreign mercenaries whose nationalities mirrored Spain's former European possessions and her revitalized relationship with Austria: three battalions of Walloons (Flemish-speaking Belgians); three battalions of French-speaking Belgians; four battalions of Irish Jacobites (Irish Catholic supporters of the Stuart pretender to the English throne); two Savoyard battalions; two Neapolitan, one Swiss, one Corsican, and one Sicilian. A truly polyglot mixture that only presaged a series of disastrous communications breakdowns.

Serving as commander of the Irish Jacobites and as Las Torres's *aide-de-camp* was the scandalous Philip, Duke of Wharton—the English peer who had seduced Walpole's sister. Despite his own good advice, he had been ruined by reckless speculation during the South Sea Bubble and, pursued by his creditors, had turned against King George and fled the country to fight for Spain. Brilliant, dissolute, when sober a canny politician and eloquent pamphleteer, he was unfortunately most often drunk. His wild antics had even managed to scandalize an age used to alcoholic escapades and aristocratic excesses. Alexander Pope called Wharton "the scorn and wonder of our days." He was, the poet said, a walking paradox, a man "too rash for thought, for action too refined." In England, Wharton had been one of the founders of the infamous Hellfire Club, a secret society open to iconoclastic, hard-living aristocrats. Among other picturesque debaucheries they indulged in blasphemous parodies of Anglican religious rites, performed by naked prostitutes.

The death of Wharton's young son from smallpox in 1720 threw him into the arms of his worst impulses and caused a rupture with his first wife—his last link to what might be called normal life. More than £120,000 in debt—an astronomical sum, the modern equivalent of tens of millions—Wharton first sought refuge in Italy. There, he had offered his services to the Pretender, James III, who ran a tinsel parallel court in Rome. The exiled Stuart, impressed with Wharton's energy and title, awarded him the coveted Order of the Garter, which only the rightful King of England could bestow.

The rogue duke's abandoned first wife died—some say from drink, others from despair—and he married again in Spain, the beautiful daughter of an Irish soldier who was one of Queen Isabela's maids of honor. At the wedding, Wharton, drunk as usual, exposed his penis—apparently of an impressive size—to the assembled company, just to show what his wife "would have this night buried in her gutts."

By the time Wharton reached the Spanish lines at Gibraltar, he had become an embarrassment. Perpetually drunk, and with no previous military experience, he led suicidal charges straight at the British fortifications, daring the soldiers of his own country to fire at him: "whereupon the soldiers," wrote an early twentieth-century biographer, "being far from desirous to kill a madcap nobleman of their own nation held their fire and suffered him to return uninjured to his trenches."

But Wharton's bravado eventually caught up with him. As an eyewitness reported:

The day before yesterday, the Duke of Wharton insisted on going to a Battery to show his Garter-Riband, crying out a thousand times "Long Live the Pretender," and using a quantity of bad language. They represented to him repeatedly that he ought to withdraw, but he refused to do so. At last, he was struck by a piece of shell on the toe. He had been drinking Brandy, otherwise perhaps he would have been wiser.

This injury, significant enough to lead military surgeons to contemplate the amputation of his foot, sufficed to invalid the Duke out of active service. Shortly thereafter, Parliament declared him an outlaw and confiscated his estates and property in England. A few years later, broke, drunk-sick, and sick at heart, the one-time roguish bon vivant, nursed by his long-suffering second wife, died in the Royal Cistercian Monastery at Poblet in Spain. He lies there still, buried beneath a crumbling, vine-covered slab, its inscription barely legible.

3.

The 13th Siege of Gibraltar dragged on, measured in the parabola of each falling cannon ball.

The Count de Las Torres pounded British fortifications with his artillery to no avail. Many of his guns, poorly cast, "drooped at the mouth" from overheating or burst after repeated use. Attempts at undermining also failed. Spanish miners clambered up the cliff face to dig a gallery large enough to contain four hundred barrels of gunpowder. They endured withering fire from a British naval squadron riding the bay below but it was the tough fiber of the rock and not British guns that ultimately doomed their effort: the hard granite of Gibraltar refused to yield to Spanish pickaxes. To mine a gallery of sufficient size, Spanish engineers estimated, would take eight-to-ten months of constant labor. The plan was abandoned after several fruitless weeks and many pointless casualties.

Meanwhile, in the battered town of Gibraltar, the usual drama played out: rationing, sickness, cruel punishments meted out to deserters, hoarders, thieves, profiteers, and anyone else who violated the rules of behavior during a state of siege. Time passed slowly between the nearly unendurable cannonades of what one participant dubbed a "gunner's war," in which the danger of being killed by one's own guns exploding was as great as being killed by enemy fire. Two British officers committed suicide out of sheer ennui, another was killed in a duel. In April, torrential rains made life miserable for the defenders and for the besiegers, whose zig-zag trenches, inexorably approaching, filled with mud. Then the days grew long and hot; bodies stank in the rubble.

All the Spanish residents of Gibraltar had been expelled at the beginning of the siege, their loyalty suspect, leaving two hundred Genoese and one hundred Jews to assist the British garrison with the defense of the town. Spanish shells destroyed British fortifications daily; at night these were rebuilt with grueling effort. According to an unnamed British officer—identified only by the initials S. H.—who kept a diary of the siege, later published, the Jews at first balked at the demands of their unending labor:

"A body of the Jews desire to leave to retire to Barbary, because commanded to work for the common Preservation," S. H. observed, "but answer'd by the Governor that as they had enjoy'd safe and plenty during Peace, if they will not assist for their own safety, they shall be turned over to the Spaniard." With this rebuke, their attitude soon changed, and another siege diarist later noted "the Jews were not a little serviceable, they wrought in the most indefatigable manner and spared no pains where they could be of any advantage."

A shipment of prostitutes arrived from Ireland in mid-May, conveyed by a Royal Navy corvette for the diversion of the garrison. From these unfortunate women, came, says S. H. "a great number of necessary evils." Some of them proved not-surprisingly unruly, drinking and soliciting in the streets. By way of discipline, they were subjected to an odd contraption called the "Whirligig." The Diarist comments:

A poor lady, by name Chidley . . . was most formally conducted to a pretty Whim or Whirligig, in the form of a Bird Cage, for the greater benefit of air. It contains Room enough for one person. . . . It is fixed between two swivels, so is turned around till it makes the person, if not us'd very gently, a little giddy and Land Sick. This Office was performed by two of the private Gentlemen of the Garrison, for the space of an hour in the Market Place, being well attended. All this was to oblige her for the following good qualities, which she had the goodness to make frequent use of, such as giving soft words in smooth language, beating

better manners into several men, and a too frequent bestow-
ing of other favors.

The effect of this "whim" was actually more punishing than the
Diarist allows: after a few minutes, "the centrifugal action caused
the victim to empty through every orifice."

The cruelties of the age were not of course confined to women.
Random cannon balls took off the heads and limbs of garrison
troops. Moors, coming and going from across the straits to Africa
in small boats sold necessary provisions at exorbitant prices that
could only be afforded by officers. Two of the former, exposed as
spies in the pay of Spain, were "put to death and afterwards flayed,"
reports S. H. "Their skins were then nailed to the gates of the town,
where they appeared in the same proportions when alive, and being
large, gigantic fellows, as the Moors in general are, they were horrid
ghastly spectacles." He adds:

> The best part of them were remaining when we came away.
> Nature had sent them into the world with their hides tanned,
> so that the heat of the sun, which is very intense at Gibraltar,
> could add but little to their original dusk; but it had so hard-
> ened them that they soon seemed equally solid with the gates
> themselves. After the siege they were much lessened by the
> curiosity of our people, who cut out a great many pieces of
> them to bring to England, one of which, to gratify our readers,
> may be seen at Mr. Warner's, the publisher of this treatise.

Yellow fever, a relatively new scourge in Europe, brought on
slave ships—Gibraltar being one of the ports involved in the triangle
trade—eventually felled more than five hundred of the defenders
and an unknown but probably greater number of Spaniards, given
their position in wet, mosquito-ridden trenches.

At last, in the penultimate week of June, the Spanish bombardment ceased all at once, and the hot blue sky above the Rock, so
recently ripped by cannonballs, cleared. The Count de Las Torres
sent a fatted calf to the governor, Lord Portmere, long since returned
from England to organize the defense. With this ironically biblical
gift, Las Torres acknowledged his defeat. His remaining engineers,
consulted at last, had advised him that Gibraltar could not be penetrated with the forces available, especially in the absence of naval
control of the Straits. The Count's vehemence and bellicosity had
failed to deliver the promised outcome. Now he blamed his chief
engineer, Verboom—who he claimed had worked against him—and
who had decamped weeks before to Madrid to protest to King Felipe
the futility of the siege. Las Torres also blamed the poor quality
of his own soldiery; most of them foreign mercenaries with more
allegiance to their pay than the Spanish cause. In any case, he had
been remarkably spendthrift with their lives.

The 13th Siege ended in a British victory against overwhelming
odds, which only served to bolster their growing reputation as an
obstinate and warlike people. The Rock would remain in British
hands—as it does to this day, over Spain's unending objections.
At no point during the Siege had the defenders been in any real
danger of losing Gibraltar. They were, in fact, better supplied by
sea from England, than the Spanish in their own country—the
latter had found it necessary to bring all provisions slowly overland
from Andalusia in primitive carts on rough roads. Also, fresh water
ran clear and potable from various places on the Rock; the Spanish
had to content themselves with barrels of water "black as a hat and
stinking."

When the firing stopped, official Spanish casualties stood at
1,500 killed, 2,450 wounded, with more than 3,000 deserting to
British lines; on the British side 118 killed, 207 wounded—though
the numbers who succumbed to disease on both sides were no

doubt far greater. According to S. H. "we begin to find our soldiers sicken very much into fluxes and gripes of the bowls, which the physicians attributed to the too frequent drinking of new wine, and a great deal of which was sour . . . the disorder of the gripes and flux"— probably dysentery and the flu—"became at length so epidemical that our hospitals were all filled with the sick, five or six of a night almost constantly dying for a considerable time together."

The siege had lasted more than four months during which 24,000 shells and 53,000 round shot had been expended: "We laughed at the Spaniards for fools," concludes the Diarist, "to throw away their Powder and Balls and Shells. . . . Thus ended the famous siege which made rather more noise in the world in preparation than when undertaken."

Meanwhile, the war continued across the Atlantic, with rather different results.

4.

Admiral Hosier's martyred ghost haunted the British imagination for generations: Wrapped in a dingy hammock, with four thousand other ghosts similarly attired at his side, all pointed spectral fingers at Robert Walpole, whose craven, short-sighted foreign policy had assured their deaths. The eighteenth-century balladeer Richard Glover memorably illustrated this spectral nightmare:

> *On a sudden, shrilly sounding*
> *Hideous yelles and shrieks were heard;*
> *Then, each heart with fears confounding*
> *A sad troop of ghosts appeared;*
> *All in dreary hammocks shrouded,*
> *Which for winding sheets they wore;*

and with looks of sorrow clouded
Frowning on that hostile shore

This stanza, plucked from Glover's lengthy ballad *Admiral Hosier's Ghost*, was written a dozen years after the Admiral perished along with his command, cruising the fetid, mosquito-infested waters off Porto Bello, entrepôt of the Spanish Treasure Fleet, on the Caribbean side of the Panamanian isthmus. The ballad from which it was taken resides among several dozen pieces collected in one of the best-selling anthologies of the era, the *English Reliques*, a volume of popular English songs and ballads, supposedly transcribed from an elusive, handwritten manuscript rescued from the fireplace at a country house: The chambermaid had been using its stiff age-spotted pages as kindling, so the story goes, until the manuscript was recognized, just in time, as a national treasure by an antiquary visiting for the weekend.

Historical consensus blames the foreign policy failures of the king and his ministers—and the Royal Navy's criminally bad hygienic practices—for Hosier's disaster. The British public at the time chiefly blamed Robert Walpole: Walpole, now the preeminent Whig, First Minister, wily politician, corrupt, corruptible, a man of business, a compromiser, a deal-maker. Trading nations, Walpole maintained, need never go to war. A deal and greater profits could solve any international problem. He was at heart, a vulgar but peaceable country gentlemen, like Squire Allworthy in Fielding's *Tom Jones*—the racy, literary masterpiece of England's mid-eighteenth century. Portraits of Walpole (now dubbed the "Great Man" by the London press, both for his size and his influence) show a hearty man of enormous bulk, always outdoors, dressed in country clothes with a couple of hunting dogs at his side, a rifle slung casually over his arm. All in all, Walpole seems to say to us across the years, "I'd rather be out huntin'." In fact, he was the preeminent politician of his era, his hunting grounds the drawing rooms and coffee houses of London.

Spain's renewed alliance with Austria and the growing problem of depredations of the *guarda costa* on British shipping in the West Indies gave Walpole a case of political indigestion. He knew a full-scale war with Spain and her allies loomed; he wished to avert it at all costs, but could not be seen as an appeaser. Spain's attack on Gibraltar would soon force his hand in the Mediterranean. Still hoping to avoid an all-out war inimical to British trading interests, his ministry dispatched a squadron to the West Indies, with the capable, doomed Rear Admiral Francis Hosier in command.

Hosier, aboard his flagship *Breda* dropped anchor off the Bastimentos Islands, near Porto Bello, Panama, on June 6, 1726. He was eventually joined by sixteen other ships serving on the Jamaica Station and a few from England, bringing his squadron up to twenty. Limited rules of engagement imposed by the Walpolian government ensured military disaster: Hosier was instructed to blockade the port city of Porto Bello, but not to make any move to take the town itself, nor any vessel riding in its harbor. His squadron, encompassing 4,750 men, would instead cruise up and down endlessly, allowing no Spanish ships to proceed without first examining their cargo for treasure. If found, this might be confiscated.

The strategists at the Admiralty knew that Spain's economy relied on the annual shipment of silver from the famous Potosi mines and other sources. Porto Bello, protected by three impressive fortresses, with its stone warehouses and garrison troops, operated as one of the chief transshipment points. Silver came up the Pacific coast by sail and across the isthmus by mule train where it met, at Porto Bello the galleons of the Spanish treasure fleet. These were laden for the final leg of the journey to Cádiz.

Hosier would seize these galleons should they emerge from their protected anchorage; if they did not emerge he would do . . . nothing. A deadly waiting game ensued. The Spanish, as it turned out, knew how to wait better than the British Navy, "forced to loiter and cruise off a mosquito-infested coast."

5.

At first, the Governor of Porto Bello pretended to be baffled by the presence of Hosier's squadron at his doorstep. He sent a carefully worded dispatch enquiring politely the reason for the blockade—as far as he knew, England and Spain were not at war. As it happened, a South Sea Company "permission ship," the *Royal George*, London-bound and laden with a rich cargo of raw materials from the Spanish colonies, lay refitting for the journey home in Porto Bello harbor. Hosier, using the *Royal George* as a pretext, informed the governor that his entire squadron had been sent as an escort for this single trading vessel. The governor quickly saw to it that the *Royal George*, loaded and ready, sailed unmolested across the bar to join its supposed escort. Of course, Hosier did not call off his blockade once the *Royal George* had sailed for home. Now, what had been painfully obvious became utterly clear: Hosier was after the treasure galleons, the economic lifeblood of Spain. Their cargos now unloaded and stored for safekeeping in Porto Bello's warehouses, the galleons still failed to emerge.

Week after week, all through the sweltering hot months of the tropics, Hosier's squadron sailed up and down, helpless to pursue their prey, tantalizingly close but untouchable. Gradually, the British sailors and officers began to sicken and die from the same yellow fever that had made a brief appearance at Gibraltar. It is a mosquito-borne tropical disease, a fast killer to which Englishmen had no resistance.

Shipboard hygiene at this period, notoriously lax, only increased the morbidity of the contagion. Sailors lived in airless galleries below decks, amid their own slops. The ships stank of feces and decay; the "iron rations" of salt pork and hardtack became rotten and vermin-infested in the tropical heat.

"It is doubtful whether any other British fleet had ever suffered from disease so severely as Hosier's suffered in 1726–1727," says naval historian William Laird Clowes in his magisterial seven-volume *The Royal Navy*. After six months of aimless cruising, officers and crew became "daily more distressed by the ravages of the epidemic" to the point where their large, complex warships could no longer be sailed properly. At last, blockade duty became impracticable, and Hosier ordered a retreat to Jamaica. Here, he hoped that he and the remains of his crew might recuperate, his vessels would be refit, and new sailors be recruited. Meanwhile, he applied desperately to the Admiralty for a release from his inhibiting orders. Porto Bello itself might be taken with a mere seven ships, he insisted, and he commanded twenty. The Admiralty's response is not recorded, but Walpole's strategy remained in place—to harass Spain up to the point of engaging her in all-out war.

What do we know of Hosier? He was a competent and coura-geous officer of a relatively advanced age (fifty-four) when sent by his government on the fruitless and deadly mission to Porto Bello. He had been a young lieutenant at the Battle of Barfleur in 1692—a decisive naval engagement that had prevented France from aiding the restoration of the ousted Stuart monarch, James II to England's throne. Hosier came from a naval family. His father had been a close associate of the great diarist and "Savior of the English Navy" Samuel Pepys. No portraits of Hosier exist, but we can imagine the wig rising over his forehead, the expression of steely resolve in his eye, the velvet coat with extravagant cuffs, perhaps a breastplate, as military fashion dictated, one hand on the pommel of his sword.

After a few weeks of R&R in Jamaica, Hosier returned doggedly to his blockading duties off Porto Bello, cutting a line between the Bastimentos and the Bay of Sharks. This water had always been fatal to English seamen: the renowned Sir Francis Drake had died thereabouts in 1596, aboard his famous ship the *Golden Hind*. The lead coffin bearing the remains of the famous Elizabethan pirate and circumnavigator clutching his jeweled sword still lies somewhere on the ocean floor off the Panamanian coast, the unfound Holy Grail of Caribbean sport divers.

6.

On March 10, 1727, Admiral Hosier at last surrendered to the disease that had killed so many of his men:

"His death has been attributed to anxiety and chagrin," Clowes says, "but was in fact caused by fever. Nor is it astonishing that the fleet was then little better than a floating charnel house. The most elementary prescriptions of sanitary science seem to have been neglected."

They buried Hosier, wrapped in a bit of sail cloth, in the bilge of his flagship, where no doubt, it began to stink and fester, and "where it remained, a necessary source of danger to all on board." Eventually, he was disinterred and transported aboard the ironically named vessel *Happy* for a martyr's burial in England. Unfortunately, Hosier's death did nothing to change government policy regarding the blockade. He was replaced in command by acting senior naval officer Edward St. Loe, until this gentleman was superseded by Vice-Admiral Edward Hopson, fresh from the Siege of Gibraltar. Hopson arrived at the Jamaica Station on January 29, 1726; he lasted until May 8, when he too died of yellow fever, aboard his flagship. St. Loe once again took command until—after outlasting his two superior officers, the odds caught up with him on April 22. He was buried at sea, wrapped in the Union Jack.

7.

With negotiations between Britain and Spain reaching for a temporary resolution at peace talks held at Soissons in Northern France, the mission to Porto Bello was at last called off. It had been a strategic failure. More than 4,000 of Hosier's squadron had died out of an initial strength of 4,750—including two rear admirals, eight captains and forty lieutenants. The operation had also been a tactical failure: taking advantage of Hosier's absence in Jamaica, in January 1727, the Spanish Admiral Antonio de Gaztañeta slipped through the British blockade and led the Spanish Treasure Fleet, bearing 31 million pesos worth of silver, back to Spain.

Echoes of what the British public rightly saw as a national tragedy reverberated for the next dozen years. Though Britain had not exactly lost the Anglo-Spanish War of 1727–1729 (they had retained Gibraltar against a numerically superior Spanish army) and though Spain had not exactly won the war (they had not retrieved Gibraltar from the hands of Protestant heretics), the waiting game played at the blockade of Porto Bello had essentially defeated the vaunted British Royal Navy. (This lesson would be applied by Blas de Lezo a dozen years later to greater effect.) And treasure, ripped from the back of the Indies, had reached Spanish shores unseized and undiminished. Meanwhile, Britain ached for the loss of her sailors, their lives spent for nothing "as the eccentricities of British Foreign Policy and their own wandering natures had directed them," their corpses "picked white by fishes as the tides rolled them among the treetops of a submarine forest," so Evelyn Waugh puts it in his *Vile Bodies*. In any case, it had been "a horrible experience that made a deep and lasting impression on the nation."

More impressed than most by the horrors of the Porto Bello disaster was an irascible half-pay naval officer with several years of experience in the West Indies, where he had seen action during the 1718–1720 war against Spain. This conflict had taught him to hold the Spanish navy in contempt—it had on every occasion refused to fight, remaining in sheltered harbors, or running at the sight of a British sail. He also knew from hard experience that Spain's greatest ally in the Caribbean was time and disease. Porto Bello, he asserted, should have been quickly taken, and could have been, with far fewer ships than had been present under Hosier's command.

But he was no longer a naval officer; he had become a politician and was now an MP representing the borough of Penryn, Cornwall. In this capacity he gave many fiery speeches in Parliament, advocating what was then called a "Blue Water" policy: In short, a strong navy would ensure domestic liberty by negating the need for a standing army that could, in the hands of a despot, be used to oppress the people. That navy would also protect British maritime trade abroad and act as a counterweight against the despotic land-based powers of Europe. And while a Whig, this ex-naval officer was a "Patriot," or "Country Whig," that is among those Whigs in opposition to Walpole, who believed his ministry corrupt, interested only in profit and at odds with Britain's best interests and national honor.

The name of this semiretired officer was Edward Vernon. His time would come. Meanwhile, the nation could only lament her losses, best expressed in Glover's ballad, later published and illustrated with the image of a destroyed ship and a crew of accusing, skeletal sailors, Admiral Hosier chief among them:

Heed, oh heed my fatal story,
I am Hosier's injured ghost:

You who now have purchased glory
At this place I was lost . . .
Think on revenge for my ruin,
And for England shamed in me.

8.

Soissons, an obscure, attractive city in the département de l'Aisne, in the green heart of France about sixty miles northeast of Paris, has found itself at the crossroads of world events several times in its 2,500 year history.

In 57 B.C.E., Caesar led his ironshod legions to the foot of its defensive palisades; the Suessiones, the Celtic tribe inhabiting the area, promptly surrendered their capital, thus beginning a long French military tradition. In 300 C.E., Soissons became one of the first Christian dioceses in Northern France, and acquired the "shoes of the virgin," a precious holy relic soon housed in the Abbey of Notre Dame, founded by France's pious Merovingian kings. Hopscotching across the centuries to the Hundred Years' War, in 1327 the city became the site of the notorious "Massacre of the English Archers," during which far more than the archers were killed: the King of France's army, breaching Soissons's walls after a lengthy siege, ran amuck, pillaging, raping and killing indiscriminately. French soldiers massacring the English was to be expected; French soldiers massacring other Frenchmen shocked France and the rest of Europe. Shakespeare references this lamentable event in *Henry V*: the king's famous speech "Once more unto the breach, dear friends . . ." was delivered to the English troops at the Battle of Agincourt, purposely fought on St. Crispin's Day, October 25, 1415—Saints Crispin and Crispianus being Soissons's patron saints.

More than three centuries later, in June 1728, representatives of Britain and Spain met in the Palace of the Counts of Soissons to resolve the inconclusive Anglo-Spanish War then still raging. They had already tried, unsuccessfully, in March of that year, at the El Pardo Palace in Madrid. That time, after some hard bargaining, the British Ambassador to Spain, Sir Benjamin Keene, and representatives of Spain's King Felipe, had arrived at terms later considered too lenient. These terms were repudiated by Walpole's ministry. Hence, this second attempt, eight months later, in a series of lengthy diplomatic meetings that became known as the Congress of Soissons.

Now on the British side we find a duo of sharpers—diplomat Sir Stephen Poyntz and Robert Walpole's younger brother, Horatio. Negotiations continued for another year, this as Hosier's fleet languished in the poisonous waters off Porto Bello, its British sailors dying by the dozens each day.

First, Horatio Walpole sought to impede the Spanish-Austrian alliance, already solidified in the Treaty of Vienna. In this, he was not successful. Then, he sought to confirm Spain's recognition of British possession of Gibraltar and Menorca; this he achieved at the price of acknowledging Spanish territorial rights in Sicily and Parma—Queen Isabela's cherished ambition for her sons. Trade issues, however, proved intractable. Britain wanted fewer restrictions on trade with Spanish colonies in the Americas and an end to the search and seizure of British merchant ships in West Indian waters by *guarda costa*. These seizures had already led to claims and counter claims sufficient to perplex both governments. But Spain held firm to the terms agreed upon in the Treaty of Utrecht. Of course, underlying Spanish obstinacy lay the vast amounts of contraband goods, carried by English ships and flooding their American colonies.

Horatio Walpole chose to pretend the extensive, organized smuggling now carried on by the South Sea Company and numerous private traders didn't exist. Spain knew better, having been briefed by two English traitors, whose testimony survives in the Spanish archives at Simancas.

"The Spanish archives are naturally richer in materials for the study of contraband trade than are the English repositories," wrote the distinguished Canadian historian Vera Lee Brown in 1924:

> While the English government wished to remain in official ignorance of the contraband activities of its subjects, the Spanish government was willing to pay well for circumstantial information which they realized would strengthen their position. . . . Much of the material is from English sources, the English company having been particularly unfortunate in faithless servants.

The "faithless servants" in question were two turncoat employees of the South Sea Company who, independent of each other, betrayed their country and sold themselves into the service of Spain: Dr. John Burnet and Matthew Plowes. Burnet, a South Sea Company factor at Cartagena had been financially ruined by Spanish seizures of Company property during the 1718–1720 war, and needed money. Plowes, highly placed in the Company— he was its recording secretary and chief accountant—may have had more complex reasons for betrayal, but money was also undoubtedly a prime motivator.

Negotiations at Soissons, seemingly endless, wound on through the winter of 1728 and into the following year. Spanish negotiators presented their list of grievances concerning British smuggling and violations of trade restrictions; the British pressed their claims regarding unjustly seized trading vessels, imprisoned sailors and lost merchandise. Overeager *guarda costa* captains, from the British point of view little better than pirates, seemed to be pushing the two countries toward yet another inconclusive war.

In August of 1729, in the middle of this mess, in the middle of the night, the chief Spanish negotiator at Soissons, the Marquis de Barrenechea, awoke to an insistent knocking at his door. It was Secretary Plowes, wearing a suitably rococo disguise and wrapped in a voluminous cloak, bearing a cache of forty-two documents stolen from South Sea Company vaults which would do great damage to his country's cause. The astonished marquis examined this trove as Plowes explained himself: his price for this information was £60 immediately, Plowes said, followed by asylum in Spain and a state pension of 500 doblones per year for life.

9.

The stolen documents fell into two general categories: the first described in detail the various subterfuges whereby the South Sea Company concealed contraband cargo in their vessels; the second provided lists of corrupt Spanish colonial officials who had been bribed to look the other way as the Company pursued its illicit activities. These officials included, astonishingly, the Viceroy of Mexico, who along with regular cash payments, had received "a sword garnished with diamonds and a very exquisite musical clock." The supercargo of the *Royal George*—the same ship that had been stranded in Porto Bello harbor at the beginning of Hosier's blockade—had paid out 118,000 pesos in bribes to the governor of that town to secure the release of his ship without the requisite examination of cargo called for by Spanish regulations.

Corruption ran very deep on the Spanish side. In one of Plowes's documents, a South Sea Company factor complained to his superiors, illustrating the typical sort of bribes necessary to do business in the Spanish Americas:

It is with great concern that we are obliged to tell Your Honours that we have been compelled by threats and menaces of having the intervention put upon us, to regale the Governor of Panama with 6000 *pesos de ocho*, the fiscal with 1500 and the two other Royal Officials with 1000 each and as Your Honours never sent a present to the General we were forced to purchase a ring for him with 2400 *pesos de ocho*, the same demands Your Honours must always expect from the Governor and royal officials.

Another choice document described secret contracts between Don Francisco de Alcibar, a prominent Spanish official in Buenos Aires, and Jesuit missionaries, then in the midst of their ill-fated civilizing mission to the Indians of Paraguay—all of whom were engaged in the illegal export of silver in exchange for British manufactured goods. Two Jesuit fathers made the trip to England aboard a South Sea Company vessel with over 400,000 pesos in silver concealed in their baggage.

But, perhaps the most damaging document of all implicated the Spanish representative to the South Sea Company in London charged with enforcing the regulations of the *Asiento*. This person can be counted among the greatest double agents of the eighteenth-century. Among his corrupt practices, the consistent undercounting of allowable trade cargo in the annual permission ships, which had cost the Spanish government thousands in lost revenue.

The Marquis de Barrenechea's eyes must have bugged out as he read over the stolen documents brought in by Plowes and similar material provided later by Dr. Burnet. The marquis judged them so important to ongoing negotiations at Soissons that he eschewed the usual practice of having all diplomatic material transcribed into French (then the lingua franca of diplomacy) and sent them on to the ministry in Madrid in the original English, endorsed and stamped by Plowes and Burnet and another turncoat, a South Sea Company ship's captain named Opie. They were later deposited in the Spanish Archives at Simancas. This is where Vera Lee Brown found them in the 1920s and became the first to read their bald account of corruption and diplomatic intrigue in two hundred years.

10.

Until Brown's discovery, the intractable position of Spanish negotiators at Soissions in 1728–29 seemed yet another example of Latin obstinacy in the face of a superior British bargaining position. Further digging in the archives turned up an accompanying report, authored by Dr. Burnet, that explored the depths of British smuggling activities and the consequent corruption of Spanish officials and offered a stern condemnation of the trade practices of the South Sea Company condoned, however tacitly, by the British Government: no ship sailing from England to the West Indies since 1715, Burnet charged, had failed to carry contraband—this included Royal Navy warships and every one of the slavers delivering the *piezas de Indias* under the *Asiento* Contract. South Sea Company ships in particular were riddled with secret compartments concealing manufactured goods, a far more lucrative trade than the transportation of slaves.

Burnet also explored the South Sea Company's practice of allowing its individual servants to engage in private side-deals, turning every factor, no matter now insignificant, into a smuggler.

"In this fashion," Brown asserts, "the Spanish American dominions were kept awash in illicit goods and legitimate traffic by the Spanish galleons suffered heavily."

The list of stolen documents still extant at Simancas also includes a copy of the English code cipher used by diplomatic representatives in communications with the Foreign Office; a variety of shipping invoices listing contraband goods going back to 1715; and even a copy of the secret instructions recently issued by the Spanish government to its own delegation at Soissons. This last document had been acquired for a stiff price from a corrupt naval officer at Madrid.

"Taken as a whole," comments Brown, "the documents secured from the South Sea Company secretary constituted as rich an assemblage of facts damaging to that organization as could well have been gathered from any quarter."

The impact of this trove on the negotiations at Soissons and their role in contributing to the war of 1739–1742, later named after the unfortunate Jenkins and his severed ear, cannot be overestimated. They immediately stiffened Spanish opposition to Horatio Walpole and the other English negotiators. As talks continued, the Marquis de Barrenechea smothered his rage at British duplicity under an exterior of aristocratic calm. But he refused to bend on the most contentious matter under discussion: the search and seizure of British ships in West Indian waters. He now knew with certainty they nearly all carried contraband goods. The South Sea Company had been cheating since the beginning, with the connivance of their government.

One of the documents, signed by the second mate of the *Royal George*, detailed a complex smuggling operation that occurred even as the delegates sat at Soissons:

The *Royal George*, while anchored at Porto Bello just before Hosier's blockade, had taken on an illegal treasure amounting to 386 chests and fifty-five cases of Spanish silver. Upon the vessel's release—after pressure from Hosier and the judicious application of substantial bribes—the ship was met by a sloop containing an additional 136 chests, two cases and one cask of silver. All this was speedily transferred to the *Royal George*'s hold. The presence of such riches in a single company ship might have raised eyebrows in England; rumors would certainly have reached the ears of the Spanish ambassador. South Sea Company officials hatched a plan to avoid this scrutiny: The *Royal George* sailed to the British island of Antigua and was there falsely condemned as unseaworthy. Crews then shifted its treasure to a waiting Royal Navy warship which sailed for England, transforming itself briefly into a smuggling vessel.

Spain had been a dupe, her honor insulted. The stolen documents illustrated her humiliation. At Soissons her representatives suddenly became truculent and unwilling to compromise. British negotiators began to suspect that Spain had somehow acquired secret information—though they didn't know its source. In the meantime, Plowes and Burnet continued to operate as double agents, feeding information to Spain. Because of them, the negotiations at Soissons ended in an inconclusive fizzle.

The tepid agreement called the Treaty of Seville that resulted, signed by the delegates on November 9, 1729, returned international matters to the status quo pre-1727, which is to say it reconfirmed the unworkable situation laid out in the Treaty of Utrecht. In the end, nothing got resolved. An outcome that can be laid directly at the feet of the two spies who sold out their country for cash.

So what happened to these two "faithless servants?" It is a sad truism that traitors generally finish well. Both Burnet and Plowes escaped judgement and hanging, though in Plowes case, just barely: information only he could have provided accusing the directors of the South Sea Company of vast frauds, used injudiciously in a letter published by the Spanish ambassador in the London press, clearly implicated the corrupt accountant. Plowes was in Soissons at the time; the directors ordered him home for questioning. Plowes panicked and threw himself at the mercy of the Marquis de Barrenechea. Thinking fast, the marquis arranged for Plowes to see a physician who then confirmed that an emergency surgery was necessary and that Plowes could not possibly travel. His medical condition was so grave, in fact, that he might be obliged to resign his post with the Company and retire to private life.

Around this time Dr. Burnet received a letter from a friend in London, reminding him of his duty to the Company and to the king. Clearly, he was also under suspicion. And yet neither Plowes nor Burnet lost their positions of trust. Plowes value to Spain, initially greater than Burnet's, faded out after the Congress disbanded. Two years later, we find him in Paris, unemployed and friendless "without the resources to supply the needs of himself and numerous family."

A final piece of correspondence in the Simancas archives shows him begging the Spanish government to make good on the pension they had promised him. They probably did; but no further records of the matter has been found and Plowes voice echoes no more. He disappears from history, a traitorous drop in the ocean of the past.

11.

Burnet, however, continued to be of service to Spain and seems to have been made from sterner stuff than Plowes. He wrote a damning and detailed report for his handlers. Burnet's nongrammatical Spanish necessitated the intervention of a Spanish official, a certain Don Andre de Otamendri who transcribed and organized the material. This report must have become required reading for all Spanish government officials serving in the American colonies. Divided into six detailed sections, it can still be found in the Simancas archives.

Section 1, *Sobre Commercio Ilicito*, describes every trick the British employed in secreting contraband goods aboard their vessels: the hidden compartments built into ships meant to carry African slaves; the false bills of lading; the fast local sloops adding to the legitimate cargos of the permission ships at a prearranged rendezvous, some isolated lagoon or desert island; the unmarked cargo loaded and unloaded in the dead of night; such operations, Burnet adds, usually supervised by Jews in the Company's employ, who knew "very well how to handle goods at our wharfs in the night time without any notice being taken of them."

In one memorable instance, sailors aboard an English ship supposed to be carrying *piezas de Indias* for the market at Cartagena, but in fact carrying manufactured goods, were ordered by their captain to paint themselves up in blackface and pose as slaves exercising on deck—an absurd camouflage to deter passing *guarda costa* cutters. That this ploy apparently worked stands as an indictment of the nautical telescopes of the day.

In much of the smuggling activities, Burnet continues, the Royal Navy was deeply involved—as seen with the *Royal George* incident. The navy provided protection for Company ships from both *guarda costa* privateers and pirates of the more conventional sort, with navy captains receiving a percentage of the profits of smuggling runs. Less than half the silver exported from the Spanish colonies left the West Indies legally, Burnet says. Contraband trade was ruining the Spanish colonial economy; dealers in such goods, immune to all customs duties, undercut legitimate merchants at the trade fairs of Porto Bello and Cartagena by fifty percent or more.

To support his incendiary charges, Burnet enlisted his wife. He had most recently been the South Sea Company's factor at Cartagena. His wife had remained there during his sojourn at Soissons. Now he sent her special instructions: she was to pack up all his personal papers, company documents, bills of lading, and other documents and ship them to him in Madrid, where he had gone to consult with his new masters. She did as he asked—and took ship with the chests of pilfered documents to join him. With this new information in hand, Burnet concluded his damning report, its penultimate section *De Contravenciones* offering a fatal prescription to end contraband trade that would lead directly to war in 1739. He called for the maintenance of "an adequate number of *guarda costas* capable of seizing whatever foreign vessel might appear on the coast."

The Spanish government took this draconian recommendation to heart—though they ignored his more reasonable suggestion that to truly end smuggling "a frequent and abundant supply of goods from Spain . . . should reach American shores." But totalitarian governments, then as now, will choose enforcement (more prisons! more police!) over amelioration in most circumstances.

In the decade following 1729, Spanish *guarda costa* seizures of British merchant vessels increased in number and viciousness. The incarceration and mistreatment of British crews also increased along with official encouragement of vicious semipiratical *guarda costa* captains like Juan de León Fandiño, villain of the attack on the *Rebecca* and Captain Jenkins in 1731. The violated Welshman's severed ear stands as a vivid symbol for what had become, by 1738, a "Depredations Crisis" for British merchants dealing in the West Indies.

The British government wanted a free exchange of British goods for Spanish silver; the rigid mercantile system adhered to by Spain did not allow for such an exchange—even though they could not supply their own colonies with those goods needed to maintain a decent standard of living. But the inhabitants of the Spanish Colonies were, in the end, the arbiter of world events: smuggling will always exist where there also exists an appetite for what is smuggled—viz the "War on Drugs" of our own era.

As payment for betraying his country, Burnet asked he be made an inspector general of the Caracas Company, a Spanish trading concern modeled on the South Sea. This request was denied. He'd betrayed his own people in a similar position, why would he not do so again for the right inducements? Desperate and short of funds he then asked that he be appointed *médico de cámara* to the Spanish Navy. He was a doctor, after all, a graduate of the University of Edinburgh, and had been a medical adviser to Hosier's doomed fleet. He also asked for an officer's appointment for his nephew.

Despite Hosier's fate and the horrific deathrate on Royal Navy ships in 1727–29, both these requests were granted.

Like Plowes, Burnet then vanishes from the official record. No one knows where their bones lie or their ultimate fates, beyond that which awaits all men. Then end results of their treachery, however, would have shattering consequences—and result in the war after which Captain Jenkins's excised auricular appendage is perhaps unfairly named.

12.

July 1737 finds the melancholic Spanish King Felipe V once again abed in his palace in Madrid. Wallowing in his own filth, clinging to his wife's tattered nightgown, visited alternately with vivid night terrors and deep, days-long lethargies. He refused to shave or bathe and would only eat a few spoonfuls of tepid soup daily and only if served by his wife's own hand. This had been going on for half a year. The affairs of Spain, both domestic and international, had suffered from his incapacitation. Even his wife, Queen Isabela, de facto ruler of the Spanish Empire, could not quite do without him. When clean and sober and temporarily dispossessed of his madness, he showed a shrewd grasp of state matters as befits a nephew of the great Louis XIV.

And there was something more: In the hierarchical, deeply conservative Spain of the Grandees, the king, mad or not, sat at the top like God in Heaven. All power emanated from the throne. Lying in bed, nearly catatonic, he was useless to his country and his queen. Something had to done. The power of her sexual blandishments had faded with age; though the king, even semitorpid as he was, still sought his release with unusual frequency in the sanctioned joys of marital embrace, sex failed to rouse him as before.

The court physician, Dr. Giuseppe Cervi, a man ahead of his time, recommended music therapy as a cure for melancholia in general, and he now prescribed it for Felipe. But to cure a king would take a very great musician indeed. Only one, Cervi believed, might be equal to such a task, the great Italian *castrato* opera singer, Farinelli, who was just then in Paris on a European tour and would soon be coming to Madrid. After a recent performance at Versailles, King Louis XV had presented the castrated wonder with a golden snuff-box emblazoned with the royal portrait surrounded by diamonds.

Carlo Maria Michelangelo Nicola Broschi—stage name Farinelli—born near Naples in 1705, is the most famous representative of a bizarre tradition in Italian sacred music, going back centuries. Choirboys, caught before their voices changed, were shorn of their testicles. This act of mutilation preserved the vocal range initially shared by both sexes before it succumbs to the corrosive effects of testosterone. Castratos maintained a prepubescent flexibility of voice, combined with the lung power of a mature male, and were much sought after by opera directors, when that genre became popular in the seventeenth-century. According to contemporary listeners the effects were otherworldly, like listening to the angels, themselves unsexed, sing in heaven.

Farinelli's fanatical admirers in England, where he performed under contract for a company called the Opera of the Nobility, were mostly aristocratic and female; they swooned over his performances and showered him with cash and expensive gifts. He had just completed two triumphant seasons there. With Farinelli mania at its peak, one enthusiastic patron, said to be a certain Lady Rich, loudly declared from her box at the opera during a Farinelli performance "One God! One Farinelli!" The audience gasped, but this blasphemous phrase became a sort of eighteenth-century meme, depicted on snuff boxes, and mocked in the satirical prints of Hogarth. Farinelli was the rock star of his day, complete with groupies and sycophants—albeit one lacking the ability to shag them Mick Jagger-style.

The physical side effects of castration at an early age are both debilitating and strange. The absence of testosterone keeps bone joints pliable; oddly long limbs and a massive rib-cage results, giving castrati a gawky, alien look. Pulmonary development allowed them to maintain notes as high as C6, the top of the range, for literally breathtaking lengths of time. Composers treasured this ability; operas were composed specifically with castrati in mind. The practice of mutilating boys for musical effect mercifully ceased in the mid-nineteenth century. A creaky recording exists of the last castrato, Alessandro Moreschi, taken in 1902 at the Vatican; the poor fellow was by then middle-aged and no longer at the peak of his powers but the sound he produces is entrancingly strange, neither male nor female; the voice of an androgynous, aging cherubim.

Italian authorities exhumed what remained of Farinelli's bones from a cemetery in Bologna in 2006 and subjected them to a pitiless examination. The soil was acidic, the bones in poor condition, but the odd elongation of limb and insect-like jaw could still be discerned. A few critical accounts in the eighteenth-century London press describe Farinelli's absurd, awkward presence on the stage: he barely moved, they complained, he could sing but dramatic skills eluded him completely. A contemporary sketch shows him in a dress, playing a woman's part, looking like a cross between a praying mantis and a marionette, invisible strings moving his flexible joints from the rafters. Nonetheless, Queen Isabela now pinned all her hopes on the great castrato.

On August 25, 1737, just a few days after Farinelli had begun the Spanish leg of his European tour, Queen Isabela brought him to the antechamber just outside the king's bedroom. There, the castrato sang five or six Italian arias, his personal favorites. This performance repeated over several nights managed to rouse the king from his mental slumber. At last, Felipe emerged, bleary-eyed, bearded, and stinking, as usual, wearing his wife's cast-off night-gown. He praised Farinelli's wonderful singing and, per tradition, granted any reward the castrato might ask as compensation for his performance. Later in life Farinelli told the English musicologist Charles Burney that he had been coached by Queen Isabelala to ask the king, as a special favor, to bathe, shave, dress, and join the Queen for dinner.

This request, Felipe reluctantly granted. Over the next few days he once again took his place as the King of Spain—though the cure remained incomplete and constantly in need of renewal. Felipe insisted that Farinelli accept a position in the royal house-hold as *musico de camera* and *familiar criado*, which is to say the king's personal musician. Farinelli had no choice but to acquiesce, became indispensable to the royal household, and never again sang in public. But with these appointments he and his family rose in society; extravagant gifts and estates were showered upon him. Aristocratic antecedents somehow discovered in the Broschi family tree, Farinelli was made a Spanish knight and his scheming brother Riccardo eventually became Spain's Minister of War.

Meanwhile, the castrato sang for King Felipe every evening at dinner, always the same four or five songs sung that first night. Though, as the British ambassador Sir Benjamin Keene remarked, these performances had unintended side effects. In a letter to the Duke of Newcastle, Keene describes the surreal scene at the royal table:

> Your grace must smile when I inform you that the King himself imitates Farinelli some times air after air, and some-times after the musick is over, and throws himself into such Freaks and howlings, that all possible means are taken to prevent people from being witness to his Follies.

There was, however, a more serious consequence to Farinelli's command position at the Spanish court. He had been effectively removed from his adoring London public, his ironclad contract with the Opera of Nobility broken. Given the sensitive Anglo-Spanish situation and the escalating seizures of English merchant ships by *guarda costas* in the West Indies, Farinelli's "detention" by Spain took on vivid political overtones. Farinelli, the London papers said, had been stolen in the same way their ships were "detained in the Caribbean by the Spanish Guard Coasts." Here was yet another example of illegal Spanish appropriation of British property.

The directors of the Opera of Nobility naturally objected to the "theft" of Farinelli, which to them would mean an entire season's revenue lost, not to mention production costs already invested, and thus, probable bankruptcy. In an open letter to King Felipe, the directors "unanimously resolved" that they could not release Farinelli from his contract, "considering the great loss, they must sustain by his absence, all the Operas being performed this season, so far advanced that it is absolutely impossible to supply his place."

But their protests, at once angry and impotent, failed to influence the Spanish king who refused a single peso of compensation for his appropriation of their star.

The castrato would stay in Madrid for the rest of his professional life—though his performances were now limited to King Felipe, his wife, and a few hardy courtiers. Farinelli eventually retired to Bologna where he died in 1782, Carlo Broschi again, lonely and embittered, having out-lasted all his friends and admirers, reliving in memory the years when he had been worshipped as a god by opera lovers, one of the first pan-European celebrities.

13.

The appropriation of Farinelli by Spain became the talk of London in 1737–38 and the source of much indignation. A conversation overheard by Sir Thomas Geraldino—an Irishman in the Spanish service, then Spanish ambassador to London—characterizes the English attitude: "That the King of Spain did not let Farinello return; and that it is Farinello who wants to remain because of the 3,500 Doblones—" though his compensation has been reported at considerably more than this, up to £14,000 per year, including a mule drawn coach, gold, diamonds and other blandishments.

Spain, her king, and Farinelli herself were denounced in mock-heroic style articles and letters in the London press. Walpole himself was blamed, the opera singer's defection to the Spanish court seen as a living symbol of Spanish attacks on British shipping in the Caribbean.

"The coincidence of Farinelli's detention in Spain with the increasing captures of British shipping was too obvious to miss," writes musical historian Thomas McGeary. "Journalists and satirists of the opposition quickly put the Farinelli affair to political ends. The opposition periodicals . . . regularly returned to [it] to score political points at Walpole's expense. . . . Images of London enchanted and enraptured by Farinelli's singing symbolized a lethargic and enervated Britain under Walpole's pacific policy of submitting to Spanish depredations; and the Spanish court's 'detention' of Farinelli and breach of the opera director's contract was a convenient parallel to Spain's capturing British merchant ships, violating treaties and depriving the South Sea Company of its commercial rights."

The anti-Walpole journal *Common Sense*, writing of Farinelli's defection to Spain, reported that "several pretty Gentlemen and Ladies, whom the Depredations in America never in the least affected were Thunder-struck at the fatal Report, and were no sooner recovered from their Surprize, but several indecent Expressions were thrown out against his Spanish Majesty for this unheard of Outrage. . . . Cries a Lady of exquisite Taste 'What are the taking of a few Ships, and the cutting off the Ears of the Masters of our Merchantmen, to the loss of our dear, dear Farinello?'"

The anonymous author of this piece kept both feet firmly planted in the waters of sarcasm, after the fashion of the times, but behind the satirical tone loomed an international imbroglio the "Depredations Crisis" which would at last, inevitably, lead to the wider war everyone dreaded.

14.

One imagines Captain Robert Jenkins knocking around London coffeehouses and Bristol sailors' taverns and the seas of the world for seven more years with his ear "preserved in a bottle" or some say in a small box swathed in cotton wool. For the price of a pint or a tot of rum he displays this grisly artifact and tells his oft-repeated tale of Spanish barbarity on the high seas, the same story he had once told to the king himself. When would justice be done?

True, the famous ear, removed by the brutal *guarda costa* captain Fandiño, had initially inspired a flurry of sternly worded diplomatic correspondence. But by 1737, the "ear matter" had receded into the past, forgotten as other more recent and more outrageous incidents came to replace it in the public imagination: Captain Thomas Weir, "Maimed of Both Arms," bedbound murdered along with eight of his crew by Spanish officials; Captain King of the *Runslet*, tortured with gunlock screws and lighted matches. . . .

In the intervening years, Jenkins went back to sea on the West Indies route and later for the East India Company, haunting his own life like a ghost missing an ear. Justice had eluded him along with any sort of compensation for his stolen property or battered and mutilated body. Walpole's ministry, committed to peace above all, sought to downplay Spanish atrocities. Walpole himself still believed firmly that a government interested in making money could negotiate or buy itself out of any crisis. His attitude might be described as affably corrupt or perhaps inadvertently humanitarian; war's ultimate cost in British lives and treasure would always outweigh any injury to national honor, the sacrifice of a few ships and cargos, the imprisonment of a few dozen sailors, the severing of an ear. These things were just the cost of doing business.

Meanwhile, British losses in the West Indies mounted. Spanish *guarda costas* had grown increasingly aggressive. The presence of a single Spanish piece of eight, standard currency throughout the Caribbean, found aboard an English ship was enough to condemn it as a smuggler, with its cargo seized and its crew imprisoned in the dungeons of Havana's Morro Castle. At last the growing political opposition to Walpole in Parliament took up the debate regarding Spanish depredations with a new intensity: Spain must be made to pay damages or war would result.

A petition seeking "to procure speedy and ample satisfaction for the Losses . . . sustained and that no British vessel be detained or searched on the High Seas" sent to King George in October 1737 bore the signatures of 149 prominent merchants. To this document they had affixed a list of ships ransacked or seized by *guarda costas* in the West Indies. This list went back several years and was accompanied by details regarding each incident. Toward the bottom could be found the case of the *Rebecca*, Captain Jenkins, and his severed ear.

Unusually, upon receiving this petition, the ministry acted quickly. The king himself had taken an interest; perhaps he remembered that poor fellow Jenkins whose ear had been cut off, and who had petitioned him personally for redress back in '31 and never got any. The merchants' new petition was then examined by a Special Committee of the King's Privy Council:

"His Majesty was so sensibly touched with the losses and sufferings of His Trading Subjects," Secretary Newcastle commented, "that he was pleased immediately to direct a Memorial to be prepared."

The resulting "memorial"—or diplomatic memorandum—
more sternly worded than usual, forwarded to the Spanish court via
Ambassador Keene in Madrid, kicked off a new round of intense
negotiations. Both nations, apparently, hoped to avoid another war.
But this was also an era of nostalgia for a glorious past inimical to
such negotiations: Spain hankered for the deeds of the Conquistadors; England for Drake and Sir Walter Raleigh and the Great
Elizabeth.

The Spanish government had now fallen into the hands of a
quartet of hard-liners: Ustaritz, first commissioner of the War Office;
Commercial Minister De la Quadra; Marine Secretary Quintana; and
Montijo, president of the Council of the Indies, all united under the
authority of Queen Isabela, the king too busy howling at dinner
to Farinelli's tunes to pay much attention to the affairs of his
country. Within the Queen's often mercurial and whimsical oversight,
this Gang of Four ruled Spain. "The country is at present governed
by three or four mean, stubborn people of little minds and limited
understandings," Keene complained from Madrid, "but full of the
Romantick Ideas they have found in old Memorials and Speculative
authors who have treated of the immense Grandeur of the Spanish
Monarchy, People who have vanity enough to think of themselves
reserved by Providence to rectify and reform the mistakes and abuses
of past ministers and ages."

The Spanish Gang of Four at first tried to reject British claims.
Many of the claims had passed their expiration date, their details
vague, documentation and ship's manifests lost. Jenkins's and
Rebecca fell into this category. But Parliamentary pressure on
Walpole to do something became impossible to ignore. The multitude of older claims, unresolved and nearly forgotten, merely under-
scored the opposition's point: that only long delays and oblivion
could be expected from Spanish justice. The merchant's petition
of October now inspired a series of increasingly urgent diplomatic

memorandums all sent to the Spanish ministry through Keene. Each detailed more unresolved claims. The harried ambassador presented an additional twenty-eight bundles of claims and depositions. The Gang of Four regarded this welter of paperwork with disdain. Keene reported Montijo's words on the matter to Secretary Newcastle:

"If Spain would accumulate her grievances," Montijo said, according to Keene, "she might make as much to do as England did . . . that there were Faults on Both Sides; England's contrabandists ought to be punished as well as some of the Spanish Governors Hanged."

Still, Montijo, generally regarded as the most conciliatory of the four, was willing to negotiate. Meanwhile, the mood in England, hardening, edged toward war, with the London press and the pamphleteers, all members of that "malicious tribe of writers," beating the drums. Now an ocean of verbiage poured from the pens of Grub Street—plays, ballads, masques, satires, articles, editorials—all advocating war with Spain. The anti-Walpolean journal *The Craftsman* led the opposition press in its vehemence and powers of invention: it accused Wapole of failing to protect English trade from "Pyratical Depredations and cruel treatment of our Seamen," and reported a particularly incendiary story that was at best half-true. English sailors "enslaved" in Havana, *The Craftsman* said, were forced to work on labor gangs in chains, "ragged, meager, and half-starved."

"Are our brave English Mariners to be thus abused, who have committed no Crime, and whom the Spaniards durst not look in the face upon equal Terms, were their Hands unty'd?" went a typical *Craftsman* editorial.

The sailors in question comprised the crew of two ships, the *Loyal Charles* and *Dispatch*, both of London. These vessels were well known to the merchants of that city; the imprisoned sailors in effect, native sons. The opposition press got busy pleading the sailor's cause. Popular prints—the political cartoons of the day—showed them skeletal and beaten, laboring under the Spanish lash. But this was mostly eighteenth-century "fake news." The British Consul at Cádiz, appointed to look into the matter, eventually found the sailors under house arrest in that city, not laboring in chains, being fed, given clothes and shelter, and treated reasonably well. This intelligence was largely ignored. The image of free Englishmen tortured and enslaved at the hands of cruel Spanish papists could not be dislodged from the popular imagination.

15.

More vicious parliamentary debates followed. Merchants and sea captains who had been brutalized by *guarda costas* in the West Indies were asked to testify before a special committee of the House.

Historians agree that Captain Jenkins, his case singled out, perhaps for its picturesque qualities (what's not to like about a severed ear?) was among those called to tell his tale of woe. The *House of Commons Journal*, official record of the doings of the legislature, listed the following item on March 16, 1738: "Ordered, that Captain Robert Jenkins do attend this House immediately." Apparently, Jenkins didn't show. The next day came a second summons: "Ordered that Captain Robert Jenkins do attend on Tuesday morning next, the Committee of the Whole house to whom the Petition of divers merchants interested in the British plantations in America and many others is referred." Similar orders, though Jenkins is not mentioned specifically, followed on March 21, 22, 23, and 30.

Did Jenkins appear or not? Here's where things get tricky. Unfortunately, transcripts of House testimony from this period have not survived; controversy over this point still rages. In fact, nothing certain is known of Jenkins's movements between 1738 and 1741 when he was appointed temporary governor of the island of St. Helena, then an East India Company refueling station in the South Atlantic. Some historians, crediting contemporary press accounts, assert that Jenkins answered the summons and made a dramatic, epoch-making presentation before the House, brandishing the blackened remnants of his ear:

"Jenkins was examined before a committee of the House of Commons," says the account in the Dictionary of National Biography, (DNB):

> His story lost nothing in the telling; he produced something which he asserted was the ear that had been cut or torn off, and being asked "what were his feelings when he found himself in the hands of such barbarians," he replied (in what became a famous phrase), "I committed my soul to God and my cause to my country." The report roused the utmost public indignation.

Other historians insist that Jenkins never uttered this rousing response, that the patriotic sentiments ascribed to him, first reported in the *Gentleman's Magazine*, had been invented by MP William Pulteney, one of Walpole's most vocal and nimble-tongued parliamentary opponents. They generally place Jenkins out of England at the time of the debates, hence his failure to respond to the initial summons.

For roughly 150 years, historical consensus—which had come to see the war given Jenkins's name as wholly unnecessary and a national tragedy—doubted his story altogether. The man probably never existed! The tale of the severed ear was a fiction, or at least heavily embellished by opposition politicians seeking to destroy Walpole's successful and peaceable ministry. A few admitted the reality of Jenkins himself and even that his ear might had been severed but suggested the unfortunate mariner had lost it the pillory, to which he'd been condemned for various petty larcenies.

Archdeacon William Coxe, one of the earliest historians of the Walpolean era, writing in 1796, credited Jenkins's appearance before the House with great reluctance and looked with a jaundiced eye on the inciting ear-severing, which he called "this ridiculous story."

"According to contemporary accounts," Coxe wrote, emphasizing the element of hearsay, "[Jenkins] related the transaction with many additional circumstances of insult and barbarity, and displayed the ear, which he had preserved, as some assert in a box, and others in a bottle."

Coxe passed on his skepticism to historians of the next generation who came to regard the severing of Jenkins's ear as a complete myth, no more than anti-Walpolean propaganda, invented by the *Gentleman's Magazine* and repeated by other opposition journals. A peculiarity of press censorship of the times added greatly to the confusion: newspapers, prevented by law from printing House debates verbatim, resorted to a variety of creative subterfuges. The *London Magazine*, for example, reported on the speeches of a "learned and political club," in which prominent MPs were given Roman names—behind which the actual figures might be discerned lurking by contemporary readers, like Polonious behind the curtain in *Hamlet*. The euphemistic Senatorial debates of "Magna Lilliputa" featured in another publication.

The early twentieth-century historian William Thomas Laprade blamed such tactics for misconceptions, exaggerations and outright lies—often resorted to when "a publication was in a pinch" for news. Laprade numbered among those who considered the tale of Jenkins's eloquent testimony before the House as wholly untrue. Laprade believed that though summoned to testify, Jenkins never did, that he was "otherwise engaged and did not go." In the late 1940s, historian A. J. Henderson supported this view, asserting a new narrative he presented as "the truth":

"Jenkins was not in London, nor even in England at the time of the investigation (March 1738)" Henderson declared. "He was aboard his ship, the *Harrington*, homeward bound from a voyage to the West Indies; and he did not arrive in London until May 25, which was five days after Parliament had been prorogued for the summer."

However, against this debunking, it must be remembered that until the dogged researches of naval historian J. K. Laughton in 1898, the existence of Jenkins and his ear was utterly dismissed by nearly every reputable historians. These men were apparently not aware of—or had rejected—the early account published in Franklin's *Pennsylvania Gazette* in 1731. Laughton, during the course of an exhaustive investigation, discovered a cache of letters between Rear Admiral Charles Stewart, commander in chief at the Jamaica Station, his superiors, and several Spanish colonial officials. In his groundbreaking article published in the *English Historical Review,* Laughton wrote:

Whilst recently making some researches into the admiralty records, I came accidentally on a correspondence which seems to have hitherto escaped notice, which is interesting from the very clear light it throws on the state of our naval and mercantile relations in the West Indies for some years previous to the declaration of war with Spain in 1739. Incidentally also it confirms the story of Jenkins's ear, which for certainly more than a hundred years has been generally believed to be a fable.

Laughton then prints, for the first time, several of these records, silencing the ear-doubters for good.

In a letter from Laughton's trove, dated Oct. 12, 1731, Rear Admiral Charles Stewart first mentions Jenkins:

"I was a little surprised to hear of the usage Captain Jenkins met with off the Havana," he writes to Secretary of State Newcastle, "as I know the Governor there has the character of being an honest good man, and don't find anybody thinks he would connive or countenance such villainies."

To this letter Stewart appends a copy of his letter of protest, written in quite a different mood and sent to "his Excellency Dionisio Martinez de la Vega, Governor of Havana." This one reads in part:

> I have repeated assurances that you allow vessels to be fitted out of your harbor, particularly one Fandiño, and others who have committed the most cruel piratical outrages on several ships and vessels . . . particularly about the 20th April last sailed out of your harbour in one of those Guarda Costas, and met a ship of this island bound for England; and after using the captain in the most barbarous inhuman manner, taking all his money, cutting off one of his ears, plundering him of those necessaries which were to carry the ship safe home, without doubt with the intent that she should perish in the passage.

Laughton rescued Captain Jenkins and his ear from the realm of politically motivated fairy tale. Post-Laughton historians, now unable to deny that Jenkins lost his ear to Fandiño's cutlass, maintained instead that the incident really didn't matter that much. Philip Woodfine, writing in the 1980s, suggests that Jenkins's mutilation had no role in inciting the war that bears his name. The *Craftsman*'s account of the enslaved British sailors, Woodfine says, held more weight in parliamentary debates and with the public. By 1738, Woodfine concludes, "the episode of Jenkins' ear was an old one, not unique in its cruelty, not refreshed by any recent publication, and not supported by any appearance before the House."

And yet the wealth of surviving cultural evidence stands against this view. In the journals, newspapers, popular prints, and dramatic presentations of the years 1737–39, severed ears abound. They seem to appear just about everywhere. Allegorical dramatic pieces, often satirical in nature, portrayed Jenkins and his ear. One memorable masquerade performed in February 1739 featured, according to a contemporary account a "Spaniard, very richly dressed, who called himself knight of the Ear; as a Badge of which order, he wore on his Breast the form of a Star, whose Points seem'd ting'd with Blood, on which was painted an Ear, and round it, writtin in Capital letters, the word Jenkins."

Popular ballads sing of English merchants losing their ears; prints show an aggrieved Jenkins, ear in hand, trying to interest an indifferent government in his cause. (Cartoon-like and often brilliantly colored, political prints were collected with avidity by the average citizen in eighteenth-century England, as comic books were collected by most American kids in the 1950s and '60s.) One of the most popular prints of 1738 depicts a chaotic scene in Walpole's ministerial office:

There's the Great Man himself, the "Skreenmaster General," at his desk offering a "talk to the hand" gesture to a distraught Captain Jenkins displaying his piece of ear as a black servant removes the mariner's wig to show the healed-over stump. In the foreground a small dog tears up the *Asiento* contract and another minister obliviously pays court to a seated lady. In the background, a Walpolean flunky shows the door to a London merchant bearing a long list of English ships seized by *guarda costas*. No one in this scene pays any real attention to the injured and outraged Jenkins, symbol of Spanish cruelty and English national dishonor.

Also, there's just something about a severed ear. It has a kind of psychological power not easily dismissed, existing on a shadow line between the funny and the horrible. A severed ear sticks to the ribs of the imagination—think of Van Gogh's famous act of self-mutilation, or the bloody ear found in the grass in David Lynch's seriocomic *noir* thriller, *Blue Velvet*. And of course, there's the ear struck from the head of the High Priest's servant by the Apostle Peter in the New Testament: "Thus Simon Peter, who had a sword, drew it, struck the high priest's slave, and cut off his right ear. The slave's name was Malchus." (John 18:10) Here's Luke's version: "His disciples realized what was about to happen, and they asked, 'Lord shall we strike with a sword?' And one of them struck the high priest's servant and cut off his right ear. But Jesus said in reply, 'Stop, no more of this!' then he touched the servant's ear and healed him." (Luke 22:49–51)

Indeed the tale of Jenkins's severed ear made such an impression on the historian Carlyle that—in keeping with his famously arch literary style—he named the war after it and the name stuck, to the dismay of later, sober-sided modern historians like Woodfine.

16.

As public opinion called for war—fanned by the opposition press and by London theaters—complicated negotiations to avert it continued between Britain and Spain. Meanwhile, Walpole's ministry, recognizing its own precarious hold on a restive populace, shaded into tyranny: censorship became the order of the day. Walpole began to shut down the most vociferous opposition journals and those Drury Lane theatres where anti-government sentiment ran hottest. Walpole invoked the "Stage Licensing Act" passed by Parliament in 1737, a draconian piece of legislation that allowed for the suppression of theatrical pieces critical of government policy. With its usual sarcasm, *The Craftsman* made the point that such suppression of free expression was the chief attribute of tyranny. In a much read satirical piece they demanded certain passages decrying bad government in some of Shakespeare's famous plays be excised— and then quoted the passages verbatim, all of which might be easily applied to Walpole's regime.

Though *The Craftsman*, backed by powerful opposition politicians, could not be shut down outright, its print-jobber, a certain Henry Haines, was promptly arrested and thrown into jail. This unfortunate contractor was held without bail awaiting trial for two years.

Also, around this time, an actor named James Lacy produced an "oratory" (a kind of staged reading performed in a rented hall) on a historical subject that bore a strong resemblance to the Depredations Crisis. The plot of this oratory followed the true story of a fourteenth-century mayor of London and merchant named Philipot. In 1378, Philipot outfitted a private navy, recruited over one thousand sailors and went after a nest of Spanish pirates then preying on English shipping. Philipot's navy engaged the pirates in a pitched battle off the Spanish coast; fifteen pirate ships went to the bottom, thus putting an end to a threat the king and his ministers

106

had failed to suppress. But upon returning to London a hero, the bold and enterprising Philipot was arrested for "waging war without official authorization." Public outcry eventually secured his release and a knighthood.

Parallels between Philipot's story and the political situation of 1738 could not have failed to strike the audiences of that year. The first performance of Lacy's Oratory was interrupted by constables. Nine actors ran; only Lacy held the boards to insist on his rights as an artist and a patriot to perform the piece. Arrested and "condemned without trial to Bridewell Prison for six months of hard labor," he was soon sprung by opposition politicians. But opposition assistance to Lacy and a few other actors did not preclude other forms of Walpolean oppression: an entire issue of *The Craftsman* supporting Lacy's cause disappeared. Confiscated and carried off in coaches, not a single example survived the censoring fires lit by authorities.

The press might be muzzled by actions such as these, but Walpole could not squelch the increasingly bellicose mood of the people, nor silence Hosier's ghost, crying out for vengeance. The country moved inexorably toward war—or as Temperley has it, by early 1738: "The atmosphere began to grow dark, the thunder to mutter and the storm seemed on the point of breaking."

17.

In Madrid, Ambassador Keene, who felt a genuine affection for the Spanish people, was determined to prevent the "storm from breaking." Unfortunately, the Spanish Gang of Four remained unmoved on the subject of compensation for seized English ships and abused crews. English West Indian merchants continued to demand swift action from Walpole's government; the opposition press continued to agitate on their behalf. At last, on March 2, 1738, Secretary of State Newcastle wrote to Keene with stunning news:

> His majesty has thought fit to declare that he will grant Letters of Reprisal to such of His Subjects whose Ships or effects may have been seized on the High Seas by Spanish garda costas or ships acting by Spanish Commissions, which is what His Majesty thinks he could not in Justice any longer Delay.

The letter of reprisal, an ancient tool, allowed hundreds of Philipots to muster their own navies. Aggrieved merchants were now urged to arm their vessels and turn themselves into privateers. That none did emphasizes the practical, not the piratical: the age of Philipot had long passed; without the support of a professional navy, such a move against another sovereign nation only invited disaster. It did, however, send a message to Spain. Two weeks after the granting of reprisals, on March 17, "the inimitable Captain Jenkins is believed to have presented to a sympathetic House of Commons his tale of woe together with his ear in a bottle." Two weeks after this semimythic appearance, on March 30, Captain Clinton, commander in chief of the Mediterranean Fleet received secret orders to take his ships from Gibraltar to Menorca and prepare for war. And in an even more provocative gesture, Commodore Charles Brown was sent to Jamaica with a squadron of ten war ships. His instructions: "to seize such armed vessels of Spain that cruised and lurked about under the notion of Garda Costas in order to take the ships and vessels of His Majesty's subjects."

The dispatching of Brown to the West Indies is seen by many as the true opening salvo in the as yet undeclared war.

Meanwhile, aided by Walpole's ministry, peace still threatened to break out. Ambassador Keene wrote to Newcastle on April 18, 1738: "I have omitted no occasion of setting this [Spanish] Court right in its notions about the Motives of the present general dissatisfaction in England, and of convincing them that it does not arise from any Intrigues of Party, but from the just resentment of the whole Nation occasioned by the cruel treatment His Majesty's subjects have received from the Spaniards."

Keene was an amiable fat man, a life-long bachelor, fond of fancy clothes and parties, and liked by many in Spain where he had lived for years; but beneath his pleasant rotundity, lurked a first-class diplomatic mind. He now made another vigorous appeal to la Quadra in Madrid: "As yet, the whole matter was *dans son entier* . . . absolutely in the hands of Spain to put a happy conclusion to it," he pleaded to the grandee.

To everyone's surprise, the usually haughty la Quadra relented. He was a proud man but not stupid. The letters of reprisal and Clinton's naval maneuvers had shaken him. He knew Spain, with its half-destroyed navy and nearly bankrupt treasury could ill afford another war. The payment of reparations perhaps offered a cheaper solution. At last la Quadra sent instructions to the Council of the Indies to draw up documents "in a manner to let them perceive that His Catholick Majesty's Intentions were to cultivate a good Understanding with the King of Great Britain and to render justice to such of his subjects as had been injured by the guarda costas." At the same time a separate set of instructions, sent to the Spanish colonial governors and other officials tasked with investigating British claims, ordered them to skew the numbers in favor of Spain.

Secretary of State Newcastle, forecasting just such Spanish foot-dragging, initiated more preparations for war. Another British squadron under the veteran Admiral Nicholas Haddock, consisting of nine ships and two fireships, was now dispatched to the Mediterranean with instructions to menace the Spanish coasts. Here was a vital instrument—perhaps the most efficient war-making machine in the world at that time—poised to fire a shot into the heart of Spain. By June 1738, war again seemed a moment away as parliamentary debates raged on:

"War is called for without Doors," cried Walpole apologist MP Henry Pelham, "it is called for within Doors; but Gentlemen don't consider how little you can gain by War."

"Let us exert the Courage that our Wrongs have inspired us with: In short, let us tread in the Steps of Former Ages," responded the silver-tongued Pulteney, conjuring the glories of the Elizabethan sea dogs, victors over the Spanish Armada in 1588.

South Sea Company factors in the Spanish ports now received covert warnings to evacuate with their families and merchandize. Meanwhile, the Admiralty issued orders for the press-ganging of sailors sufficient to crew a substantial naval force. (This brutal practice—essentially kidnapping legitimized by the government—persisted into the nineteenth-century: gangs of navy toughs armed with clubs and pistols roamed the port cities and the countryside miles inland, seizing able-bodied men walking down the street, working in the fields. These unlucky bastards, forcibly "recruited" on the spot, were dragged off to serve in the navy—often to their doom. Those who refused were beaten insensate and taken anyway.)

With England's finger hovering over the trigger, with Haddock cruising the Mediterranean ready to strike, and Brown on his way to the Jamaica Station, Walpole himself stepped in to take control of the flagging negotiations with Spain. The presence of Haddock's squadron in Spanish waters was now said to be causing Queen Isabela the sort of night terrors usually reserved for her husband. For her, this war seemed like "the Big One," with the fate of Spain's overseas empire at stake. Negotiations to avoid war on the part of Spain suddenly moved forward with renewed vigor. Spain had been building coastal fortifications; she now turned her full attention to diplomatic solutions. At last, in October 1738, with the help of the

Spanish ambassador to London, Don Geraldino, Spain and Britain reached a workable compromise.

Negotiations dragged into January 1739, through the drafting of proposals and counterproposals, the ironing out of details. At last, on January 27, Keene and la Quadra signed an agreement that came to be known as the Convention of El Pardo, named after the palace in Madrid where the negotiations and signing took place. In this document, Spain agreed to satisfy all outstanding British claims against the *guarda costas*, up to December 1737, for a total of £95,000, to be paid out in full within four months. Walpole breathed a sigh of relief. The Great Man had prevailed, saved his ministry from the opposition, and war had been averted. He immediately instructed the Admiralty to send orders to Haddock to cease his cruising and return home. Spain, anticipating war, had been meanwhile desperately building up her navy; as a gesture of conciliation, la Quadra ordered ship builders to back off from any new construction.

"They have unarmed the greater part of their Ships," Keene, now jubilant, wrote to Newcastle, "given liberty to their Officers to leave their Regiments and their Destinations."

The Convention of El Pardo had seemingly disposed of the immediate causes for war—compensation for British ships and cargo seized by *guarda costas*—but there remained three other important issues, as yet unresolved: 1) The British colony of Georgia, recently established for the benefit of "sturdy debtors" by the redoubtable James Oglethorpe on land la Quadra insisted—rightly—that by treaty belonged to Spain ("I fancy," Newcastle commented, regarding Spanish claims, "however the right may be it will now be pretty difficult to give up Georgia"); 2) British logging in what had become a de-facto British colony in Campeachy Bay—later called British Honduras, now Belize; and 3) the inalienable right to "Free Navigation," for British shipping in West Indian waters and elsewhere. This last matter was nonnegotiable: The chant of "No

Search! No Seizure!" had become the rallying cry of the London mobs. But none of these nuts were too tough for the nutcracker of diplomacy, so Keene believed. All would soon be settled by a comprehensive treaty to which the Convention of El Pardo was merely a preamble.

War averted for the moment, negotiations now entered a second phase: what would the new treaty look like? Inevitably, everything began to slow down. The diplomats quibbled. la Quadra remained stubborn; his colleague Montijo conciliatory. But even this comparatively mild-mannered gentleman could not stomach the rampant smuggling which had brought both nations to the brink of war.

"What would it avail if we should hang up a dozen of our Governors in America to please You," Keene reports Montijo complaining bitterly, "if you, the English, do not treat your Contrabandists with equal Rigour; You only hear of your Ships being taken, but you give no attention to the damages we suffer by Interlopers." In the same letter to Newcastle, the ambassador explains the situation further: "Besides, My Lord, no one who has any experience of this Court will ever believe they will come to any solid agreement, or any favorable extension of the American Treaty on their side, if they have not some apparent condescension on ours. The art and Difficulty will be to know when to yield, in order to get an advantageous Bargain."

Keene knew a reasonable compromise regarding smuggling and interdiction would ensure the success of the proposed treaty; Newcastle concurred. Articles detailing a plan to suppress illegal trade drawn up by Keene and his Spanish counterpart, the Marquis de Castres reached Newcastle on May 19, 1738. Their plan would include close supervision of all West Indian private traders (men like Jenkins and the shipowners out of Glasgow he worked for) but did not include in this scrutiny any vessels owned by the South Sea Company. Too many government officials, courtiers and indeed

King George II himself maintained a financial interest in this private-public smuggling leviathan.

18.

Unfortunately, over the years since it had inherited the *Asiento*, the South Sea Company had failed to pay the King of Spain his lawful percentage of the *pieza de Indias* trade as specified in the contract. This amount, Spain now calculated at £68,000—which la Quadra suddenly declared must be subtracted from the £95,000 it had just agreed to pay in claims resulting from the *guarda costa* depredations. The amount specified and agreed to in the Convention of El Pardo had now been reduced to a paltry £27,000 by Spain. Independent British merchants calculated they had lost at least £140,000 worth of cargo, not to mention compensation for the physical sufferings of brutalized crews. The South Sea Company one-upped this claim: Spain owed Company investors more than £210,000 in property confiscated at her factories in the Spanish colonies during the two previous Anglo-Spanish wars. This amount, vast and largely unsubstantiated, Spain immediately rejected.

King Felipe, entering one of his lucid phases, instead of falling back into a fit of royal madness, now indulged himself in royal outrage. He pushed aside all South Sea Company claims and instead demanded the £68,000 owed to him. When the Company refused, the Spanish King did the unthinkable and the world held its breath: he canceled the *Asiento* Contract in a fit of pique. This action proved fatal. Here was an immediate and undeniable cause for the war all the diplomats had been seeking to avoid. The *Asiento*, established by international treaty and confirmed by more than twenty years' usage had just been suspended by Spain "in deference to a private quarrel with the merchants of the South Sea Company," as Temperley puts it. This action, he concludes laconically, "irritated the English government."

War once again became inevitable. Spain now flatly refused to pay the £95,000 agreed to at El Pardo. Haddock's orders calling him back from his menacing cruise of the Mediterranean rescinded, his squadron returned to glower at the Spanish coast. The clamor for war among the English public had never really died down, anyway. It now returned with a deafening roar—so loud that no member of the government, none of the king's ministers, not even Walpole himself could safely ignore it. Still, the Great Man held out. War, he knew meant unforeseen disaster, unmeditated loss of life, and huge financial losses for all sides. The situation might be retrieved through skilfull negotiations, war might yet be avoided!

No, it was too late.

The entirety of the press advocated for war, along with the most of the people. After nearly twenty-five years of general peace, Britain felt herself ready for a fight. Hosier's ghost, spectral finger raised in a gesture of imprecation now pointed toward the West Indies.

Walpole, despairing, threw up his hands. War was declared between Britain and Spain on October 19, 1739, the proclamation nailed at crossroads throughout the land. Bonfires cast a ruddy glow on jubilant mobs as Royal Heralds proclaimed war at the Temple Bar. Vaguely Spanish looking individuals were attacked and beaten in the streets; most were French or Italian or just had dark hair. In a tavern among the common people, to the thunderous peal of all the church bells in London, the Prince of Wales drank to the success of British arms. These spontaneous celebrations, however, plunged Walpole into the deepest melancholy. War, he knew, probably meant the end of his long and prosperous ministry: the opposition had wanted it and the opposition had got what it wanted over his objections. He had ruled the nation with a skillful combination of corruption, common sense, and tyranny since the South Sea Bubble and she had recovered from that fiasco and prospered. All that was finished now.

Listening to the bells ringing in London that night, the Great Man uttered the "brilliant and immortal sentence" for which he is perhaps most remembered: "They are ringing their bells," he lamented, nearly in tears. "Soon they will be wringing their hands."

Admiral Edward Vernon

FOUR

Admiral Vernon

1.

Edward Vernon, the "Hero of Porto Bello" and briefly one of the most celebrated English admirals of the eighteenth century, was known from an early age for his violent temper and all-around pugnaciousness. A hagiography written shortly after Vernon's death in 1758, with the memory of his glory still fresh in the English imagination, illustrates his early years in a series of fanciful vignettes emphasizing the young Vernon's fighting spirit and tenacity. Young Vernon is portrayed doing battle single-handed against a gang of bullies at the venerable Westminster School (where he has supposedly already been nicknamed "the Admiral" for his precocious love of the Royal Navy); arguing in Latin couplets with tyrannical schoolmasters; and in a dispute full of classical allusions with his father, who opposes a naval career for any of his progeny. The old man wanted his favorite son to follow his footsteps into politics and the law. But once the tough and patriotic Edward's mind was set on something, he would not give it up.

More recent biographers, however, are less indulgent regarding Vernon's character. He is described as "choleric," "hot-tempered," affected by "an impatient temper which did not permit him to suffer fools gladly," and as a person with "an extremely low tolerance of being opposed." *The Angry Admiral*, title of the last biography of Vernon, written by Cyril Hughes Hartmann in 1953, says it all. But it must be remembered that Vernon lived at a time when combativeness paid off, compromise being a weakness reserved for other generations.

Later in Vernon's career, during the parliamentary debates of the Depredations Crisis and leading up to the declaration of war against Spain in 1739, his voice was the loudest and most obstreperous heard on the hawkish side. Now a middle-aged semiretired captain on half-pay—Vernon had at last followed his father's footsteps into politics, representing the borough of Penryn in Cornwall in the House of Commons, a seat to which he'd been elected in April of 1722. In Parliament, Vernon quickly distinguished himself as one of the most vociferous members of the Opposition, a prominent member of a group of breakaway Whigs, fiercely critical of Walpole's pacific policies toward Spain.

But unlike most other Opposition MPs, Vernon could support his opinionated outbursts with years of active-duty experience in the West Indies: he had chased the Spaniard into his own lair, so to speak, and baited him there. In one famously fiery speech in January 1729, Vernon denounced Robert Walpole in terms bordering on the subversive. The Great Man's policies were at odds, Vernon insisted vociferously, with the country's best interests. The First Minister's determination to maintain peace with Spain came at the price of Britain's merchant service; more, her national honor. Vernon also accused Walpole of supplying false and misleadingly edited documents to the House regarding Hosier's fatal expedition of 1726–27. The blockade of Porto Bello had been a sham, Vernon thundered; Hosier's death and the death of his crews a tragic, unnecessary waste. All to pacify cowardly Spain which would only respond to overwhelming force—any fool could see that. Porto Bello itself might have been easily taken with three hundred men.

Vernon's passionate, over-the-top rhetoric had by then become notorious in the legislative body. Lord Egmont, one of Vernon's chief parliamentary critics, commented that in one typical speech, the Angry Admiral "brought up the Pope, the Devil, the Jesuits, the Seamen, etc. so that the House had no patience to attend him. . . . He quite lost his temper and made himself hoarse again."

By the mid-1730s, Vernon had already earned several official censures from the Speaker of the House and the enmity of Walpole's ministry. He had, for example, personally insulted the Scots—whom he characterized as a bunch of hypocrites for declining to pay their fair share of the salt duties imposed on everyone else; he had called the Stuart pretender a "Son of a Whore," and used a similar "warmth of expression" unbecoming a gentleman in speeches on other matters. He called the slippery, popular Lord Bolingbroke "a complicated villain," and added that "if acts of infamy were the way to recommend him to the king, he had done it effectively."

Once, during a heated debate, Vernon rushed forward to seize documents for copying from a table at the center of the cockpit; this after having been ordered not to do so by the outraged Speaker.

But the public loved him. He seemed to have their best interests at heart. He was a salty old sea dog, who would tell the truth to anyone; a plain-speaking sailor not impressed by the Great Walpole, or by extension, the king himself.

But Edward Vernon did not come from a particularly seafaring family, though his great-grandfather had been the captain of a merchant ship and a "victualler" (supplier of provisions) to the navy in 1628. The

Vernons, an ancient Suffolk clan, claimed descent from a Norman knight who had crossed to England with William the Conqueror. From about the fifteenth century, they had sought their fortunes in the political world. The Admiral's father, James Vernon, educated at Oxford, had been private secretary to the rebel Duke of Monmouth. The illegitimate son of Charles II, Monmouth, a Protestant, had led the 1685 revolt against his Catholic uncle, James II, last Stuart king of England. With the collapse of the Rebellion and Monmouth's beheading, the Vernons' fortunes went into temporary eclipse, reviving with the "Glorious Revolution" and the accession of two acceptable Protestants, William and Mary, to the throne of England in 1688.

James Vernon eventually became "Dutch" William's secretary of state. As is often the case with many successful men, James sought to pass his ambitions on to his children. His second son, Edward, born November 12, 1684, was sent to study under the famous Dr. Busby at Westminster though the results were not what the father had hoped. Edward proved a bright pupil, becoming proficient in Latin and Greek and absorbing the classical history and literature that formed the common culture of the upper classes. He was, if anything, overeducated for a career in the navy.

"[Vernon's] writing is the formed hand of an educated man, and his letters display an insight and thoughtfulness which are not to be found in the same degree in those of the majority of his contemporaries. . . . His outlook was wider than that of the greater number of the officers of the day." So writes Admiral Sir Herbert Richmond, distinguished naval officer and historian, in his definitive three volume study, *The Navy in the War of 1739–48*. Published as part of the "Cambridge Naval and Military Series" in 1920, this work is still the go-to source on all things Jenkins' Ear.

But, he adds "Vernon's early education may possibly have contributed to his defects as well as to his qualities. . . . He who saw so clearly the essentials of a situation, who could pierce through superficialities and reach main principles, found himself unable to sit silent while he observed an Administration blundering in the mires created by its own lack of foresight. He could not resist the temptation, which a certain facility in expressing his opinions encouraged, of putting forward his views and criticisms with a directness which no Ministry at that time appreciated."

An unforeseen danger comes with possessing a top-notch intellect honed by an excellent education: the world is full of too many glib idiots who will resent the hell out of you.

Good student though he was, Vernon's heart wasn't exactly in his studies at Westminster. His dreams lay elsewhere, beyond schoolroom walls. Westminster School, one of the oldest and most prestigious institutions of its kind in England, lay not far from the Thames. The river's shoreline was then festooned with numerous docks and boat yards and sailor's taverns haunted by the maimed old tars who had served England's navy through many wars. According to tradition, the young Vernon frequently cut class to spend time down there, absorbing sailors' talk of furious sea battles and foreign shores. Many had fought at La Hogue, a decisive victory over the French Navy in 1691.

From Westminster, Vernon went on to Oxford where he studied mathematics, navigation, and astronomy under the venerated Dr. John Keill. Isaac Newton also supposedly had a hand in Vernon's education, teaching him how to gauge latitude by calculating the relative position of the pole star. One imagines the great scientist and the gawky teenager in the Greenwich observatory, eyes toward the heavens, as the stars wheeled in their courses over England.

2.

Though Vernon's father still insisted his son choose a legal career as a stepping-stone to politics, the young man would not abandon his nautical dreams. He would enter the navy against all opposition. It was an unheard-of rebellion in those patriarchal times. The furious father-son disagreements that ensued were eventually mediated by Edward's mother, the daughter of a baronet. She must have been a formidable woman: her arguments in favor of her son's choice of career prevailed. Edward went aboard the legendary Admiral Rooke's flagship, *Shrewsbury* on May 9, 1700 as a King's Letter Boy. He was sixteen.

The War of Spanish Succession had just begun. The *Shrewsbury*, part of a combined Anglo-Dutch-Swedish fleet, had been sent to chastise the Danes at Copenhagen. Vernon's early hagiographers placed him at the forefront of every major sea battle for the next twelve years of war, first in the Baltic, then the Mediterranean. He is supposed to have been commended for gallantry by Rooke, been given a diamond ring and a hundred gold sovereigns for services rendered to the Archduke Charles, Hapsburg pretender to the Spanish throne, for assisting that hopeful Austrian on his way to Lisbon. He was also supposedly present at the famous Battle of Vigo Bay in October 1702 aboard Vice Admiral Thomas Hopsonn's flagship, the *Torbay*.

A Franco-Spanish fleet had taken refuge in the protected anchorage of Vigo Bay on the Galician Coast behind a nine-foot deep boom of masts, chains, and cables. The *Torbay*'s sails filled with a sudden gust; Vice Admiral Hopsonn crashed through the boom, only to be abandoned by the wind almost immediately. Becalmed and stranded beneath Spanish guns, the *Torbay* caught blasts of enemy fire from stem to stern. Adrift, ablaze, she seemed in danger of sinking. Then, a Spanish merchant vessel anchored nearby caught a stray shell. Her hold was packed full of a cargo of snuff for the noses of Europe; the subsequent explosion sent a massive cloud of snuff raining down on the battle like fine-grained sand. Fires suddenly extinguished, the *Torbay* fought on.

At last, the wind picked up and the other ships from Hopsonn's squadron eventually followed, crashing through the boom to the

Torbay's rescue. The Franco-Spanish fleet was destroyed; more than a dozen vessels went to the bottom. A victory snatched from the jaws of defeat, but Vernon wasn't there. Rather, the ship on which he was then serving, the *Lennox*, had been detached from the squadron and sent on a mundane mission to escort a convoy of empty victuallers back to England for more supplies.

This episode neatly illustrates the many near-misses of Vernon's early career. He grew into a skilled and dutiful officer whom fate always placed just a little to the left of the main action. Others took the glory that Vernon coveted, even as he helped maintained the wooden machine that made that glory possible. His unblemished record at sea remained undistinguished by a major victory and blighted by his increasingly notorious temper. As Clowes puts it, Vernon was "blunt, well intentioned, honest and very popular . . . whose chief service faults were that he could not always control either his tongue or his pen, and that he was too fond of vulgar applause."

Over the next few years, Vernon served variously in the Mediterranean and the Baltic—notably under the euphoniously named Admiral Sir Clowdesley Shovell at the Siege of Barcelona, though he just managed to avoid Shovell's sad fate, when the latter's fleet wrecked on the reefs off the Scilly Islands during a storm. Shovell had miscalculated his longitude; he and everyone aboard his flagship, the *Association*, and a thousand other sailors perished in this preventable disaster. The wreck of Shovell's fleet eventually led to the invention of the naval chronometer, which would fix the longitude of any vessel within a few seconds accuracy.

Vernon aboard his own ship, the *Rye*, managed to weather the storm.

In 1706, Vernon earned his first independent command with the frigate *Dolphin*; in 1708 he participated in the scattering of the Pretender's Franco-Hibernian invasion fleet in the Firth of Forth, one of the many efforts to restore the Stuarts to the throne of England. In 1709, as captain of the *Jersey*, Vernon made his first voyage to the West Indies. There, over the next four years, at the Jamaica Station and elsewhere, he acquired first-hand knowledge of Caribbean waters, its islands, currents, hurricanes. And its pirates and *guarda costas*, whom he regarded as one and the same.

In 1716 Vernon was in an uncharacteristic diplomatic role: he accompanied the new British ambassador to Constantinople. This was a prickly assignment involving much careful diplomacy, the Turks being addicted to colorful ceremonies and sticklers for protocol. On the return leg of this tour, he also negotiated with the Grand Duke of Tuscany and the Venetian Doge for the return of British sailors impressed or swindled into the service of these foreign navies in the clipjoints and unsavory dives of the Italian Port of Leghorn. Vernon wrote in another one of his hectoring letters to the Admiralty:

The seamen are more corrupted and debauched in this port into foreign service, than in any other port in the world, in my opinion, nothing contributes more to debauching them, then the great number of Public tippling houses kept in the town by His Majesty's subjects, there being said to be forty to fifty of them, who are a great many employed as crimps by foreigners to debauch the English seamen into other services.

During this period, perhaps, Vernon conceived his antipathy for rum, which he regarded as the ruination of many a decent sailor. It was then allotted to them in their rations aboard ship at the rate of three-and-a-half pints weekly—and in unlimited quantities until their pay ran out ashore. His concern for the health of his men later became legendary. Though it is hard to imagine such a "choleric" and "dicta-torial" man worrying in a motherly fashion about his crews, he did. A ship was useless without the men who raised the sails. It is also hard to imagine Vernon succeeding at diplomatic missions but his assignment with the Turks and the Italians went off well. He certainly found the gaudy atmosphere of foreign courts stimulating; the pomp and display, particularly of the Turks, must have touched something in his soul.

3.

In 1727, with the 13th Siege of Gibraltar underway, England was again at war with Spain.

Ordered once more to the West Indies, Vernon took numerous Spanish prizes in small actions involving a ship or two and along with these captured vessels learned contempt for the Spanish foe. The Spaniards were, in his estimation, cruel and cowardly at once, always ready to avoid a fight with a British ship—however outgunned. During this tour, Vernon first caught sight of the walled city of Cartagena de Indias, then one of the stopover ports of the Spanish treasure fleet, and capital of the Province of New Granada. It is now one of the major cities in Colombia. This walled city was ideally situated for defense, nestled securely at the far end of a bay whose two entrances—Boca Chica and Boca Grande—were guarded by strong forts and batteries. Vernon also saw there that the Spanish would not risk an encounter with the British at sea; they preferred to run their warships aground rather than fight. They had in this manner, blocked seaborne approaches to the city—an effective tactic Vernon would come to know too well in the War of Jenkins' Ear.

All Vernon's experiences in the West Indies during this conflict showed him, according to Admiral Richmond that "the Spaniards had little appetite for a fight. The larger Spanish Barlovento Squadron at Havana had not ventured leeward [from Havana] nor sought him out. Their privateers attacked commerce and had instructions to raid isolated plantations. [This] confirmed his belief that although sea power was a fragile instrument, the Royal Navy possessed a general superiority over the 'Bully Don.'"

But perhaps the most important lesson Vernon learned during this period in the West Indies concerned the necessity of decisive military actions of short duration in the tropics. British sailors and soldiers possessed no immunity to mosquito-borne tropical diseases. Lengthy campaigns, either at sea or on land in the tropics would lead to disaster. Swiftness of execution was an imperative; blockades and long sieges not advisable, almost always fatal to the besieger. Vernon's prescient views were unfortunately confirmed by the grim fate of Hosier's fleet.

"In my judgement, I should limit all expeditions to this country," Vernon wrote in one of his pesky letters to Secretary of State Newcastle, "to be entered upon immediately on their arrival, and to be executed within the first six weeks, before their men would begin to fall sick."

"The history of West Indian operations shews how well judged was this advice," confirms Admiral Richmond. "The life of a battalion in the West Indies averaged two years . . . the proportion of sick in the West Indian garrisons might be taken as fifty percent at the least. In reading these almost prophetic opinions of Vernon's it is not difficult to appreciate his impatience."

After the Anglo-Spanish war of 1727–29, Vernon's navy career stalled. He went on half-pay—a sort of Naval Reserve service for officers—and entered parliament. Many officers on half pay tended to go to seed. They drank too much, dueled, gambled. In 1729, Vernon, levelheaded in most practical matters, married a woman named Sarah Best, the daughter of a wealthy brewer. They had three sons on whom Vernon doted. But he was a man who could not live without a fight, if not against the Spaniards then at home in the cockpit of politics. All through the 1730s he embroiled himself in the most controversial issues of the day—with a special focus on the continued *guarda costa* attacks on British merchant shipping. He was an obstreperous voice, an advocate of the vigorous "Blue Water" policy and for naval reform. Well-spoken and quotable, he became one of the most prominent members of Walpole's Parliamentary Opposition. But he was not generally known by the larger public until he vaulted to national prominence with a single speech delivered in July 1738.

Again, because of contemporary press strictures against reporting parliamentary debates verbatim, the exact words of Vernon's famous speech are hard to ascertain, but the substance has survived. Both "boisterous and bellicose" it challenged Walpole's ongoing careful negotiations with Spain to avoid war. Vernon had witnessed firsthand the Spaniard's reluctance to fight against the British Navy in the last war. They key to smashing Spanish power, he asserted, lay in seizing just a few of their strong points in the West Indies— Havana, Cartagena, and Porto Bello. The latter, whose blockade had destroyed Hosier and his men, was not impregnable, as suggested by its reputation.

Protected by three sturdy *castillos*—the *Todo Fierro* (or Iron Castle), the *Santiago de la Gloria*, and the *San Jerónimo*—Porto Bello lay at the far end of a deep bay and could not be taken, so people said, except by a major amphibious operation. Vernon now insisted at the top of his lungs that not only could Porto Bello be taken without the aid of substantial land forces, he himself could take the city "with six ships only!" fourteen fewer than the ill-fated Hosier had at his disposal in 1727.

"Vernon said, moreover," Clowes adds, "that he would gladly venture his life and reputation upon the success of such an enterprise, if only he were permitted to attempt it."

Vernon's "six ships speech" had an explosive effect. He spoke with the authority of one who had been there and with ultimate contempt for Walpole and the ongoing complex diplomatic negotiations to avoid war with Spain. From the comparative obscurity of a half-pay naval officer and back-bench politician Vernon became a national figure overnight. The Opposition had found it's champion; the nation clamored for Vernon's six ships to be sent against Spain. Before a shot in the pending war had been fired, the press and the people extolled him "as another Drake or Raleigh," said the acerbic English novelist Tobias Smollett, who would eventually serve under Vernon's command as a surgeon's mate. "He became the symbol of a party and his praise resounded from all corners of the Kingdom."

4.

What did Edward Vernon look like?

Because of his later fame, several contemporary portraits exist, including one by the great Thomas Gainsborough. The portrait that hangs in the British National Maritime Museum, by a little-known painter named Charles Philips is often reproduced. It shows a mild-looking man with smooth features, perhaps around forty—never mind that Vernon was well into his fifties during the War of Jenkins' Ear. This Vernon wears a fine velvet coat and lightly grasps the staff of authority. On his head, the usual mass of ringlets that passed for a manly wig in those days. In the background his flagship sails toward a destination that might be Porto Bello. The Phillips portrait, like others of the time, even Gainsborough's, possesses a generic quality, a kind of blandness that tells us almost nothing about the man.

A better rendering of Vernon belongs to the French sculptor, Roubillac. Vernon's bust, executed in marble in the 1740s shows perhaps a truer likeness. This Vernon, blank eyes staring toward an unseen horizon is strong-featured, his jaw set, his brow creased with lines of determination and worry. Roubillac renders this confident, tyrannical seaman in three dimensions; here's someone who expected obedience from his subordinates, always knew he was right, and deplored a world in which his judgement might be questioned. Here we see a man capable of the towering rages attributed to him by biographers.

Not long after Vernon's Six-Ships Speech, Felipe V of Spain refused to pay the first installment of the £95,000 sum agreed to in the Convention of El Pardo. War now became inevitable. Walpole, finally despairing of peaceful solutions, called a military council to explore how that war might best be conducted. Among the naval officers summoned to testify, we find the surprising presence of Vernon—heretofore one of Walpole's greatest adversaries. Now well known for his aggressive stance and already a kind of hero for his sheer obstreperousness, Vernon stressed a few of the points he had already made in parliamentary debates: An invasion of Spain itself would most likely bring France into the fight against England, both Continental powers united by their Bourbon kings, common religion, and a mutual defense treaty signed in 1733 called *Le Pacte de Famille.*

"I can never be the adviser of land expeditions especially into this country, [Spain] that may drain the Royal Treasury, and, in case of a French war, disable His Majesty from keeping a superiority at sea, on which, in my apprehensions, both the security and the prosperity of the Kingdom depend," Vernon wrote in yet another less-than-diplomatic letter to Secretary of State Newcastle. Between them, Vernon pointed out, France and Spain could summon a massive standing army of over 500,000 men. Britain at that moment could only account for around 40,000, already spread thinly around the world. Though, of course, he added, the British navy was superior in number of vessels, armaments, and critically, professionalism, to the navies of both continental powers.

At Walpole's council of war, Vernon outlined what he thought as the proper strategy for the coming war. Spain must be attacked through her American colonies. This was her soft underbelly. She was a nation that manufactured nothing and relied too heavily on the proceeds of the silver mines of Peru and Mexico—which acted as a kind of opium on the Spanish economy. Seizure of key ports involved in the "galleon trade" of South American silver would lead to the collapse of Spain's overseas empire and ultimately of Spain herself. "If only Porto Bello and Cartagena are taken," Vernon concluded, "then all will be lost to them."

The council of war ended that day, with Vernon supposing his evidence had been ignored by a hostile Walpole. "Indeed," comments naval historian Harding, "on the surface his naval and political career seemed over."

That evening, Vernon packed his belongings and left for Chatham, a town about thirty miles distant where he had established his residence a decade earlier, no doubt eager to see his wife and sons. Tradition has it that around 2 A.M., just after Vernon had tucked himself into bed, a loud knocking came at the door. An insistent visitor at that time of night in that part of the world could mean only death or disaster. It was neither and both: a messenger dispatched from the ministry in London politely commanded Vernon to return to Whitehall for a private meeting with Walpole. Vernon quickly dressed, heaved himself into the carriage supplied and met the Great Man early the next morning.

Expecting the worst, baffled, Vernon instead received astonishing news: Walpole informed him that he had been appointed vice admiral of the "Blue" Squadron of the Royal Navy—in those days divided into three squadrons, the Red, White, and Blue in that order of precedence, each with its own pennants and flags and traditions. In his new capacity as a vice admiral, Vernon would jump three orders of magnitude from Captain, semiretired. He would now take command of a squadron of nine ships and set sail as soon as possible for the West Indies. Once there, he would determine on his own initiative what actions might be taken against the Spanish colonies. He was ordered to "commit all sorts of hostilities against the Spaniards in such a manner as you shall judge most proper."

War had come for the old sailor. Vernon was fifty-five, a considerable age for the time. He had thought his career as an active-duty seaman behind him. But he had just received a monumental commission, the greatest of his life, and from the hands of a political enemy. Walpole's sentiments at this meeting can only be imagined. Some historians have suggested that the First Minister secretly hoped Vernon would fail in his mission, that he rejoiced at the prospect of sending this parliamentary gadfly to the other side of the world where he might suffer Hosier's fate. Others insist that Walpole was too great a man for such pettiness, that he was at his core a dedicated English patriot. Who can say? Who can plumb the murk at the bottom of a politician's heart?

After meeting with Walpole, equerries hustled Vernon off to the royal presence of King George at St. James Palace. There, the old sailor "kissed the ring" and received the king's blessing for an expedition whose goals and parameters had not yet been clearly established. Many supposed Vernon's instructions included orders to take Porto Bello and that he would be forced to stand behind his famous speech. This was not the case. His instructions, of a general nature, included no such specifics. In fact, the story told above of Vernon's appointment as reported by his hagiographers is not the whole story. Parts of it might not even been true: Vernon had, apparently, already solicited a commission in the coming war. In June he had paid a visit to the Admiralty and his "steady friend" First Lord of the Admiralty, Sir Charles Wager, under whom he had served at Gibraltar—both during the taking in 1704 and the siege of 1726–27. During this meeting with Wager, he had thrown his hat into the ring for a major commission in the war against Spain.

Wager knew Vernon—infamous temper aside—for a well-liked, dogged, and supremely competent officer with an intimate knowledge of the West Indies. He recommended Vernon for the job to Secretary Newcastle.

"We are all for Captain Vernon," he reported to the Duke. "Who in this case would be made a vice admiral and restored to his rank. Our master is a little averse to it, but we hope it will do."

The master Wager refers to is King George II who had resented the tenor of Vernon's attacks on Walpole's Spanish policy—by extension the policy of the king himself. But Wager persisted, calling Vernon "much properer than any officer we have to send, being very well acquainted in all that part of the West Indies, and is a very good sea officer, whatever he may be, or has been, in the House of Commons."

Unwilling to share Hosier's fate, other flag-rank officers had already refused this hazardous commission. The West Indies with it's dreadful tropical diseases and awful heat remained the least popular of assignments. At last, on July 10, 1739, with no other reasonable prospects to choose from, the king reluctantly approved Vernon's commission.

Vernon felt himself matched with his hour, commenting, only: "I pray God grant me a happy meeting with the Spaniards."

5.

The newly elevated Vice Admiral Edward Vernon had never been a man to waste time. Securing the king's blessing, he returned briefly to Chatham and his wife and sons for what must have been a fraught parting. Vernon had trained all his life for a commission of this magnitude, an expedition from which, like Hosier, he might not return. After Chatham, he departed for Portsmouth, where his little fleet had been assembled. Nine ships: *Burford*, seventy guns; *Lennox*, seventy; *Elizabeth* and *Kent* carrying sixty; *Worcester*, *Stafford*, and *Princess Louise* each carrying sixty; one fifty, the *Norwich*, and the *Pearl*, forty.

Vernon chose the *Burford* for his flagship. From its tall central mast, he flew his admiral's pennant for the first time—a broad gonfalon of navy blue. Final instructions, received from the Admiralty on July 19 reiterated the injunction to destroy Spanish shipping and installations but also contained a set of new "secret orders" under the king's seal: upon arriving in the West Indies, he would "procure the best intelligence as to where a descent (invasion) could be made on the Spanish dominions in the West Indies which would be of prejudice to Spain and of advantage to England." He was to state the number of troops that would be required, and so soon as he had ascertained these matters, "to send the information home with the utmost dispatch by a sloop."

With these "secret orders" the war's strategy had changed, for the worse, Vernon felt. Destroying Spanish shipping and harrying her colonies—perhaps capturing a city or two—were suddenly no longer adequate compensation for all the British merchantmen seized by the *guarda costas* over the last few decades. A much grander kind of war was now anticipated by Walpole's ministry and the king: a war of conquest, the object of desire being Spain's overseas empire in its entirety. Vernon must have trembled with anger and apprehension when he read his new instructions. They ran counter to everything he knew about making war in the tropics, and everything he had repeatedly advised.

Vernon and his squadron set sail from Spithead on July 23. Delayed by contrary winds, he and his nine ships malingered for days in the vicinity of the Isle of Wight. The new vice admiral took advantage of this caesura to assess the condition of his ships and his men. The ships were fine; the men not so much. The manning of the Royal Navy, a perennial problem for England in the eighteenth century, reached its nadir in the 1740s: the press gangs were at their most vicious, their victims all the more reluctant to serve in a navy where discipline was harsh, conditions terrible, and life short. Vernon fired off another one of his critical letters to superiors at the Admiralty complaining that he'd been given "unfledged mariners who had to be instructed in everything."

Returning to Plymouth on August 7, he wrote yet another letter on the subject to the secretary of state: well-trained men were an absolute necessity, "being strongly convinced in my own judgment that preserving a superiority at sea is the best security for His Majesty's Government, as well as the trade and prosperity of the kingdom." In this letter, Vernon also suggested that "marching regiments" (infantry) be converted into marines, a contingent of which would serve aboard each vessel in the navy.

He had meanwhile begun training his own men. He ran endless gunnery drills, executed complex sailing maneuvers, and took time to observe the reactions of his captains. In these men, professionals, raised in the service as he had been, he was not disappointed. In them he placed ultimate confidence. Now began the first of those innovations for which he is best remembered by naval historians. This was his "Addition to the Fighting Instructions" which allowed his subordinates to act on their own initiative during the heat of battle. Before Vernon's "Addition" captains were forced to adhere to a rigid preset battle plan, regardless of changes in circumstance. Vernon now allowed his captains to make decisions based on the unpredictable ebb-and-flow of the fight. This sort of freedom of action was almost unheard of in the tightly choreographed naval engagements of the day.

"And as it is morally impossible to fix any general rule to occurrences that must be regulated from the weather and the enemy's disposition," Vernon wrote, "this is left to the respective captains' judgement that shall be ordered out of the line to govern himself as becomes an officer of prudence and resolution, and as he will answer the contrary at his peril."

It is from such simple, commonsense concepts that revolutions are made.

Vernon's other innovation—one that contributed a new word to the English language—began in his concern for the health of his men. He was religious and abstemious and desired his men to be so. From his previous West Indian experience, he knew that one of the common sailor's greatest enemies resided in "Jamaican punch houses and the formidable Dragon, drunkenness." Rum and other strong alcoholic concoctions, in Vernon's view, accounted for countless desertions, discipline problems, and premature deaths. Now, he decided to do something about it.

Over the course of the preceding decades, the British sailor's weekly rations according to the Victualling Board of the Admiralty consisted of "7lb of biscuit or bread, 4lb of beef, 2lb of pork, 2 pints of pease, 3 pints of oats, 12 oz of butter or cheese, 7 gallons of beer or 3½ pints of rum or brandy." On the ships of his squadron, Vernon now diluted this standard rum ration with water at a ratio of 1:8. Lime or lemon juice, some sources say, was occasionally added when available, thus having the accidental effect of preventing scurvy—though no doctor of the era had knowledge of this cure for what was then the scourge of the British sailor.

"You are hereby required and directed as you tender both the Spiritual and Temporal Welfare of His Majesty's Service," so Vernon's famous order ran, "to take particular care that Rum be no more served in Specie to any of the Ship's Company under your command, but that the respective daily allowance of Half-a-Pint a man for all your Officers and Ship's Company be every day mixed with the proportion of a Quart of Water to every Half-Pint of

Rum." Vernon also insisted that these watered-down rum rations be consumed daily, putting an end to rum hoarding and end-of-the-week drunken binges.

Admiral Vernon was then known throughout his squadron as "Old Grog" after the foul weather gear he wore on the quarterdeck, some say a "sea cloak," others trousers—made from "grogram," a sort of waterproof fabric composed of heavy silk and mohair imbued with wax. His sailors, outraged by the dilution of their rum rations, derisively called the new concoction "Grog" after their nickname for the man himself. The word soon entered the language. The *Oxford English Dictionary* defines grog as "any admixture of rum or other strong spirits with water or fruit juices."

Vernon's sailors both loved and hated their commanding officer. He was a stern taskmaster and disciplinarian, but also one of the few flag officers who cared for the welfare of the average seaman. Not only did he establish onshore hospitals for the sick and fair hearings for the accused, he extended his reforms to moral matters. He outlawed swearing aboard ship and reinstituted obligatory daily prayers, which had been absent since the days of Cromwell's Puritan Navy. With his reforms, says Harding, Vernon helped "develop and improve the public image of the seaman." As for the sailors themselves, they "at first repined at this care of them," says an Admiralty report, "but by degrees were reconciled to it."

The drunken swearing British sailor was, for the moment, no more.

6.

At last, with favorable winds billowing the *Burford*'s sails, Vernon's squadron left Spithead in the first week of August 1739. After all the training in gunnery and sea maneuvers and the absence of copious amounts of rum, "there is little doubt that under Vernon's direction, this small squadron rapidly became, for its size, the most efficient that Great Britain has sent to sea for many years," says Admiral Richmond.

Vernon's instructions first directed him to cruise the Galician coast of Spain to intercept the Spanish *Azogues* fleet. The *Azogues*—small, deep-keeled merchantmen—ferried quicksilver (liquid mercury) from mines in Spain to the silver mines in Mexico and Peru, where this toxic substance was used in the refining process. They also carried cloth, olive oil, raisins, and other consumables to the Spanish colonists, returning with holds full of refined silver ingots. Vernon cruised up and down the rugged coast in vain for two weeks. The *Azogues* did not appear; they had in fact already arrived safe and sound at the Spanish port of Santander. He then detached the Pearl to continue the fruitless hunt for the *Azogues* and proceeded with the rest of his ships to the West Indies.

The squadron reached Port Royal Jamaica on October 12 and immediately Vernon presented himself to Governor Trelawny, an old acquaintance from Parliament. The two men eyed each other warily. Vernon had the usual suspicion of the military man for the civilian authority, but Trelawny was a man of Vernon's type: the son of a dissenting bishop who had defied the authority of the last Stuart king, he possessed strong opinions and had also represented a Cornish borough in the House of Commons. Here was a man the new vice admiral could reason with and whom he respected.

Meanwhile, Commodore Charles Brown who had been sent out six months earlier during the "reprisal" phase of negotiations with Spain did not get along with the governor. The two men had fallen out over Brown's injudicious use of press gangs on Jamaica. Unfortunately, Vernon told Trelawny, press gangs could not be avoided— they would later literally come to blows later on this issue. The Navy was as always critically understaffed and now the nation was at war. Vernon promised to give fair warning and use the gangs sparingly.

But Brown had loosed what amounted to roving gangs of bravos in the streets of Kingston. No male between the age of fifteen and fifty of any class was safe. Brown soon arrived at the governor's palace to a stiff reprimand from an irritated Vernon who had expected him there to greet his squadron upon arrival. But at last, the two naval officers and the governor sat down to discuss strategy.

What would be the first war objective? Vernon's orders leaned toward Havana. With Havana taken, Admiral Wager believed, Cuba would fall in its entirety to the British crown. But Wager had left ultimate decisions regarding the campaign to Vernon's discretion with the following caveat:

"You know as well as I," Wager wrote in a private letter to his chosen commander, "that whatever is determined to be put in execution must be immediately proceeded upon; for soldiers, no more than other people, cannot do anything when they are dead, and that will be their fate if they stay too long in Jamaica." "But," he added, "you will be the best judge, who are upon the spot, what shall be most advisable to undertake."

To Vernon the choice was clear, and he soon convinced Governor Trelawny and the chastened Brown. The death of Hosier and his men would be avenged.

7.

Port Bello, Panama, twenty degrees north of the Equator, is today a weedy exurb of Colón, capital of the province that bears its name. A few houses, sunstruck and ramshackle straggle down to the glassy waters of a bay hemmed in by a hilly shoreline covered with thick vegetation. Sellers of fruit ices perspire beneath ragged umbrellas on the street corners; the occasional window air-conditioning unit leaks moisture down peeling plaster walls. The commercial bustle of

Colón spreads a brown smear of exhaust above the trees. Tankers, big as apartment buildings, inch across the isthmus through the canal. Over all, a white-hot Caribbean sky, bleached of color by the tropical sun.

Little now remains of the Porto Bello of Vernon's day, except perhaps the heat, thick and pestilential, especially when it rains. And of course, the mosquitos. The mossy ruins of the San Jerónimo fort, now a UNESCO World Heritage Site, is a later iteration from the one that threatened Vernon's tidy squadron in 1739. Even in the pre-industrial eighteenth century, before the advent of "Global Warming," Porto Bello was considered "owing to the great heat and the moisture of the climate . . . so unwholesome a place that none who could help it would live there."

Founded in 1597 as a way-station for Peruvian silver, the town had been chosen for the defensibility of its excellent anchorage. Supposedly, Christopher Columbus himself had first recognized the value of its protected deepwater harbor and bestowed the name Porto Bello, Beautiful Port. Nombre de Dios, an earlier settlement a dozen miles to the west, had proved unfortunately vulnerable to pirates and hurricanes and was abandoned.

Perhaps because the great Francis Drake—"El Draque the Scourge of God" the Spaniards called him—had died aboard his ship in nearby waters and was laid to rest there beneath the waves, Porto Bello had always held a fascination for the English. Most Englishmen of the eighteenth century knew that the galleons of the Spanish treasure fleet filled their holds with silver in its harbor and from there sailed for Old Spain. Porto Bello had become synonymous in the English imagination with fabulous riches, the unimaginable wealth of the New World.

Lured by this golden legend, Englishmen had captured the place three times before 1739. The Elizabethan sea dog William Parker took the nascent town in 1601; finding nothing much there, he quickly sailed away. In 1668, the famously brutal buccaneer Henry Morgan seized a flourishing port. His pirate crews spent fourteen days raping and pillaging, leaving a burned-out ruin in their wake. Twenty years later, another buccaneer, John Cockson, repeated this performance. It seemed the English would never stop coming to kill and burn and steal the treasure the Spanish stole from the Indians. But unlike Nombre de Dios, Porto Bello possessed too fine a harbor to be abandoned. At last, in the aftermath of Cockson's attack, Spain decided to build up the town's puny defenses. Between 1690 and 1710 they erected the three impressive forts—*Todo Fierro, Santiago de la Gloria*, and *San Jerónimo*—that would menace Vernon's squadron in 1739. And because no Englishmen had laid siege in more than fifty years, Porto Bello eventually gained its aura for impregnability.

Heated Parliamentary debates during the Depredations Crisis had focused on Porto Bello's fierce reputation. But those who had seen it, Vernon among them, doubted this assessment. Vernon knew from experience that Spanish infrastructure in the West Indies languished in a state of critical disrepair, and that most Spanish colonials lacked the will to fight.

In truth, despite the galleon trade, Porto Bello in 1739 wasn't much more than a minor settlement. It consisted of roughly five hundred houses, inhabited, according to contemporary reports, "mainly by negroes and mullatoes." The town's chief merchants, public officials, ranking officers and wives and families thereof lived in airy bungalows in the surrounding hills. Porto Bello's chief buildings, a half-dozen large, unkempt stone warehouses, stood empty most of the time, waiting to receive the limitless bounty of the Americas: indigo, cochineal, sugar, cocoa, emeralds from the Amazon, gold from Mexico, and silver from Peru. Once a year, anticipating this fabulous ingress, the town swelled into a minor metropolis, its population increasing tenfold. These new arrivals, however, stayed only a few weeks. They were merchants and traders and curious visitors come to attend the *Feria*, an annual commercial fair that coincided with the arrival of the galleons from Spain.

The galleons arrived in late summer or early fall, fat and wallowing, stuffed with what manufactured goods Spain could produce (cloth and lace and tanned leather, sword blades and gunpowder) and the preserved produce (olives, pickled fruits, wines, brined hams, aged cheeses) of the Iberian Peninsula. These goods and comestibles would be exchanged for silver and gold. The South Sea Company's *navio de permisso* as stipulated by the *Asiento* Contract was also permitted to trade. Along with the legal tonnage of superior English manufactured goods she brought, smuggled in her hold and between her false decks, a greater amount of contraband.

At fair time, not a bed could be found in the vicinity of the town. The locals charged exorbitant rates for a bit of floor space and lived, it was said, off a few weeks rent all year long. Also, local Indians traveled from up and down the coast bringing rare animals and birds and the occasional precious stone to trade for rum and weapons. But they camped frugally in the outskirts beside their cookfires, pack mules set loose to forage in the thick woods that pressed on all sides in arboreal gloom.

Such was Porto Bello on the eve of the British attack in 1739. Not much more than a sleepy village that perked up once a year for the fair. But the fair had been canceled that year on account of war.

8.

Vernon's squadron, now consisting of exactly six ships—this number certainly no coincidence—dropped anchor just outside the narrow mouth of Porto Bello's protected bay late in the day on November 20, 1739. The six ships with which he intended to capture the town were

Burford—his flagship—*Norwich, Worcester, Stafford,* and *Princess Louisa*, with Commodore Brown's *Hampton Court* detached and serving under his command. The expedition's manpower amounted to 2,495 sailors and 200 marines, these last supplied by Governor Trelawny of Jamaica under command of a reliable officer, Captain Newton.

Last sunlight gleamed on a calm sea and on the formidable battlements of the Iron Castle, high on a rocky promontory at the entrance to the harbor in the distance. The wind blew gently out of the west, as it usually did in the fall in these latitudes. At 5 A.M. the next morning, the Admiral called a council of his captains to discuss plans for the upcoming attack and to emphasize his new "Addition" to the traditional "Fighting Instructions" that had more often than not hampered the maneuvering of British naval vessels in battles at sea.

"It is from my knowledge of the experience of my captains," he later wrote, and my confidence in their resolution, that I have my chief reliance successfully to execute his Majesty's orders."

The Fighting Instructions now delivered to each captain contained the following:

Upon making the land at Puerto Bello, and having a fair wind to favor them, and daylight for the attempt, to have their ships clear in all respects for immediate service; and, on the proper signal, to form themselves into a line of battle, as directed; and, being formed, to follow in the same order of battle to the attack, in the manner hereafter directed. And as the north shore of the harbor of Puerto Bello is represented to the Admiral to be a bold steep shore, on which, at the first entrance, stands the Todo Fierro, or Iron Castle, Commodore Brown, and the ships that follow him are directed to pass the said fort within less than a cable's length distant, giving the enemy as they pass as warm a fire as possible, both from great guns and musketry. Then

Commodore Brown is to steer away for the Gloria Castle, and anchor as near as he possibly can to the easternmost part of it, for battering down all the defenses.

But Vernon also ordered his captains to ignore these instructions if necessary and hew themselves to changing circumstances. In the age of sail all battles at sea were naturally subject to the vagaries of the wind. Vernon's new Addition allowed his captains to take advantage of whatever wind prevailed. They were no longer required to maintain the strict battlelines previously mandated by naval regulations. The Admiral also arranged for a signal—a blood-red pennant—to be hoisted from his mainmast when another ship should take the lead. This practice later became standard throughout the navy.

Submerged rocks called by locals the Salmandinas and a small thickly jungled islet—Drake's Island on the charts—now stood between the squadron and the mouth of the bay.

"Vernon's plan of attack," his last biographer explains, "had been based on the reasonable assumption that the prevailing wind in the harbor would be westerly . . . but even as the first ship entered the harbor it turned easterly and it became manifestly impossible to carry out the Admiral's original intention."

Brown's *Hampton Court* took the lead as instructed. Guided by Captain Renton an experienced pilot, Brown weathered the Salmandinas around 2 P.M., sailing directly down the deepwater channel toward the Iron Castle. But coming abreast the castle, the wind deserted his canvas, shifting abruptly from west to east. Suddenly becalmed, *Hampton Court*—like the *Torbay* at Vigo— lay exposed to enemy fire. Brown conformed his tactics to these changing circumstances, quickly dropping his anchor a half-cable's length from the Iron Castle's lower battery, close enough to make easy targets of the Spanish defenders hunkered down behind their guns. Now began a furious cannon duel, with *Hampton Court* initially taking a beating until she could run out her guns to the proper elevation. The roar of the cannons of both sides shattered the afternoon peace of the harbor; the atmosphere around the Iron Castle filled with acrid clouds of thick white smoke.

Brown's decision to stand and attack the Iron Castle at the first pass might have been considered controversial, might even have earned him an Admiralty Court of Enquiry and a court-martial in a naval battle fought before Vernon's "Addition." It had just become nothing more or less than good sense:

"The wind being far easterly which obliged me to anchor as it was right down the harbour," Brown recorded tersely in his journal. "Ordered a spring on our cable and fired several shots."

"Commodore Brown discharged his duty like an experienced good officer," Vernon later wrote, commending his subordinate's action. Commodore Brown had in fact obeyed Vernon's orders by ignoring them. He could not have done otherwise without losing his ship: with no easterly wind he couldn't advance to his assigned target, the Castillo Gloria, and decided to battle alone against the Iron Castle, which he did for nearly three-quarters of an hour. Fortunately for Brown, *Hampton Court*'s well-trained gunners soon proved themselves far more capable than their opposite numbers in the fort, firing off more than four hundred shots in twenty minutes, pummeling the Iron Castle's walls and batteries at a furious rate.

Naval artillerists of the day operated by the following formula: one gun ashore equaled four afloat—a calculation based on the advantage bestowed by heavier cannons made possible by a fixed position on solid ground. According to this reckoning, the Iron Castle far outgunned *Hampton Court*. The fort officially mounted thirty-two big guns, generally speaking firing between twenty-four and forty-two pound weight of shot to *Hampton Court*'s seventy guns of smaller displacement.

But only nine of the Spanish guns were in good working order that day. Negligence and the incompetence of the Spanish governor, Don Francisco Javier Martínez de la Vega y Retes had seen to the others. Most of them were missing gun carriages, though a few of these crucial mountings had been hastily knocked together from scrap timber the night before upon the approach of the English squadron. Worst of all, the Iron Castle lacked a sufficient quantity of dry powder. The extreme humidity of the tropical climate made it necessary to dry all powder in the sun on a piece of canvas—an old sail, a discarded campaign tent—before it could be of much use in the guns. The fort's commander had several times previously begged the governor for this simple scrap; Don Francisco had repeatedly ignored the commander's requests. Now Spanish cannonballs couldn't be fired with the force necessary to do much damage to the British ships below.

Brown's gunners continued to pound the Iron Castle's lower battery. Soon they brought down a portion of the heavy timber roof, knocking out three of the fort's nine functioning guns and killing their crews. At this point, the Spanish garrison of about three hundred men began to melt away. They scurried across the parade ground and out the land gate to hide in the surrounding woods, no doubt still feeling the reverberation of British cannon fire in their bones. Soon, only five officers and thirty-five marines remained to defend the fortress. This remnant was commanded by a brave officer, Don Juan Francisco Garganta, off one of the two Spanish navy vessels anchored in the harbor. He had been sent the night before to reinforce the garrison with ninety fresh men and a sufficient quantity of arms and ammunition to put up a decent fight. A few of his men had perished in the bombardment of the lower battery; the rest had joined the fleeing garrison troops before Don Garganta could stop them.

Now, with only six remaining Spanish guns and thirty-five stalwart men, Garganta maintained what fire he could on the *Hampton Court*. A lucky shot severed her anchor cable and she drifted back with the current. Vernon in the *Burford* immediately moved forward to take Brown's position. The wind had shifted slightly, allowing *Burford* to anchor fifty feet off the Iron Castle's thick stone walls. Vernon now fired at point blank range with both cannons and small arms from the "fighting tops," that is positions on the masts and in the rigging. Still Garganta managed to return fire. A Spanish ball took off the stern of the Admiral's barge in a shower of splinters; another smashed into the upper deck, knocking out a gun and killing three sailors. Yet another came within a few feet of Vernon himself, to be found as always, where the battle was hottest.

For a brief moment, the fight for the Iron Castle seemed to hang in the balance. Had Garganta a few more brave men, a few more cannons, and sufficient dry powder at his disposal, the Iron Castle might have resisted the British siege for days. Its walls were nine feet thick; its defenses laid out according to sound principles devised by Vauban, the great French military architect of the previous generation. But, without a Catholic miracle or a hurricane, thirty-five obstinate Spaniards cannot hold out for long against six British warships. The lower battery, roofless and half-wrecked, which Don Garganta continued to command, now became untenable, blasted to rubble by cannon fire and covered by a hundred English sharpshooters. Garganta now ordered a retreat to the upper fort, where he and his men would make their last stand.

Vernon, watching from the deck of the *Burford*, judged this the right moment for a landing party and sent forty sailors and marines in two longboats. But the combined firepower of *Hampton Court* and *Burford* had failed to make a breach in the Iron Castle's walls. The landing party clambered atop each other's shoulders into the lower fort through the gun embrasures, over the barrels of still-smoking Spanish cannons. Meeting no resistance, they advanced to the battlements and there pulled down the Spanish flag, tattered but still flying. In its place, to a hearty cheer from the ships, they raised the Union Jack.

This sight must have demoralized Garganta, preparing to defend the fort's upper battery. Reinforcements, he knew, would not now come from the town or anywhere else. The governor hadn't bothered to keep the Iron Castle properly garrisoned or its defenses in good repair. The king for whom they fought languished a madman in his palace in Madrid five thousand miles away from this fortress at the edge of a jungle. The smoke cleared. The moment of silence came that signifies the end of a battle. Reluctantly, Garganta gave the order and a white flag fluttered from the upper fort. Signal acknowledged, the last Spanish defenders of the Castillo de Todo Fierro emerged blinking into the sunlight, with a defeated but dignified Don Garganta in the lead.

By this time, more Englishmen had scrambled up the mole from the ships, including Commodore Brown. To Brown, Garganta tendered his sword as a gesture of surrender. Brown, however, refused the honor: according to military tradition, the sword of the commander of a captured fortress might only be accepted by the officer in command of the victorious attackers—in other words, Vice Admiral Vernon himself. Brown escorted Garganta aboard the *Burford* and into Vernon's presence. Garganta again insisted on surrendering his sword to Brown. Overwhelming and accurate fire from the *Hampton Court* alone, he explained, had won the battle for the Englishmen. Vernon, always eager for glory was however never loath to share it. Impressed by Garganta's gallant gesture, he allowed the Spaniard to present his sword to Brown—who would keep the weapon as a memento of the battle.

9.

The Iron Castle had fallen.

About a dozen British sailors and marines had been killed or wounded in the action, along with an unknown number of Spanish defenders. But the battle for Porto Bello was far from won. There remained two other fortifications, the Castillos Santiago de la Gloria and San Jerónimo and of course the town itself. Night descended, the swift green sunset of the tropics giving way to a reedy, unquiet darkness. Spanish gunners in the Castillo Santiago de la Gloria began to lob random cannon balls into the night in the general direction of the British ships across the bay—though they were too distant to do much damage and couldn't exactly see their targets. Still, a stray shot shattered the *Burford*'s foremast, bringing it down in a mess of rigging.

The *Burford* and *Hampton Court* had now been joined by the rest of the squadron: *Worcester, Stafford, Princess Louisa,* and *Norwich. Burford*, armed with the biggest guns, returned the *castillo*'s fire. One of her balls crashed through the governor's palace in the town; another sank a Spanish sloop in the harbor. But, as darkness thickened, Vernon ordered his squadron out into the bay, beyond cannon range. As they withdrew, the Castillo Santiago de la Gloria kept on firing—pointlessly—into the tropical night. A critical account of the battle written later for the Marqués de Villa Garcia, Viceroy of Peru, by a Spanish official, Don Francisco de Rovina, blamed the Castillo Gloria's commander for what he called "wasting powder and shot and making themselves the laughingstock of the enemy."

Vernon slept fitfully that night aboard the *Burford*.

The town had not yet surrendered. Unknown trials awaited the dawn. At 5 A.M. on November 22, 1739, Vernon assembled his captains for another council of war. They would move up the harbor in order of battle to bombard the uncaptured fortresses. At 6 A.M. the squadron began "warping" into the bay, a difficult process involving heavy ropes and block and tackle fixed to ships' bow at one end and on the other to points on land. The ships moved forward by a sort of painfully slow winching.

An hour later, a launch approached, bearing a white flag and the corpulent figure of the governor, Don Francisco Vega y Retes. This Spanish official was of a different type altogether than the valiant Don Garganta: lazy, unctuous, and cowardly, Don Francisco had taken advantage of the siege of the Iron Castle to move his wife and valuables to his residence up in the hills. Rovina later reserved the most scathing language in his report to the Viceroy for this incompetent and craven official. The governor of Porto Bello, Don Rovina wrote, was "supremely unfitted for such employment, of scanty talent and cowardly disposition, outward physical signs being the only evidence that he was a man at all."

Admiral Vernon received Porto Bello's governor aboard the *Burford* with all the military courtesies of the day. Sweating in his gold-trimmed gubernatorial finery and massive wig, Don Francisco offered to surrender his town under the following conditions: the Spanish garrisons still defending the Castillo Gloria and the Castillo San Geronimo must be allowed to evacuate the forts with the honors of war; this meant colors flying, drums beating and in possession of personal arms. The inhabitants of the town and their property must not be molested—this included especially all Catholic churches, priests, and nuns. Lastly the Spanish crown would be allowed to retain all vessels anchored in the harbor, including two *guarda costa* cutters of twenty guns each. (These vessels had already proved troublesome to the residents of Porto Bello: the night before, under the cover of darkness, their crews had mutinied and pillaged the town before disappearing into the jungle.)

Vernon readily agreed to the first two of the governor's terms but expressed outrage at the third. Had he not come halfway around the world to capture predatory Spanish ships, especially the vessels of the *guarda costa*? And had the rapacious captains of this odious service not been the chief cause of war in the first place? One can easily imagine the "Angry Admiral" barely managing to conceal his famous rage at the governor's temerity as the oily Don Francisco trembled and sweated beneath his wig. Vernon dismissed the Spaniard with the warning that Porto Bellow must surrender unconditionally and completely or the attack would continue. He would be given until 3 P.M. that afternoon to accept these terms.

Don Francisco sailed away, disgruntled. Vernon continued to warp his ships into position for the final assault, which some sources suggest he now intended for the following morning—unwilling to expose himself to daylight fire from the Castillo Santiago de la Gloria's gunners who had smashed his mast the previous night. An hour passed, two. The day ticked on, Vernon's squadron advanced with excruciating deliberation, equatorial sun bearing down, the water hot as a baking sheet. At last, another launch approached from the direction of the town. This time it bore not the governor himself but one of his minions. All of Vernon's terms had been accepted by Don Francisco, who was even then fleeing into the hills.

Two hours later, Captain Newton, in command of the Jamaican Marines, observed with satisfaction the evacuation of the remaining two *castillos*. The Spanish garrison marched out, arms shouldered, drums beating, fifes tootling, and headed up the road connecting Porto Bello to Nombre de Dios and Panama on the Pacific shore. Newton's marines then took possession of the forts. The Castillo Santiago de la Gloria they found well provisioned and armed with 120 cannons, sufficient balls, and dry powder. It might have withstood a protracted siege. Its officers had wanted to defend the place but had been ordered to stand down by the timid Don Francisco Vega y Retes. In the Castillo San Jerónimo, however, not a single cannon was mounted on a gun carriage. This fort, with its sturdy walls, sally ports, and corner bastions might as well have been made of paper.

For an anxious moment the now defenseless civilian inhabitants of Porto Bello, those who could not afford to abandon their homes and livelihoods, must have held their collective breath. In this part of the world the English were known for brutality and love of plunder. A few oldsters still alive perhaps remembered the terrible Morgan who had reduced their town to ashes and raped their women, sacking it as thoroughly as the Visigoths had sacked Rome. Many still told horror stories of how these vicious pirates had tortured people to reveal the whereabouts of hidden valuables.

But Vernon was no pirate. Rather, a gentleman soldier, and servant of the king upon whom any cruelties perpetrated by Englishmen would ultimately reflect. He now gave stern orders that the inhabitants of Porto Bello should not be molested, nor their personal property seized without compensation.

In this manner, Porto Bello, Panama, became, however briefly, the newest outpost of an expanding British Empire.

10.

Admiral Vernon soon realized that with the limited forces available to him—his famous six ships—he could not hold Porto Bello for long. Spanish armies might even then be assembling in Panama to besiege the fortresses he had just taken; Spanish fleets might just now be sailing from Havana to blockade *him* in Porto Bello's excellent harbor.

Ever the bold strategist, Vernon considered preempting a Spanish attack by attacking himself: he would march on Panama and lay siege to the city. After all, Morgan and a few hundred buccaneers put it to the torch in 1671. But a fearsome reputation as torturers and barbarians had preceded Morgan's expedition—a psychological weapon worth two or three thousand men. Vernon on the other hand played by the wars of "civilized" warfare: a delegation of Porto Bello's citizens later thanked him for the "humanity and justice" shown during the British occupation of their town. Also, the road across the isthmus to Panama, open and paved with cobbles part of the way, nevertheless wound through thick jungle in other parts, ripe terrain for ambush.

Vernon considered his options. The Spanish treasure fleet might still be in Panama, bearing millions of pounds in gold and silver. Capturing such wealth—of which he would receive a healthy percentage as prize money—would make him a very wealthy man. He lingered for a few days in the governor's palace in Porto Bello making up his mind, consulting intelligence reports, the promise of wealth and fame tempting him to rash action. Meanwhile, he oversaw the orderly ransacking of the town. Ten thousand silver pieces of eight intended to pay the Spanish garrison turned up buried beneath a mound of shit in a *necessaire*—outhouse. This sum he distributed among his men as a sort of combat bonus.

Finally, he came to a decision: Panama could not be taken without a major expeditionary force and so Porto Bello must be evacuated. Three more ships soon arrived from Jamaica, *Windsor*, *Aglesea*, and *Diamond*, their crews small, their armaments limited—but the latter was commanded by a competent, energetic officer, Captain Charles Knowles. Beside him on the quarterdeck stood Captain Edward Boscawen, another fine officer. Boscawen's ship was under repair in Jamaica; hungry for action, he had volunteered to serve under Knowles. Unfortunately, when *Diamond* sailed into the harbor on November 29, the battle for Porto Bello had long been won.

To these officers, Admiral Vernon entrusted his plans. Since he could not keep Porto Bello, he would destroy its strategic value by razing its forts and leaving its protected harbor an "open and defenseless bay." Knowles and Boscawen and the men off the *Diamond*, fresh from R&R in Jamaica, would undertake this act of destruction. The proud *castillos* would be reduced to piles of rubble, their nine-foot-thick walls undermined and blown up with tightly packed barrels of gunpowder.

Vernon then stripped the forts, taking possession of their brass cannons for the Royal Navy's arsenal. The inferior iron cannons, most of which lacked trunnions anyway, he ordered spiked. The demolition began the next day, an operation that occupied Knowles and Boscawen for the next two weeks. The Spanish built excellent fortresses, with finely cut stones stuck one to the other by a kind of dense, super-adhesive mortar composed in part of crushed shells. 120 barrels of gunpowder were required, in the end, to bring down the three forts, this work completed by December 12.

The governor of Panama had a month or so earlier taken hostage a brace of English South Sea Company factors—Mr. Elias Humphreys and Dr. Wright. Vernon now threatened to lay siege to that city—though he had no intention of actually doing so—to secure the return of these British subjects. Diplomatic letters flew back and forth between Panama and Porto Bello. The governor temporized; Vernon grew impatient and demanded the immediate release of Humphreys and Wright; the governor refused outright. At last, the Angry Admiral fired off what he called a "Thunderer." Unless these men were released, he would attack Panama immediately, with an invasion force eager for more action. Panama's walls would be knocked down, its public officials hanged:

"Health and Prosperity to all true Spaniards that may lament sacrificing the true interests of their country to the ambition of an Italian Queen," Vernon concluded, this last bit a swipe at Isabela, the wily Parmigiana who now ruled Spain through her deranged spouse.

Two days after this letter had been sent, the South Sea Company factors appeared on the Panama road, mounted on donkeys—disheveled and disgruntled but alive.

By the second week of December, nothing more remained to be done in Porto Bello. Vernon had proved his point, taking the place with six ships, as he had promised Parliament. Had the *castillos* been properly garrisoned and defended, the outcome might have been different. Vernon gambled on Spain's state of readiness for war, on the element of surprise and above all on Spanish troops' willingness to fight—and he had won.

This time.

11.

Vernon's squadron departed Porto Bello's beautiful harbor on December 13, 1739—its six ships now augmented by two Spanish *guarda costa* cutters and a snow (a kind of small, fast sloop) renamed *Triumph*, sailing under the British flag. In this swift vessel on December 28 Vernon dispatched the squadron's pilot, Captain Rentone, to England with news of the victory. This was an honor bestowed upon the man for skillfully leading the *Hampton Court* past the Salmandinas Rocks and into the harbor for the opening attack on Iron Castle on November 21. Rentone reached Bristol on March 12, 1740. Another vessel, a merchantman from Jamaica had put in to Dover the day before bearing the same news, but Rentone brought official dispatches.

To say England went mad upon hearing of Vernon's exploit vastly understates the degree of national frenzy. Englishmen had long felt themselves humiliated by Spanish depredations and longed for the great days of Marlborough or Drake. They had hungered for an impossible victory and here it was. Spontaneous celebrations erupted as word spread. Fireworks and bonfires lit the skies of cities from Bristol to London to York. Balls in Vernon's honor and more fireworks illuminated the splendid country houses of the Whig gentry. For a party at Cliveden, country house of Frederick, Prince of Wales, composer James Thomson wrote a martial ditty that remain's Great Britain's unofficial anthem to this day "Rule, Britannia!": "Rule, Brittania! Brittania rule the waves!," the song goes. "Britons never, ever, ever shall be slaves!" This last line supposedly referring to those half-true reports of English mariners forced by tyrannical Spaniards to labor under the lash on the defenses of Havana.

As the weeks rolled into the spring and summer of 1740, England's Vernonmania only increased. Towns and streets all over the English-speaking world took the name of Porto Bello to commemorate the victory. These include Porto Bello Road, now home of the London flea market; the Porto Bello district of Dublin and Porto Bello in Virginia, (now part of the city of Williamsburg.

Walpole, who still retained his increasingly tenuous hold on the ministry, sought to take credit for the Admiral's victory. Had he not appointed the man to lead the expedition? Parliament, upper and lower houses together—an unusual alliance—forwarded a unanimous address to King George, commending "the glorious success of your Majesty's arms in the West Indies, under the command of Admiral Vernon, by entering the Port and taking the town of Porto Bello, and demolishing all the Forts and Castles belonging thereto, *with six ships of war only.*" This last bit added, it is said, by Opposition politicians as a jab at Walpole's erstwhile pacifist policies: after all the Great Man had been one of those insisting the reduction of Porto Bello would take nothing less than an armada and 8,000 men.

King George II, formerly one of Vernon's detractors now supported the man's immediate promotion to Admiral of the more prestigious White Squadron. Captain Rentone who brought the glad tidings from the West Indies received two hundred gold guineas and a promotion from pilot to post captain. Meanwhile, the Aldermen of London voted Vernon the Freedom of the City, which took the form of a gold key traditionally supposed to open any door, presented in a solid gold box—an honor reserved for conquering heroes. It was all a bit hysterical.

Vernon had suddenly become the most celebrated military man in half a century. But it is the common people alone, remarked the venerable French historian, the Abbé de Vertot, "who dispose absolutely of glory." They now disposed of it like a crown on Vernon's head. The London press filled sell-out editions with panegyrics to the victorious Vernon; the printmaking industry worked overtime, churning out hundreds of images of the six ships, the fight for the Iron Castle, the submission of Governor Don Francisco, the demolition of the *castillos*. Portraits painted of Vernon before the war were now repainted with the capture of Porto Bello in the background. And—as great an indicator of popularity in England then as now— the names of inns and taverns, some still extant, lost their previous identities in favor of the Admiral.

This phenomenon was later taken by Horace Walpole, the Great Man's son, as an illustration of the fleeting nature of fame. In the aftermath of the Battle of Culloden, won by the Duke of Cumberland six years later, Horace wrote the following to his friend the poet Thomas Gray:

> I was yesterday out of town and the very signs as I passed through the villages made me make very quaint reflections on the mortality of fame and popularity. I observed how the Duke's head had succeeded almost universally to Admiral Vernon's. . . . I pondered these things in my heart and said unto myself, Surely all glory is but a sign.

But the surest sign of Vernon's popularity, lay in the medal-makers art: Christopher Pinchbeck, inventor of the cheap alloy that bears his name and an energetic manufacturer of novelty medals—one of the most popular collectibles of the eighteenth-century's emerging middle classes—now released thousands of hastily struck Vernon medals. Competitors quickly followed suit. Some of these medals showed Vernon rampant, sword in hand, some the six ships, guns blazing; some Vernon with his arm flung around Commodore Brown's shoulder. Hundreds of varieties, perhaps thousands, were produced of varying degrees of quality. They still turn up everywhere, in flea markets, in coin shops—even, as previously noted, on Etsy—with the best examples still eagerly collected by numismatists.

Vernon, still aboard the *Burford* in the West Indies, remained perhaps fortunately unaware of all this furious celebrating. Only a single battle had been won. A battle, as the novelist Smollett later wrote dismissively in which "the Spaniards acted with such pusillanimity . . . that their forts were taken almost without bloodshed."

From his perch across the Channel in France, Voltaire observed the English enthusiasm for all things Vernon with his usual acerbity: "It was hoped," the *philosophe* commented "and indeed expected, that this victory would be the first step in conquering the whole of Spanish America." Voltaire as usual made a point others failed to grasp, one that had escaped the jubilant English public and the popular press and the medal makers and perhaps the ministry itself: the capture of Porto Bello by Vernon and his six ships—though it might have finally placated Admiral Hosier's waterlogged ghost— didn't mark the end of the war at all. Only the beginning.

James Oglethorpe (left) Yamacraw Chief Tomochichi (right)

FIVE

The Redoubtable Oglethorpe

1.

News of the war between Britain and Spain arrived somewhat prematurely in Savannah, capital of Georgia—last and most quixotic of the original thirteen colonies—in early September 1739. The news took the form of the rumor of a ghost "pink" said to be bearing the news. A "pink," that is a square-rigged, flat-bottomed cargo ship, called the *Tartar* would be arriving from Rhode Island, people said. Allegedly stowed aboard were letters and journals from London reporting the declaration of war. The *Tartar* pink perhaps never arrived at Savannah and might or might not have existed. In any case the ghostly news she supposedly bore was accurate only in a spiritual sense. Everyone knew war with Spain was coming; desire for it had sent England into a martial delirium. But its official proclamation wouldn't be nailed up at England's crossroads and celebrated with bonfires and beatings until October 29.

General James Edward Oglethorpe—the redoubtable Oglethorpe, philanthropist, soldier, parliamentarian, reformer, friend to the poor, father to the Indians, and founder of Georgia—missed the *Tartar's* fictitious arrival at Savannah by a few weeks. He was just then on a diplomatic mission to the Creek Indians at Coweta, capital of the Lower Creeks on the Chattahoochee River. Oglethorpe marched with a retinue of twenty-five soldiers from his personal regiment—the 42nd Regiment of Foot—and an honor guard of Indians from various allied tribes, including his half-English, half-Yamacraw Indian translator, Mary Musgrove. This mixed-race wife of an English trader, described as "a minor princess who played a major role in Trustee-era Georgia," was yet another collaborationist squaw in the long line that extends from La Malinche, right hand of Cortez, through John Rolfe's wife Pocahontas, to Sacagawea, Lewis and Clarke's indispensable guide.

Oglethorpe's Creek hosts had planted "cakes and bags of flour" in trees along the way for the encouragement of the diplomatic party, which arrived on the outskirts of Coweta on August 6, 1739. There they were met by a contingent of smiling Lower Creek youths bearing armloads of corn, a gift from Chief Chislacaliche. An exhausting series of ceremonial banquets followed over the next several days. The Lower Creeks served watermelon, squash, potatoes, and numerous haunches of venison. Oglethorpe, perhaps suffering from a touch of malaria, felt increasingly feverish. Unfortunately, neither the feasting nor the endless diplomatic parlays could be avoided; his mission to cement the Lower Creeks to the English cause must not fail. Both Spanish and French agents had been trying to woo the Creeks to the side of the Bourbon powers. A neighboring tribe, the Choctaws, teetering in their allegiance, hadn't quite declared for Louis XV of France, but rumor had them about to. All felt war imminent; it hung in the air like the smoke of a distant fire.

Oglethorpe and his settlers at Savannah and a few other scattered English outposts in the "Debatable Land"—that vast, sparsely peopled region roughly delineated by Charles Town in English South Carolina to the north and St. Augustine in Spanish Florida to the south—daily expected a Spanish invasion, launched from St. Augustine. That Spanish stronghold, protected by the massive Castillo de San Marcos had been an irritant to the Carolinians for years. Decades before, in 1695, Spain's sad and noble Carlos II had issued a proclamation offering deserters from England's armies and runaway slaves from English colonies freedom and land in exchange for a conversion to Catholicism and allegiance to the Spanish Crown.

So many of the latter had fled South Carolina's brutal rice plantations for Florida that the Conde Manuel de Montiano, St. Augustine's wily governor, had put them together in an exurban settlement called Mose—certainly the first exclusively Black township in North America. A fort had been constructed there to protect the residents and also the flank of St. Augustine from British attack. A Spanish secret agent named Pedro had recently circulated among South Carolina plantations quietly passing word of Spain's slave amnesty—a stratagem the English planters considered dastardly. War was one thing; tempting one's slaves with freedom quite another, and might have much more serious consequences: slave uprisings, massacres, the complete disruption of planter society on both sides. Caught at last, Pedro pretended to be on his way to find Oglethorpe in Georgia. He apologized, he had lost his way, he said. The South Carolinians saw through this thin excuse, arrested him and his mulatto companion and imprisoned them in Charles Town gaol—but not in time. Pedro's agitations led directly to the "Stono Uprising," the bloodiest slave revolt in what became the United States until Nat Turner's Rebellion in Virginia a hundred years later.

2.

Oglethorpe and the Lower Creek chiefs ate and talked for twelve days at Coweta. A lightly fermented beverage made from casena berries passed from hand to hand in conch shells. The Indians danced endlessly, contorting themselves in "antik postures." Oglethorpe, alternately shivering and burning, bore up under all of it with his usual fortitude. On the morning of August 11, he gave a long and impressive speech, announcing that he acted "on behalf of his Majesty, King George" who only desired peace and amity between Great Britain and the Creek Nation. Gifts were exchanged, the Lower Creeks ruminated and consulted their elders, then rendered judgement. Any nation who could produce as impressive a figure as Oglethorpe deserved Creek support; they would join with King George in the event of a war with Spain or France. As Thomas Jenys, a South Carolina legislator later wrote of Oglethorpe: "noe Man in Life is soe well Acquainted wth. the Nature and turn of the Indians." Or, as another commented: "He is like a King and a God to them."

More gifts, more dancing, more venison followed to celebrate the deal in Coweta, then the exhausted, feverish Oglethorpe and his retinue traveled to Cusseta, chief city of the Upper Creeks. There, the diplomatic feasting and dealmaking repeated itself for ten more days with the same results. The Upper Creeks would also fight for King George and Oglethorpe against Spain. Oglethorpe had successfully done what he had set out to do: he had built a Creek "Wall of Defense," on Georgia's southern border against England's enemies.

But while Oglethorpe feasted with the Upper Creeks, the Choctaws descended on Savannah, looking for hospitality and rum, the latter officially illegal in Georgia. (Oglethorpe had insisted on nothing stronger than beer in his new colony; like Admiral Vernon, he believed rum fatal in the torrid climes of the New World.) The generally impoverished Georgians, led in Oglethorpe's absence by William Stephens, representative of the Georgia Trustees back in London, did their best to entertain these new, aggressive visitors. Soon, a fundamental difference between Englishmen and Indians became apparent: the Choctaws, Stephens wrote were "troublesome and expensive to maintain" and made a habit of entering English houses uninvited and "laying their Hands on anything they liked." The concept of private property had yet to reach Choctaw country. Finally, hung over and sated, they left a message for Oglethorpe and departed, having reconnoitered the defenses of Savannah, should they decide to throw their support behind Spain.

This vital question needed to be answered by all Indian tribes of the Debatable Land: On whose side would they fight? Claimed by both England and Spain, the lightly settled region, once the Spanish province of Guale, lately expropriated by England as the site for their new Georgia colony, had gradually been abandoned by Spain and now lay mostly fallow. The question of Indian alliances was made even more complicated by internecine rivalries among the "savages" themselves. Creeks and Choctaws, traditional enemies, seemed on the brink of another war. If the Creeks fought for the English, did that mean the Choctaws must fight against them? And if the Choctaws fought for England and against Spain's allies the French, on their western border in Louisiana, did that mean they could not fight the Chickasaws, hereditary enemies, who had recently become English allies? These conflicting loyalties and the resulting diplomatic machinations were as complicated as any European treaty and accounted for Oglethorpe's desperate mission to Creek country. Luckily for the future of the Georgia colony, the entire Creek nation had fully embraced Oglethorpe and England.

"Everything is entirely settled in peace," he wrote to the Georgia Trustees. Both the Upper and Lower Creeks, he added, with his usual self-regard, loved him and had found it "impossible to Dissolve the Joy they experienced at my Arrival." But peace wasn't the point. Oglethorpe had solidified Creek support in the coming war with Spain.

Still racked with fever and recuperating in newly settled Augusta, Oglethorpe was not able to rest for long. A large delegation of Cherokees soon found him in this rough frontier village. Traditional enemies of the Creeks, the Cherokees however sought to avoid alienating Oglethorpe, the newest power broker in the Debatable Land. For his part, Oglethorpe "Received them with all Tenderness" and secured a peace treaty a few days later, after the requisite feasting and an exchange of gifts, including 1500 bushels of Georgia corn. A devastating smallpox epidemic had caused the failure of Cherokee harvests the previous spring; Oglethorpe's gift corn saved the tribe from starvation and gained him the pledge of 600 Cherokee warriors.

3.

The Georgia colony's southern, western, and south-western borders now secured by Indian alliances, Oglethorpe returned in triumph to Savannah on September 23, 1739. He arrived late in the afternoon, a cool breeze blowing up from the river, fireflies winking above the half-mown grass along the Yamacraw bluff. As the sun set over the unknown continent to the west, he retired to the campaign tent in which he still lived, situated in a grove of lofty pines. Though Oglethorpe was the settlement's First Citizen, founder, and de facto governor, he had refused to accept as his residence any of the newly constructed houses in the carefully laid-out town below. Instead, in what might be called a gesture of ostentatious simplicity, he preferred his small military tent.

Rumors of a declaration of war circulating in Savannah— supposedly bearing down aboard the *Tartar* pink—were taken for truth by all residents, including now Oglethorpe himself. He spent the following days huddling with Stephens and others, planning the defense of the colony. His regiment had already been established at the recently fortified settlement of Frederica on St. Simons Island, now a popular beach resort, days away on the coast. Thus, in the event of attack, the residents of Savannah would have to defend their city alone until reinforcements could arrive. In time of war, the people's resolve as much as their state of preparedness could translate into victory or defeat.

On October 3, to the sound of a stirring martial tattoo, Oglethorpe called all males of military age to Savannah's central square. Two hundred assembled and were counted, playing soldier in ragged ranks. Oglethorpe then blew off a few cannons and ordered the militia also present to fire muskets into the air in "three handsome volleys." As the black-powder smoke cleared, Stephens read out an unofficial, official-sounding declaration of a war that would not be declared in England for weeks and would not reach American ears through government channels for months. In Charles Town the news wasn't published until April 1740. (Carolina's planters and traders, heavily engaged in smuggling to the Spanish Caribbean, had rather more to lose than gain from another conflict with Spain.)

Oglethorpe, impatient by nature, inclined to precipitous action, shared Admiral Vernon's contempt for the Spanish. He was anxious for the war to begin. He came from a military background; the desire for martial honors was never far from his heart. Members of his family could be counted in England's armies from Saxon times nearly a thousand years earlier: Oglethorpes had fought Vikings and Danes, Normans and Celts. More recently, his father Sir Theophilus Oglethorpe had commanded a contingent of dragoons against the Scottish Covenanters at Bothwell Bridge in 1679. As a teenager, James Edward had himself served on the staff of the famous Prince Eugene, fighting against the Turks in the Austro-Turkish War of 1716–1718.

During the bloody siege of Belgrade in 1717, to the delight of Oglethorpe's sisters who loved to boast of their war hero little brother, he had "mounted the trenches," in the final night assault. This was serious business; enemy fire cut down a servant just inches from his side—one of the many "near misses" that followed Oglethorpe through life. (Ironically, as he busily negotiated with the Upper and Lower Creeks in the wilds of the Debatable Land, the Turks retook the unfortunate Balkan city in whose liberation he had assisted as a youth. They would keep it for the next hundred years.)

Now, as inspirational cannons belched smoke in Savannah's main square, and musket balls whizzed into the hot blue sky over Georgia, Oglethorpe read out the letter he had received from King George, dated June 15, 1739. After the usual salutations, while carefully avoiding any direct mention of war, the king had instructed Oglethorpe to "annoy the Subjects of Spain" by whatever means possible. This was enough of a declaration for Georgia's First Citizen. He'd already decided on the opening campaign: an army composed of Georgians, South Carolinians, and Indians would attack and seize St. Augustine. The presence of its formidable fortress and able governor, did not, he felt, offer serious obstacles. To the redoubtable Oglethorpe, St. Augustine and all Spanish Florida was already a part of the burgeoning British Empire.

4.

Hail, Oglethorpe, with triumphs crowned
That ever were in camps or sieges found,—
Thy great example shall through ages shine,
A favorite theme with poet and divine.
People unborn thy merits shall proclaim,
And add new luster to thy deathless name.

So wrote Alexander Pope in 1732, the year of Georgia's official founding, though the poet's prediction has hardly come to pass. James Edward Oglethorpe remains the least remembered of the founders of England's colonies in America. Other names readily come to mind: John Smith of Virginia; Miles Standish and Governor Winthrop of Massachusetts; Roger Williams of Rhode Island; Pennsylvania's William Penn. And yet Oglethorpe, who crammed enough experience in his long lifetime (b. 1696, d. 1785) for any number of founders, has passed into relative oblivion.

A long life, of course, can have its drawbacks. In addition to suffering the "whips and scorns of time," mentioned in Hamlet's soliloquy, the very old often have the misfortune of living from one age into the next. Oglethorpe as a youth met Louis XIV; he lived to dine with Dr. Johnson and Boswell and debate with John Adams, first ambassador from a free and separate United States to the Court of St. James. But he remained, perhaps, a creature more suited to the Sun King's magnificent seventeenth century than to the enlightened, industrializing eighteenth.

Oglethorpe's character reflects this complexity: he was at once a hot-headed duelist and a "paladin of philanthropy"; a calm and determined parliamentarian and a bold political strategist; a brave soldier and a military failure. He abhorred slavery, lawyers, rum, and Catholics and banned all of these in the colony he founded as a refuge for England's "worthy debtors." Volumes have been written detailing Oglethorpe's life and exploits, most of them unfortunately published more than a hundred years ago. The best is probably *James Edward Oglethorpe—Imperial Idealist* by Amos A. Ettinger published in 1936. A new one is needed; here however, we paint a larger canvas. A brief outline and a few anecdotes must suffice to illustrate Oglethorpe's early career and background.

His family traced its roots back to one Ligulfe, Thane of Oglethorpe in the reign of Edward the Confessor (c. 1003–1066).

Another ancestor supposedly fought "a forlorn hope" against the invading army of William the Conqueror and perished at the Battle of Hastings. The Oglethorpe family fortunes waxed and waned over the seven centuries of fraught English history that followed. They suffered under Cromwell's Puritan Commonwealth but regained influence after the Restoration of the Stuarts. Favorites of James II, England's last Stuart king, the Oglethorpes acquired a rich estate at Godalming in Surrey and influential positions at court, in Parliament and in the army. The family matriarch during this period (James Edward's mother) a beautiful, domineering Irish woman named Jenny Wall, had been, some said, the king's mistress.

Unfortunately for the Oglethorpes, upon James II's downfall everything crumbled. Overnight, they went from power brokers to hunted criminals; James Edward's father Sir Theophilus died and James Edward's siblings fled to France with the exiled king. This included his older brother Theophilus Jr. who chose life as an expatriate in France and Italy over life in an England governed by the German upstarts of the House of Hanover. James Edward's four beautiful sisters, called "the Nymphs," also fled England and married into the French aristocracy. But Jenny Wall Oglethorpe who remained loyal to the Stuart (Jacobite) cause until her death, remained in England and became an inveterate conspirator. Her youngest son James Edward was marked out by her for a life of plotting in the orbit of the Jacobite court in exile, established in the chateau at Saint-Germain-en-Laye on the outskirts of Paris. But first she set out to make of her youngest son a sort of Jacobite double agent. She sent him to Eton and Oxford, then a hotbed of pro-Jacobite sentiment, where "drinking was both an art and a sport," and "bowling, fives and cockfighting abounded," but at the same time purchased him a commission in George I's Hanoverian Foot Guard.

College life, however, wasn't for the restless James Edward Oglethorpe. And England, at peace, offered no opportunity for martial glory. He wanted action. He quit school, resigned his commission, crossed to the Continent, and joined Prince Eugene's army in time to fight against the Turks at Belgrade—one of the bloodiest sieges of the eighteenth century. He was twenty-one. Seventy years later, Oglethorpe's memory of that terrible battle remained undimmed. At dinner with Dr. Johnson in London one night in 1785, he dipped his finger into a glass of red wine and drew a map of the allied trenches before Belgrade on the white tablecloth. Dr. Johnson listened with rapt fascination as the wine dyed the cloth the color of blood and Oglethorpe told tales of that momentous siege long into the night. The carnage in the darkened city, taken after sunset, had been immense; they fought from street to street against desperate Turkish occupiers loath to pay for decades of cruel, tyrannical rule. The action, as James Edward wrote with typical understatement, to his sisters in Paris at the time, had been "very bloody and sharp."

From this siege, also, comes an episode emblematic of Oglethorpe's character. He would suffer no fool gladly, nor any affront to his dignity—rank and position be damned. In Eugene's tent, pitched beneath Belgrade's walls, on the eve of the battle, during a drinking party, a high-ranking German prince seeking to humiliate the young English ensign flicked some wine in his face with a spoon from across the table. Oglethorpe's reaction was immediate and smart, as relates Boswell in his *Life of Johnson*: Oglethorpe, "with an engaging and disarming smile, exclaimed, 'That's a good joke, but we do it much better in England,' at that moment flinging an entire glassful of wine into the astonished royal countenance, to the great amusement and admiration of the company."

Oglethorpe was even then, at twenty-one, a fine reader of the crowd and of the temper of his adversary. He had rightly judged the German prince, Alexander of Wurtemburg, a coward.

5.

During the half-dozen years following the siege, James Edward, adhering to family tradition demonstrated a "blind, unwavering loyalty" to the Jacobite cause that "often bordered on the pathetic." Bouncing around several European capitals, the young veteran could be described as a Jacobite "fellow traveler," plotting and counterplotting along with his mother and beautiful sisters. He hovered around the court of the Old Pretender (James II's son) now kicked out of France and exiled to Rome after the failed invasion of Scotland in 1715. But sometime during this period, Oglethorpe grew disenchanted with political sympathies he knew to be moribund. The future seemed to lie elsewhere, with a new, energetic Hanoverian England, busy with empire, financial speculation, and industry. The Jacobites and their lost cause belonged to a receding, mythic past.

Oglethorpe returned to England. He withdrew to the family estate at Godalming which his mother had managed to keep safe from government seizure through personal influence and the most adroit political maneuvering. For two years he waited, molting his Jacobite skin, meditating on his allegiances and on the best way to restore his family's lost prominence. He sought no action on the stage of national politics and war. Instead, he bent his intellect to the solution of local problems, to the welfare of those who lived on his estate and to the affairs of the nearby town of Haslemere. He read deeply, catching up on the education he'd missed at Oxford.

In 1717, James Edward's unwaveringly Jacobite brother Theophilus was able to write: "I am very well satisfied with him and love him the more, because I see he is entirely affectionate to the King [James] and that the Germans [King George] have not in the least prevailed on him." But by 1722, James Edward, now twenty-five, had thrown off the influence of his scheming family and made a private peace with Hanover. Emerging from the chrysalis of Godalming, he

entered public life again and announced his candidacy for the parliamentary seat of Haslemere, which had been held by the Oglethorpes
in better days. His years of absorption in local matters now paid off.
To everyone's surprise, James Edward gained the seat for the Tories
by the narrowest possible margin—a single vote. The election results
were immediately disputed by the loser and the Whig party. They
protested, demanded recounts: How could Oglethorpe, a Tory and
an unreconstructed Jacobite, possibly serve a Parliament that had been
called by King George? Opposition to Oglethorpe's election soon grew
dangerously heated.

On March 25, 1723, Oglethorpe and a friend named Burrell
encountered two irate Whigs in downtown Haslemere—a certain
Captain Onslow and Mr. Sharp, secretary to the bishop of London.
According to a report in the *London Daily Journal*, after an exchange
of insults and angry words,

> Mr. Oglethorpe drew his Sword there on Mr. Sharp . . . and
> wounded him in the belly: Which Insult being resented by
> Capt. Onslow, Mr. Oglethorpe and he Drew, and in the
> Re-encounter both being slightly wounded, the Captain
> disarmed Mr. Oglethorpe without pushing his Resentment
> so far as the Provocation deserved.

But Oglethorpe had his own version of the bloody encounter.
Three days later, he wrote a letter presenting the facts as he saw
them—and, unwittingly a portrait of himself at twenty-five: prickly,
quick to violent anger, but also quick to compassion for a defeated
enemy.

"News-Writers, in whose Power it is to blacken the most spotless
Character, would have very good Authority before they publish
Things prejudicial to any one's Reputation," he began, going on to
detail the "true account" of the encounter:

On Sunday the 25th, after Evening Service, Captain Onslow and Mr. Sharpe, meeting Mr. Burrell and Mr. Oglethorpe in the Market-Place at Haslemere, Mr. Oglethorpe tax'd Mr. Sharpe with some Stories that he had rais'd. Mr. Sharp giving him a warm Answer, Mr. Oglethorpe corrected him for it; Captain Onslow, stepping in between, Mr. Sharpe drew his Sword, on which Mr. Oglethorpe, Captain Onslow, and Mr. Burrell also drew. In the Scuffle, Mr. Oglethorpe wounded Mr. Sharpe in the Belly, and Captain Onslow in the Thigh. Mr. Burrell beating down Mr. Oglethorpe's Thrusts, of which Captain Onslow taking advantage, seiz'd on the Blade of Mr. Oglethorpe's sword with his Left hand, and said your Life is in my Power. Mr. Oglethorpe answer'd do your worst, and struggling, tore his Sword thro' the Captain's Hand which is very much disabled . . . Mr. Oglethorpe (who was not wounded) bound up Captain Onslow's Wounds and set for a Surgeon to him.

The next violent episode, however, was not so easily explained. Though perhaps an act of self-defense, it resulted from what was obviously a drunken brawl in a bar. The *London Daily Journal*—a Whig publication and no friend of the Jacobite Oglethorpes—again presents the incriminating details:

Yesterday Morning about 6 of the Clock, James Oglethorpe . . . had the misfortune to go into a Night-House of evil Repute, without Temple Bar (being overcome with Wine), where mixing with a promiscuous Company of Hackney-Coachmen, Shoe-Blackers, and Linkmen, Mr. Oglethorpe missed a piece of Gold, and charging a Link Fellow with having taken it from him, high words arose, and the Linkman struck Mr. Oglethorpe several Blows with his

Link, who resenting such usage drew his Sword and gave the Fellow a mortal Wound in the Breast.

Oglethorpe now found himself arrested and charged with murder. Somehow, through family connections or the services of a good lawyer (ironic if the latter, given Oglethorpe's antipathy for the profession) charges were dropped and he assumed his seat in the House. Though punishment might be escaped, guilt lingers: the unfortunate incident certainly had an effect on Oglethorpe's developing moral sensibilities. Perhaps Oglethorpe regretted killing the Linkman, a night bodyguard-for-hire, the aforementioned "link" being the torch with which he lit his client's way through lightless London streets. This occupation marked him as a struggling member of the working class. Whether or not the Linkman stole the gold coin was beside the point—what need would drive a man to an act of public theft?

In the aftermath of the Linkman's death, Oglethorpe matured. He experienced what might be called a political epiphany— emerging from the crisis ready to dedicate his life to improving the lot of England's poor. Over the next few years, he grew into one of the "leading members of the House," known by all for his energy, sympathetic nature, and good humor. He chaired many committees and became an eloquent political pamphleteer. In the late 1720s, concerned with conditions in the navy, he authored one of the most widely read pamphlets of his time, *The Sailor's Advocate*. This pamphlet called for an end to press gangs and improvements in what we would today call working conditions.

"It is not the Timber nor the Iron of the *Ships* of War . . . but the Sailors who mann them, who are the strength of the NATION," he thundered in what became an oft-quoted passage. The future Admiral Vernon, though Oglethorpe's exact political opposite, echoed these concerns.

But in the end, as the maxim goes, all politics are personal. The untimely death of a dear friend in debtor's prison led Oglethorpe to his greatest cause and, ultimately, the founding of the Georgia Colony.

6.

Robert Castell, an architect, artist, and dreamer, whom Oglethorpe had met at Oxford, loved classical architecture for more than just its elegant proportions. He saw in the stately columned buildings and planned cities of ancient Greece and Rome a solution for England's urban poor. Better buildings, he believed made better people. Castell, in his vision of the "social engineering" role of urban architecture, anticipated the twentieth century's great progressive practitioners—Corbusier, Mies van der Rohe, Frank Lloyd Wright—by more than two hundred years.

A man of great talent and modest means, with a young family to support, Castell nevertheless gambled on the publication of an architectural manifesto which he hoped might make his name and fortune. Entitled *The Villas of the Ancients Illustrated*, and dedicated to the Earl of Burlington, it was a "superb folio" written in both Latin and English and containing more than a dozen expensive foldout copper-plate engravings. The Earl, despite the dedication, failed to provide any financial support to its author. Castell borrowed money for the volume's publication and marketed it with a missionary zeal. Sadly, not many readers shared his mission. "Many are called, but few are chosen," as Matthew's gospel has it; the volume failed to find an audience. Oglethorpe and a handful of others accounted for a dozen copies—then the bill came due. Castell's publisher seized all remaining editions and foreclosed on the project and Castell, like Defoe before him, became a hunted debtor.

A debtor in England's eighteenth-century penal system was treated no better than a thief or murderer: Had he not effectively stolen food from the mouths of his creditors? The law allowed only one punishment for these miscreants: "The person of the debtor was the property of the creditor until the debt was discharged." Castell's creditors insisted on debtor's prison for the unfortunate architect.

Debtor's prison, absurd as the concept sounds to modern ears, was one of the cornerstones of eighteenth-century English life. Wardenships of these semiprivate and immensely profitable institutions were bought by entrepreneurs for thousands of pounds. Thomas Bambridge, warden of the notorious Fleet—so called because it fronted Fleet Street in London—regarded his prison as nothing more than a source of personal revenue. Prisoners paid £5 upon incarceration, a substantial sum for a debtor with no money at all, and numerous additional fees for food and lodging. Debtor's prison was, ironically, an expensive place to stay.

Well-off debtors could lodge in a relatively comfortable appendage called a "sponge house" for the money in fees it soaked up with alarming rapidity. Meals, bedding, rum, servants, all had to be paid for. Aristocrats might even lodge outside the prison walls in nearby apartment houses said to be "within the Rules of the Fleet." Others might ply their trade in the prison yard, with a cut going to the Warden. A few impoverished, incarcerated scribblers managed a modest income producing pornographic ballads for the scurrilous publishers of such material.

But those who could not pay the Fleet's exorbitant rates or who had exhausted all family resources, were then cast into a dungeon in chains. In these "holes" pestilence raged. Castell, meager funds devoured by the sponging house, had been ordered to a hole and appealed to Bambridge for mercy. The hole was no place for an educated gentleman, he pleaded, an artist and scholar with a family to support. He would not long survive in such conditions! Bambridge remained unmoved by the architect's pleas; he'd heard it all before. One can imagine the look of vicious disdain on his face as he threw Castell into a particularly foul hole infested with smallpox. The unfortunate architect only lasted a few weeks. He died in October of 1728 from this dreadful disease, covered in pustules, the victim of an inhumane system and his own intemperate love of ancient architecture.

7.

Oglethorpe had cherished the man; he missed his erudite and talented friend. The dead cannot be resurrected without divine intervention, but their deaths can be avenged by the living. Oglethorpe now sought to prosecute Bambridge for murder; the attempt failed. Bambridge too well connected and too canny, had spread a substantial amount of bribe money among influential judges and Government officials. But the larger issues leading to Castell's death remained: the inhumane treatment of debtors in England's prisons. Devoting himself untiringly to this cause, Oglethorpe established an investigative parliamentary commission in what became one of the world's first attempts at comprehensive prison reform. This commission eventually put the number of "total miserable debtors" in prison in England at more than sixty thousand, most confined in appalling conditions.

Along with Lord John Percival, later Earl of Egmont, James Vernon, (brother of the future admiral) and other prominent men, Oglethorpe produced a damning report. A group portrait of the committee members was done by an unknown artist in early 1729: there they sit, with Oglethorpe at the center, in a large basement room that might be part of the Fleet Prison. Barred windows let in a gloomy light; bewigged all, they wear frock coats and stockings and look very serious, as befits the seriousness of their cause.

Released on March 20, 1729, the Fleet Report described the awful conditions at that prison in particular and other prisons in general and concluded with a recommendation to prosecute the horrible Bambridge. The heartless warden, though he escaped punishment again, was at last forced to resign his lucrative post. Charging ahead, Oglethorpe then pushed through Parliament the "Insolvent Debtors' Reform Act." This piece of legislation released perhaps as many as ten thousand debtors from odious confinement all over England. Oglethorpe's biographers generally ascribe his burst of activity on the behalf of incarcerated debtors to the death of one man, his friend Cassell but some take a larger view:

"Had there been no Fleet and no Castell tragedy," writes Georgia historian Webb Garrison, "another catalytic event would have released and channeled Oglethorpe's enormous life-long drive toward benefitting the friendless, aiding the helpless, and ameliorating the conditions of the oppressed."

The release of so many debtors at once, however, presented new problems: many were utterly insolvent and long abandoned by friends and family. Their presence on the streets of the kingdom (and especially in the raffish London of John Gay's infamous highwayman-thief Captain "Mac the Knife" Macheath) only added to the number of the indigent and potentially criminal poor.

This unforeseen consequence called for a radical solution.

For some years prior to 1729, plans had been put forward by both British imperialists and London entrepreneurs for the founding of a new colony to the south of South Carolina in the former Spanish province of Guale. The Franciscans had established several missions there for the conversion of the Indians in the sixteenth and seventeenth centuries. Now called "the Debatable Land" by the English, its possession however was not a subject of debate for

Spain which still regarded it as Spanish territory. They wanted to retain this unproductive and rustic wild as a buffer between the English in South Carolina and their own capital at St. Augustine. The English wanted it for more-or-less the same reason.

In 1717, an aristocratic speculator, Sir Robert Montgomery, had received a land grant from the Lord Proprietors of the Carolinas to establish a colony in the Debatable Land. He called it, rather fancifully, the Margravate of Azilia. All colonial ventures of the era required a foundational text as both PR and mission statement. His, called *A Discourse Concerning the Design'd Establishment of a New Colony to the South of Carolina, in the Most Delightful Country of the Universe,* failed, despite its extravagant title, to attract a single colonist. A dozen years later, Oglethorpe and others from his prison reform committee, especially the Earl of Egmont, again picked up the idea of a buffer colony but to a different purpose. There, in the "most delightful country of the universe," they would establish "a charitable colony" for the settlement of those worthy debtors, recently released from England's prisons by the Insolvent Debtor's Reform Act.

The idea of a charitable colony, championed by the great eighteenth-century philanthropist the Rev. Thomas Bray, had bounced around philanthropic circles for half a generation. Now, it took on a new urgency: Oglethorpe's timely intervention in a lawsuit over an intestate will allowed him the use of £5000 for charitable purposes. This smallish sum became the seed money for a new British settlement in the Debatable Land, a colony to be called Georgia after King George II.

As always, money attracts money. Oglethorpe's energy and enthusiasm ballooned the initial £5K to nearly half a million pounds to be administered by a group of Trustees based in London. But Georgia, conceived as an exclusive refuge for paroled debtors of "good character" (like Oglethorpe's friend Cassell) soon broadened, welcoming the oppressed, religious dissenters—even Jews—almost anyone willing to work hard enough to carve a home out of the wilderness. Only Roman Catholics, lawyers, and slave owners would be excluded from the new Georgia paradise. Though Oglethorpe refused to abandon his concept of the venture as "a colony of poor and honest industrious debtors," in the end only about a dozen or so made it from the holes into which they had been cast to the wild Georgia shore.

8.

On the morning of November 10, 1733, after many setbacks and controversies, Oglethorpe and over a hundred colonists departed the Thames aboard the *Ann*, bound for Georgia. With them, they took the usual rations: hogs, sheep, ducks and geese, weapons, bibles and other religious texts, and "ten tons of Alderman Parson's best beer." This amounted to a couple of quarts per week for everyone aboard for several months. The city they founded with the consent of local Indians on the Yamacraw Bluff, at the edge of a dense pine forest overlooking the river after which it took its name, would eventually become Savannah.

The nascent settlement's town lots were laid out in 20x30 yard parcels around elegantly proportioned central squares and intervals of greenspace, a design for which it is much admired by both tourists and urban planners today. Not until 1885 did historians realize the careful streetscape of America's first planned city had been taken from Castell's *Villas of the Ancients Illustrated*. This was Oglethorpe's enduring monument to his dead friend.

The Georgia settlers began building their town on February 12, 1733. It grew quickly and at last prospered. The Yamacraw Tribe, assiduously cultivated by Oglethorpe, helped. Their chief, Tomochichi, became an indispensable ally and a good friend. A few years later the chief was taken to England along with his nephew Toonahowi and a retinue of braves to meet the king. Performing Yamacraw dances and parading around in bearskins and eagle feathers, they were the hit of the London season. Oglethorpe continued to manage his Indian affairs carefully and without prejudice, thus safeguarding Savannah from attack and wooing the various tribes away from both Spanish and French influence.

"It is also important to remember that it was due not only to his brilliant foresight but even more to his paternal kindliness," writes Ettinger of Oglethorpe's enlightened policies, "and the fact that 'he understands somewhat of their language'" which enabled him, "to win the affection of the Indians." Pastor J. M. Boltzius, leader of a group of Austrian religious dissenters known as the Salzburgers, welcomed to the colony in 1734, noted that the Indians "honor Mr. Oglethorpe as their Father, and ask his Advice in all their circumstances."

More settlers arrived. Oglethorpe ruled his new colony with an enlightened despotism many soon came to resent. Everyone hated the proscriptions against rum; his dictum against slavery was hotly resented by planters eager to make the most of land granted to them by the Georgia Trustees. (Oglethorpe had learned his precocious anti-slavery views through encounters with Ayuba Suleiman Diallo, a Muslim scholar and aristocrat captured by invading Mandingo tribesmen in Senegal and sold to the British Royal African Company. Diallo eventually ended up on a tobacco plantation at Kent Island, Maryland, where his new owners realized he could read and write Arabic. Useless as a field hand, Diallo was clearly "no common slave." A peripatetic missionary, the Rev. Thomas Bluett of the Anglican Society for the Propagation of the Gospel, subsequently discovered Diallo languishing in the Kent County Jail after an escape attempt. Bluett took Diallo to England where he enjoyed the company of the Royal Family and other prominent persons. Diallo's purchase and manumission subsequently arranged by Oglethorpe, the grateful scholar returned to Senegal where he died in 1773.)

Supremely self-confident, Oglethorpe remained oblivious to the ill will engendered by his progressive policies and praised the new city of Savannah fulsomely in all too infrequent letters to the Trustees back in London. In 1733 he wrote:

> Our people are all in Perfect Health." I chose the Situation for the Town upon an high Ground. Forty Feet perpendicular above High-water Mark; the Soil is dry and sandy, the Water of the River fresh; Springs coming out from the Sides of the Hills. I pitched upon this Place, not only for the Pleasantness of the Situation, but because of the above mentioned and other Signs, I thought it healthy; for it is sheltered from the Western and Southern Winds (the worst in this Country) by vast Woods of Pine-trees, many of which are an Hundred and few under Seventy Feet high. There is no Morse on the Trees, tho' in most parts of Carolina they are covered with it, and it hangs down Two or Three feet from them. The last and fullest Conviction of the Healthfulness of the Place was, that an Indian Nation, who knew the Nature of this Country, chose it for their Situation.

The Spanish, however, resented Oglethorpe's presence in his "pleasant situation," which just happened to be situated in a region they still viewed as belonging to the King of Spain. Though Guale had failed and Spain retained little influence in their former province, the Spanish hoped to stifle any permanent English presence in the Debatable Land. Despite various skullduggeries directed by Governor Montiano from his nest in St. Augustine, as of 1736 Oglethorpe's city had put down permanent roots. Major threats to Georgia's existence now came not from local rivalries but from international developments occurring far away from the little colony clinging to life on the salubrious bluff of the Yamacraw.

In the end, only war would settle the matter of who had the right to the place. October 1739 finds Oglethorpe, veteran of the Siege of Belgrade, donning his soldier's armor in the Georgia wilderness, about to strike the first blow.

9.

A year earlier, at rustic Fort St. Andrew on Cumberland Island, near the Georgia-Florida frontier, Oglethorpe's position had been far more precarious. In fact, he came with a quarter of an inch—literally—of losing his head; it was one of those near misses, like the cannon ball at Belgrade, that dogged him throughout his long life. Oglethorpe, recently returned from a trip to England, had been made "Commander in Chief of the Military Forces of South Carolina and Georgia," by a reluctant Walpole. With this title came a promotion to General and his own regiment of British Regulars—the 42nd Foot.

But the men of this outfit, fresh from garrison duty at Gibraltar, were a mixed bag, rotten with malcontents and Irish Catholics who had no natural allegiance to the Crown. Safe behind Gibraltar's natural defenses, they had become used to a soft, sedentary life; this hardship post in the Georgia wilderness stuck some as unmerited punishment duty. As regulars, they were maintained "on the establishment," that is, their pay and provisions came out of the Royal Treasury. This support had yet to arrive from the far side of the Atlantic. Wilderness duty and long, often deadly sea voyages were also supposed to trigger automatic hazard pay increases and extra rations, which rumor had it, they would not receive.

By November 1738, the 625 men of the 42nd Foot, already poorly fed and clothed and inadequately armed hadn't been paid in several months. About twenty-five rankers led by an unnamed Irish ringleader who "had so much of a Roman Catholic spirit as to harbor an aversion to Protestant heretics," planned to assassinate Oglethorpe and escape across the border into Florida where they would offer their services to Spain.

The appointed hour for the mutiny arrived. General Oglethorpe sat writing in his tent, flap open; he was about to inspect the men gathering on the parade ground. Suddenly, the chief conspirator took up his musket and fired into the tent at close range directly at Oglethorpe's head. So close he couldn't miss, but he did: the ball whizzed through Oglethorpe's campaign wig, singed the collar of his uniform and grazed his cheek. Another mutineer fired a second shot. His musket misfired, the flint failing to ignite the damp powder in the pan. A third mutineer drew his "hangar" (a short military sword) and charged the general, who leapt forward and drew his own, the two exchanging a dozen clanging blows before Oglethorpe, a veteran duelist, disposed of the man.

At that moment, Captain Hugh Mackay, an Oglethorpian loyalist from the regiment's contingent of Highlanders, ran forward, his own sword drawn, to defend his commander. He received a deep cut from yet another mutineer and fell back with a cry. Oglethorpe had just survived three distinct assassination attempts. He now seized the misfiring musket from the second would-be-assassin and swinging it like a club, threatened to bash the brains out of anyone else brave enough to make a fourth attempt. Those who gave up the mutiny would be immediately pardoned he announced; those who did not would be shot. The men of the 42nd, abashed, cowed by the good fortune and bravery of their commander, stepped back. How many men survive three assassination attempts in a row? Clearly, General Oglethorpe was made of different stuff than the average man. Or maybe he enjoyed some special protection you couldn't see.

Oglethorpe, once again in control of the situation, searched the barracks, a detail of loyal soldiers watching his back. He quickly turned up twenty-five muskets, loaded and primed, ready for use against him. The owners of these guns represented the extent of the conspiracy. Another commander, in accordance with the military usages of the day, would have ordered floggings, firing squads. Instead, Oglethorpe met privately with each of the mutineers. He listened to their grievances, forgave, and made up missing pay out of his own pocket. He later admitted that this nearly fatal incident, which would have shaken the resolve of just about anyone, had the opposite effect on him. "Hardships rather animate than daunt me," he told a friend on the Georgia Board of Trustees.

10.

Loyalty now assured by their General's magnanimity, the remaining mutineers of the 42nd Foot formed the nucleus of the small army with which, more than a year later, Oglethorpe planned to attack St. Augustine. It would be the first major land campaign of the war. But a regiment of 625 men was not of sufficient strength to assault the impregnable Castillo de San Marcos. More than twice as many had failed in a similar attempt in 1689. Also, Oglethorpe lacked the necessary supplies and armaments, chiefly artillery. Personal funds exhausted, he turned to the South Carolina legislature for an appropriation of money and men. Was he not, after all, the commander in chief of their military forces?

Critical months passed as the legislature dithered over Oglethorpe's request. He offered to lend South Carolina £50,000 at 8 percent interest to facilitate the expedition to take St. Augustine, but the legislature refused and kept talking. Oglethorpe's great ally and friend, Chief Tomochichi died and was buried with great pomp in one of Savannah's leafy squares. The Yamacraws would still fight with Oglethorpe against the Spanish but in fewer numbers than if their chief had been alive. The General now calculated the expedition would require £139,000 worth of supplies and at least 4,000 men.

Meanwhile, Governor Montiano, informed by spies of Oglethorpe's intentions, grew frantic. Though the Castillo de San Marcos looked impregnable from the outside, within it had decayed from neglect like Porto Bello's Iron Castle—and indeed all the Spanish fortresses in the New World. If the *castillo* fell, Spanish Florida would fall. Montiano now wrote a series of urgent letters to the Governor of Cuba. The potential loss of St. Augustine, he wrote, would be "a rebuff of His Majesty's sacred honor, a foul stain on his Catholic arms, and an insult exciting the rage of our nation." Reinforcements and aid must be sent as soon as possible to avert this disaster.

Oglethorpe grew increasingly impatient for action. Hoping to goad the South Carolina legislature into making the appropriations he needed, he now organized a commando raid into Spanish territory. On January 1, 1740 he marched out of his brand new fort at Frederica with two hundred men and a contingent of allied Creek warriors. Five days later, he reached the St. John's River, not far from St. Augustine. The mouth of this estuary was guarded by two Spanish forts on opposing banks, Fort Picolata and Fort San Francisco de Pupo. Picolata, like much of Spanish real estate in this part of the world, had crumbled and been abandoned. But San Francisco de Pupo put up a good fight, replying to Oglethorpe's demands for surrender with volleys of small arms fire. Oglethorpe had dragged a couple of small field pieces along on the expedition; he now made good use of them, battering the gates of the fort with repeated blasts.

Outnumbered, their own cannons out-of-order, the garrison of San Francisco de Pupo surrendered.

Taking possession, Oglethorpe repaired the damage he had just inflicted and seconded fifty men from his small force to garrison the place. On the way back to Frederica he wrote self-congratulatory letters to Walpole and to the Georgia Trustees, trumpeting his small victory, which he spun as "of great consequence, strategically." In his defense, the St. John's River forts stood between two centers of Spanish power in Northern Florida: St. Augustine in the East and Pensacola on the Gulf of Mexico. Holding the forts would interrupt supply lines and communication between the two settlements.

On January 9, Oglethorpe ordered the last maneuver of his little expedition, sending a reconnaissance party of Creek Indians to St. Augustine. From dense bush overlooking the Castillo de San Marcos, the Creeks observed Montiano's frantic preparations. Battlements were being reinforced, new cannon wheeled into the embrasures, provisions and personnel brought in through the landward gate. The vigilant Montiano had at last received some of the supplies and reinforcements begged from Havana and was obviously preparing for a siege. Back in Frederica on January 11, Oglethorpe was apprised of this disturbing news. Worried by these developments (he had clearly lost the element of surprise) he wrote an urgent letter to an ally in South Carolina. "The longer we delay," he warned, "the stronger they will be."

Indeed, Montiano had just summoned all available troops to the defense of the city and sent more dire letters to his superiors in Havana, now requesting naval support. The Spanish war machine, creaky, obsolete, dating from the era of the Conquistadors, moved with exquisite slowness, but apparently faster than the peregrinating South Carolina legislature. At last, after eight months of debate and delays, and after Oglethorpe had loaned £4000 to the cause (a sum drawn "upon the Credit of their Future taxes, without which the Siege could not be carried out," as Oglethorpe put it) on April 3, 1740 South Carolina came through at last. They granted £120,000 to cover the expedition's costs and found a sturdy professional soldier, Colonel Alexander Vander Dussen to command the Carolina Regiment that would join Oglethorpe in the assault on St. Augustine.

But unfortunate concessions had also been made: Oglethorpe received roughly half the troops he needed. And the Carolina Regiment would only serve for four months and not the usual six. Nor would Oglethorpe have complete military control over them. The South Carolinians, who already faulted him for his opposition to slavery and rum, had lately come to resent him for what they saw as dangerously despotic tendencies; they now insisted on a shared command. But with the army forming ranks for the invasion of Florida, Oglethorpe still appeared a savior to many. "We have nothing here but the Face of War between us and Spain," wrote one terrified resident of Charles Town. For the moment, Oglethorpe alone stood between South Carolina and Spanish domination.

11.

Accounts vary as to the composition and strength of Oglethorpe's army as it left Georgia for the invasion of Florida in late May, 1740. Some historians say Oglethorpe commanded, in addition to his own regiment of roughly 600 regulars, about a thousand South Carolina militiamen, both mounted and afoot, under Colonel Vander Dussen, and perhaps 200 Creek Indians. Others that the Creeks sent 1100 braves to assist Oglethorpe in his siege of the Spanish fortress. Thus, estimates of his full strength vary from 900 to 2,000 effectives, not counting the men aboard eight Royal Navy vessels sent by Admiral Vernon from the Jamaica Station to blockade the port city. These sailors and marines serving under Commodore

Vincent Pearce in *Flamborough*, arrived on the station June 1 to a nasty surprise.

The endless delays perpetrated by the South Carolina legislature had allowed Governor Montiano to assemble a small defensive fleet composed of six "half-galleys" (small maneuverable shallow draft vessels fitted out with sail and oars and nine-pound cannon). These half-galleys suddenly covered all water-borne approaches to the city through the shoals of the Matanzas inlet and across the St. Augustine bar, which drew only nine feet of water. They were also commanded by an able and ruthless Spanish officer: none other than Juan de Leon Fandiño, the notorious *guarda costa* captain who had cut off Jenkins's ear. Pearce's warships drawing more water than Fandiño's half-galleys, might only cross the bar into the Matanzas with difficulty and unmolested; thus the presence of these little vessels effectively neutralized the Royal Navy's threat to St. Augustine.

When Pearce dropped anchor off Anastasia Island, a sandy barrier between the Matanzas and the sea, the Spanish immediately abandoned the defensive batteries there. The Commodore interpreted this Spanish retreat in the face of a superior British force as an act of cowardice; in fact, it had been ordered by Montiano as part of a well-considered strategy. The governor had decided to concentrate all his forces and supplies behind the Castillo de San Marcos's stout walls in preparation for a long siege. He planned to rely on Florida's natural defenses (heat, hurricanes, malarial mosquitos) to defeat the British; all he had to do, he reasoned, was hold out through the summer.

Now, as seen through Pearce's spyglass, the Castillo de San Marcos presented a formidable obstacle to British siege plans. The oldest masonry fort still standing in what is now the United States, the Castillo was then also the strongest, designed by noted Spanish military engineer Ignacio Diaz, and built over a period of twenty-three years, beginning in 1695. Its star-shaped layout and deep, water-filled moat followed all of Vauban's defensive principles, with a Floridian twist. It had been constructed out of "coquina," a peculiar local limestone, half stone-half shell and quite soft, but nevertheless known for its ability to endure a serious pounding: cannon balls, impact absorbed by the spongy coquina, would simply lodge in the huge, porous blocks of its glacis and hang there like boils on a pockmarked face.

While Pearce maneuvered in the shallows beyond the Matanzas, blockading the city from the sea, Oglethorpe captured the small Spanish outpost of Fort Diego, twenty-four miles north of St. Augustine in what is now Palm Valley, Florida. This odd installation was little more than a fortified farmhouse, encircled by a capacious wooden stockade, built in 1703 by Diego Espinoza, a doughty rancher and entrepreneur. He had found an ideal landscape for stock-raising in the local terrain and put up the stockade to protect his herd from pirates and Indian raids. It proved no match for Oglethorpe's guns. The general had now accrued more than fifty-three cannon for the coming siege of St. Augustine.

Attacked on May 10, 1740, Fort Diego surrendered the following morning, providing Oglethorpe with even more cannon and a multitude of horses. Many Spanish prisoners were also taken. All of it had fallen so easily into Oglethorpe's hands he assumed the Castillo de San Marcos would fall as easily. But when he arrived at St. Augustine with the bulk of his army, he confronted an altered situation—one that made his overall strategy unworkable. He had intended to capture the *castillo* in a coordinated land-sea pincer movement, a plan formulated the year before in Charles Town: Pearce's squadron would blast the fortress from the Matanzas River while Oglethorpe mounted a simultaneous assault on its landward walls. Caught in this vice, surely Montiano would quickly capitulate. But now, Pearce's squadron could not sail close enough to the town or the *castillo* for a meaningful bombardment without being seriously damaged by Fandiño's half-galleys. Unsupported, Oglethorpe's army lacked sufficient strength to breach the walls. What would he now do? Faced with these changed circumstances, his carefully planned strategy unworkable, for the first time in his life, Oglethorpe faltered.

"It is difficult to say what happened to Oglethorpe's usually decisive manner during the first month of operations in Florida," writes the eminent Oglethorpian Phinizy Spalding. "Apparently he suddenly became irresolute in his approach to the problems which faced his expedition, for he demonstrated a lack of imaginative leadership that made some wonder if he had lost his nerve."

12.

The unraveling had begun in early June.

After taking Fort Diego, Oglethorpe marched his small army slowly through dense fields of sawgrass and Palmetto, mosquito-plagued and fever-haunted, to within nine miles of the gates of the Castillo de San Marcos. A straight road paved with shells and loud with the chatter of tropical insects led directly to St. Augustine. Guarding this approach lay Fort Mose, the "Negro Fort," and the black township Montiano had established for runaway slaves—now abandoned, all residents and troops evacuated behind the *castillo*'s coquina walls. Oglethorpe burned the unoccupied town and half-destroyed the fort; St. Augustine's defenders could see the black smoke lifting off the horizon in the distance.

With his original plan for a coordinated land-sea assault on St. Augustine thwarted, Oglethorpe cast about desperately for a new strategy and only came up with a bizarre facsimile of same: in a sort of *opera-buffa* tactic, he marched and countermarched his men hither-and-yon, around the bush, always within view of the *castillo*'s battlements, his drummers beating out a popular military tune, the *Grenadier's March*. Perhaps Oglethorpe hoped Montiano might be intimidated into submission with music and martial display; or that the *castillo*'s walls would come tumbling down at the sound of trumpets like the walls of Jericho. But Montiano was prepared to resist to the final extremity. Still, Oglethorpe kept up his ridiculous marching, insisting that "he knew what to do; that it was the Custom of Armies always to shew themselves to the Enemy first and to make a Feint."

Watching from his redoubt in the *castillo*, Montiano pronounced himself baffled at the inexplicable tactics of "Don Diego Ogletorp." Clearly, Oglethorpe hoped to goad Montiano into emerging from the *castillo* for a European-style fight out in the open, troops drawn up in even ranks, banners flying. But the ungoadable governor had now completed the careful withdrawal of his forces and would not be drawn into a fight he would probably lose.

Desperate to get the campaign moving before the hot weather set in, Oglethorpe now made a risky move: he divided his small army into three smaller forces. The first occupied Anastasia Island and repurposed the two defensive Spanish batteries. They would now fire upon the *castillo* on the other side of the Matanzas and not away from it. Here, amid the dunes and the sand fleas, Oglethorpe established his base camp. He intended to blast St. Augustine into submission; unfortunately, the distance was too great, his available cannon unequal to the task. The second force, under Vander Dussen made camp on Point Quartell across the Matanzas's mouth to the north, fronting the St. Mark's River. Here he established another battery. In ordering Vander Dussen to this position, Oglethorpe hoped to interdict supplies still reaching the besieged town from the direction of the St. Mark's.

Meanwhile, a flying squad, commanded by Colonel John Palmer of the South Carolina militia went out to harry the countryside.

Palmer and his men were ordered to keep constantly on the move; they must never sleep in the same camp twice. His corps would destroy outlying settlements and capture or kill any stragglers heading for the *castillo*.

Montiano watched and waited, kept apprised by spies of all developments in the field and especially of Palmer's maneuvers. He knew that a divided army is necessarily a weaker one. By trisecting his army, Oglethorpe had foolishly weakened his military effectiveness. Deserters to the Spanish lines also kept the governor informed of divisions and quarrels in Oglethorpe's command, and especially of the quarrel between Oglethorpe and the Royal Navy, in the person of Commodore Pearce.

Pearce had informed the general that his ships would leave off blockade duty as of July 5, which marked the start of hurricane season in Florida in those days. He would seek out a protected anchorage and rejoin Oglethorpe in November—two months after the South Carolina regiment's term of enlistment expired. The commodore then blandly recommended an immediate, all-out assault on the *castillo*'s walls, despite the fact that Oglethorpe's small army was not of sufficient strength for such a task.

Oglethorpe protested Pearce's decision to abandon station in the most vigorous terms; their conferences almost came to blows. Ultimately, however, the general lacked the clear authority to force Pearce and his vessels to remain on-station past July 5. A dispatch from Admiral Vernon giving Oglethorpe complete authority over Pearce's Florida Squadron, sent aboard the fifty-gun *Colchester*, had somehow failed to arrive. Pearce treated his squadron as an independent command because he had not heard otherwise. As far as he knew, he had been ordered to cooperate with Oglethorpe's land forces only at his discretion. At last, Oglethorpe lowered himself to begging. He now implored Pearce for more vigorous help against the Spaniards. Surely, an attack, supported by the Royal Navy could be launched against the troublesome half-galleys? Once they were dealt with, Pearce's squadron might approach the *castillo* close enough to reduce the place to rubble. Pearce refused this reasonable request, unwilling to expose his men to enemy fire in the shallows and his ships to the elements.

At a loss, Oglethorpe now turned to Vander Dussen. The South Carolinian conceived a daring plan to attack the half-galleys with longboats manned by a hundred sailors and as many troops. The commodore again refused; he would not leave his ships under-manned, at the mercy a Spanish sneak attack or a sudden gale. Undeterred, Vander Dussen concocted a second plan, this one less hazardous and perhaps just as effective. Again requesting a hundred sailors, he planned to entrench a battery commanding the St. Sebas-tian River to the south. Supplies were still reaching the beleaguered city—rumored to be on the brink of starvation—via this estuary. But Pearce, his day of departure growing nearer, refused his assis-tance yet a third time. Too risky.

Oglethorpe now utterly paralyzed with indecision returned to his tent, probably suffering from a relapse of the malarial fevers that had afflicted him the year before at Coweta. His only serious plan, a concerted land-sea attack on St. Augustine had been rendered impossible by circumstance. Nothing else, he believed, might be attempted without Pearce's enthusiastic support. Outwardly calm and stiff-backed, Oglethorpe nonetheless trembled inwardly, racked by increasingly violent fevers and chills.

A lull in the fighting followed in which neither side fired a shot. Then, on the morning of June 15, 1740, just before dawn, disaster struck. Colonel Palmer, disobeying orders to remain mobile, had camped with his men for several nights running in the ruins of Fort Mose. His force consisted of 135 men: About forty Carolina Rangers, forty Highlanders under Captain John Mackintosh from the new Georgia settlement of Scottish emigres at Darien, and thirty Regulars seconded from Oglethorpe's 42nd Foot. The rest were Creek Indians.

Only the Carolinians and the regulars shared a common language. The Highlanders spoke Gaelic; the Creeks their own tribal tongue. In Palmer's camp, all was miscommunication and internecine rivalry: The Highlanders pitched their tents together within the tumble-down walls of the fort; Colonel Palmer and the regulars without. The Creeks maintained their own camp in the surrounding fields.

Discipline had grown lax. All, including Palmer himself, thoroughly exhausted by the marching and countermarching through the Florida heat failed to take the simplest precautions against attack. The mission seemed pointless, every last Spanish soldier and homesteader, along with their sheep, pigs and cattle, had long since evacuated to the Castillo de San Marcos. Palmer had not even bothered to post pickets to watch the long, straight St. Augustine road, glowing white in the slowly brightening darkness.

Then, just before dawn, the land gates of St. Augustine creaked open. Captain Antonio Salgado of the Royal Spanish Army issued forth, leading a force of three hundred Spanish Regulars, backed by a contingent of Free Black Militia under Francisco Menéndez—a former slave from Gambia who had escaped a South Carolina plantation to serve the Spanish Crown—and a few dozen Seminole auxiliaries. This commando army advanced quickly and in silence down the shell road toward Fort Mose. They attacked Palmer's polyglot force without warning at first light.

Outnumbered by at least three-to-one, Palmer's men, taken by surprise, succumbed to a ferocious onslaught. Most didn't have time to load their muskets; many, still asleep were slaughtered in their tents. The Creeks, sensing defeat crept off into the bush; the regulars and the South Carolinians, unable to form into their accustomed ranks were massacred. Inside the remains of the fort, the fighting was fierce and hand-to-hand. The Highlanders alone put up a good fight, seizing up their "claymore" broadswords and hacking at the invading Spanish in the half-light. The battle lasted only an hour or so. Palmer himself, three British captains and three lieutenants along with seventy-five men perished in this action. Thirty-five more were taken prisoner.

With Oglethorpe's offensive stalled, the Royal Navy recalcitrant, and dissension in Palmer's camp, Governor Montiano had chosen exactly the right time for this attack. The encounter, entered into the annals of the 42nd Foot as the "Battle of Bloody Mose," destroyed what was left of the little fort and town. Spanish authorities would rebuild both and restore the black community fifteen years later. The Free Black Militia leader Menéndez, commended by Governor Montiano for his bravery during the fighting, relocated to Cuba where he founded the town of San Augustin de la Nueva—New St. Augustine. He is generally recognized as one of the most effective black soldiers who fought for Spain during her days of Empire. The site of Fort Mose, rediscovered by archaeologists in 1990, has been designated a National Historic Landmark and is recognized as the first "Legal Free Black Community" on the North American continent.

News of the massacre at Bloody Mose reached Oglethorpe languishing under the heavy hand of fever in his tent on Anastasia Island later the same day. This defeat destroyed what remained of his resolve. He could not think of what to do next. A few days later, resorting to a subterfuge born of hubris, he wrote a letter to Montiano (unintentionally comical given the circumstances) demanding an immediate surrender of the *castillo*. The prisoners taken at Mose, he added, had better be well treated! Montiano laughed off this foolish missive; only an enemy in desperate circumstances would make such absurd demands. In any case, as he said in his reply, he was prepared to resist "to the last extremity." In a siege, especially in those days, the defensive position is often the strongest. The reduction of fortresses requires much expenditure in blood and time. Montiano had only to wait; Florida's enervating heat would do the rest.

13.

A week after Bloody Mose, Vander Dussen and a subordinate in his command visited Oglethorpe on Anastasia. There, Vander Dussen later wrote, he "found Things in a good deal of Distraction; Resolutions taken and not put into Execution." Oglethorpe's men, including the Indians, wilted in the heat, eager for immediate action. The soft walls of the Castillo de San Marcos loomed tantalizingly close across the Matanzas—perhaps the place might yet be taken by a sudden assault. More reports of starvation and weakening morale had come from the Spanish side.

A few weeks earlier, Oglethorpe might have acquiesced to such a precipitous attack. But by now he'd lost the last of his gumption, sapped out of him by fever. Oglethorpe was a good actor when necessary, always careful in his appearance, in control of himself and "disdainful of physical frailty." Until now he had managed to hide the extent of his weakness from his subordinates. But Vander Dussen, with whom he now conferred daily was not fooled. The former later wrote that the General was "in so ill a State of Health . . . being reduced to an extraordinary Weakness, by a continual Fever upon him, with some Intermission, for two Months past . . . his Spirits supported him under Fatigue; but the Disappointment of Success (it is believed) now galled him, and too great Anxiety of Mind preyed upon him."

Oglethorpe was a proud a man, too proud to relinquish his command to Vander Dussen, now clearly far more capable of leading the army. Instead, he sought via urgent dispatch more troops from South Carolina and a shallow-draft schooner which would allow him to attack Fandiño's half-galleys in the Matanzas. Even his friends in the Legislature balked at this request, reluctant to throw good water after bad. At last the promised day arrived and Commodore Pearce and his ineffectual Florida Squadron decamped, a few of the vessels having already sailed off before the agreed upon date of July 5. They had done nothing. Their presence in the shallows beyond the bar had been rather more of a reminder of failure to Oglethorpe than a comforting sight.

With the Squadron now gone, Oglthorpe fretted that the entire coastline from Florida to the Carolinas lay open to Spanish attack. In his fevered dreams, he saw Charles Town aflame, laid waste by Spanish cannon fire. He now fixed on returning to Fort Frederica on St. Simons Island with his regiment. From this position, after a period of recuperation, he might rejoin the campaign against St. Augustine—or defend against any forthcoming Spanish offensive further up the coast. He also now knew that the Castillo de San Marcos would not fall to his depleted army and "resolved to abandon the siege."

Meanwhile, Vander Dussen, back on Point Quartell observed several Spanish launches carrying food and supplies down the St. Mark's, beating toward the *castillo*. He scrambled his men to intercept this small flotilla, but Fandiño's ever-present half galleys came up quickly and drove him off. This failure marked the end of the Siege of St. Augustine. Resupplied with necessities, the Castillo de San Marcos might hold out indefinitely.

Presently, Oglethorpe ordered a general withdrawal and the long, feverish march back to Fort Frederica began. Once there, he retired to his quarters and languished, according to Stephens, the colony's secretary, "on his bed", in the clutches of a "lurking fever." He lay there for the next five months, plagued by illness and by the emotional blow-back from what had been, essentially, the first great defeat of his life.

At last, in January 1741, Oglethorpe emerged strong enough to do the business of the colony, now in a state of disarray from his long absence. Recriminations over the defeat at St. Augustine had already begun. News of the disaster had hit the London press in September.

The Champion—a Whig mouthpiece—called Oglethorpe's leadership "irregular" and compared the dissentions in his small army to the Greeks' notorious ten years of infighting before the walls of Troy.

But the most vicious criticism came from those who had contributed the most (albeit belatedly): the South Carolinians. Oglethorpe had spent over £100,000 of the colony's money and lost dozens of her sons at Bloody Mose and elsewhere. His reputation in South Carolina, already mixed, had now suffered an irretrievable blow. Joseph Wragg, a wealthy Charles Town merchant blamed Oglethorpe entirely for the loss. The general, he wrote "follows no advice." Worse, he marched the men to-and-fro to no purpose, "only to harass them, without any Design of coming to Action. Our Volontiers are daily coming away as they see there is no prospect of Succeeding under such Mad conduct."

For his part, Oglethorpe blamed the legislature's eight months of dithering. Supplied and manned in time, he would have beaten Fandiño's half-galleys to the Matanzas. Without this mosquito fleet to harry Pearce's squadron, the commodore might have crossed the bar to bombard St. Augustine while Oglethorpe attacked from the landward side. The *castillo* would have surely fallen, along with all of Spanish Florida.

But this scenario fails to take into consideration Governor Montiano's able and tenacious defense of his citadel. Montiano rightly concentrated all his forces behind the *castillo*'s coquina walls and after careful planning, chose the correct moment for a sortie against Fort Mose. Then he waited. Sometimes, as the military philosopher Sun Tzu tells us, the best thing to do in war is nothing at all. Recognizing Oglethorpe's superiority in the field, Montiano refused to meet him there. He retreated, abandoning the countryside, but in doing so surrendered to Oglethorpe "only fields of Palmetto," as Spalding puts it "and with the exception of San Diego, forts with breached walls and poisoned wells."

Montiano meanwhile kept pressuring Havana for reinforcements and supplies—which arrived with excruciating slowness. Prisoners taken at Fort Mose and exchanged, reported that St. Augustine had been a mere four days from starvation when Oglethorpe evacuated. This unlikely scenario represents perhaps a bit of strategic misinformation designed to tempt Oglethorpe into an ill-timed assault. In any case, by then Pearce had ended his blockade and the South Carolina militia had decamped.

To what other factors must we ascribe the first major British defeat of the War of Jenkins' Ear? There are several to choose from, encompassing enough guilt to cover all parties. First and most basic, Oglethorpe, despite his many impressive qualities, lacked the requisite military experience leading men in day-to-day battlefield operations. His only combat ribbon had come at the Siege of Bucharest twenty-three years earlier in a subordinate capacity. He was, in the end, an intellectual. He had studied tactics and strategy at a military school in Paris alongside his friend, the famous émigré Scottish soldier James Edward Francis Keith, later *Generalfeldmarschall* in the Prussian army of Frederick the Great. But such book-knowledge often vanishes at the first whiff of grapeshot.

Second, Oglethorpe's efforts had been effectively sabotaged by the South Carolina legislature. Eight months of parliamentary debate gave Montiano, informed by his spies of Oglethorpe's intentions, plenty of time to organize an effective defense. Nor had South Carolina vouchsafed Oglethorpe enough troops and supplies to reduce the formidable Castillo de San Marcos; twice as many men serving twice as long might not have sufficed. Also, Oglethorpe's "lingering fever" must be counted a factor; surely it impaired his judgement and blunted his usually decisive nature.

A goodly portion of the blame must also fall on Commodore Pearce. The critical lack of cooperation between the army and navy in what should have been a joint amphibious operation—so typical of the British in this period—probably foredoomed the expedition. Pearce had stubbornly resisted Oglethorpe's advice, then his entreaties, when decisive action presented the only way forward. But Admiral Richmond in his magisterial exegesis of the naval war blames both men: "Oglethorpe and Pearce proved themselves indifferent leaders" he wrote. "The former though he developed the idea, was incapable of putting it into execution; the latter saw difficulties everywhere but made little effort to overcome them."

14.

The thirty-day Siege of St. Augustine, June and July 1740, left Oglthorpe's reputation in tatters, his health compromised, and his spirits at a low ebb. Failure of leadership, a divided command structure, and army–navy friction would continue to plague British military efforts in the coming seasons of war. Admiral Vernon had succeeded at Porto Bello beyond anyone's expectation, but he had acted alone, using only the resources available aboard his "six ships." The Oglethorpian debacle in Florida and Montiano's determined resistance only presaged greater disasters to come.

The last word regarding the siege must belong to the self-effacing Montiano whose "defenses were equal to the emergency, justifying the long years of preparation and suffering that had attended the construction of the [Castillo de San Marcos.]" As the governor wrote to his superiors in Havana after the siege: "My wonder at the shameful flight" of the British from beneath his walls, "is inexpressible."

Blas de Lezo

SIX

Cartagena de Indias

1.

While Oglethorpe sweated and tossed in feverish sheets in the upstairs room of his quarters at Fort Frederica, Georgia, in August 1740, visions of the disaster at St. Augustine haunting his dreams, a strange procession of worn-out, diseased, and disabled veterans, in some cases carried on stretchers, went aboard Commodore George Anson's flagship *Centurion* moored at the Royal Navy base at Spithead, Hampshire on the other side of the Atlantic. Anson, whose care for his men exceeded even Vernon's, watched aghast as these poor devils struggled up the gangway onto his ship.

The ministry's council of war—which now included Walpole, Secretary of State Newcastle, Admiral Sir Charles Wager, First Lord of the Admiralty, Admiral Sir John Norris, and other powerful naval

199

and military men—had ordered Anson around Cape Horn into the Pacific. There at the head of a small squadron, he would attack Spanish towns and shipping along the coast of Chile and Peru and, if possible, seize the Isthmus of Panama and also perhaps the Manila Galleon, the fabulous "Prize of All the Oceans," bearing the riches of the Orient to Acapulco, overland to Vera Cruz, thence, Spain. With the isthmus under his control, he would rendezvous overland with Vernon's forces in the Caribbean, thereby cutting the link between Spain's colonies in North and South America.

It was a tall order for five smallish British warships—*Centurion*, *Gloucester*, *Severn*, *Pearl*, *Wager*, and *Tryal* (a sloop), all fourth rate or below—which is to say carrying between twenty-eight and sixty guns. But this unlikely mission would change the scope of the war. What had started out as a localized conflict between England and Spain over smuggling and depredations in the West Indies had suddenly become a world war. Anson's squadron would become the first Royal Navy military expedition into the Pacific; with his arrival there the theater of operations would span the globe from the Mediterranean to the Caribbean; from the Atlantic coast of North America to the Pacific Coast of South America and the China Seas. From those distant waters, Walpole now blandly suggested, Anson might as well continue around the world to get home again, adding another British circumnavigation to the Age of Sail.

Anson's original orders had also included an attack on Manila and an occupation of the Philippines—then one of the richest Spanish colonies—but the council had dropped this suggestion, sensibly realizing Anson lacked the resources required for such a major undertaking.

Less than a year in, the war against Spain, except for Vernon's capture of Porto Bello, wasn't going well. Thus far it had been characterized by lethargy and bumbling on the part of Great Britain. Her ships lacked manpower and naval supplies for any kind of sustained campaign, but especially manpower. She was clearly unprepared for war after a generation of relative peace.

With the scheme to attack Manila now deleted, Anson, per the Council's official orders had only to "proceed with his squadron to the South Seas and distress the Spaniards by sea and land," explains Admiral Richmond. "And to attack any town or other places practicable of assault, endeavoring to get the Indians to side against the Spaniards." A council of war was to decide whether Callao should be attacked. And if the attack was made and miscarried, proceed to Panama, "looking into all the ports between Lima and Panama" and capturing shipping. On arrival at Panama, he was to "get into communication overland with the West Indies squadron, and if it were considered practicable by the commanders of the joint forces, some of the troops in the West Indies were to be landed at Porto Bello to attack Panama, both squadrons operating from the sea."

"This done, his subsequent movements were to be at his own discretion . . . he might go to Acapulco, the American port of arrival of the Philippine trade, and endeavor to take the treasure ships as they arrived, then return home by the Cape or the Horn as he desired, leaving, if he considered it necessary, two ships in the South Seas to protect trade and cover any places taken."

The Council had originally envisioned a squadron of eight ships bound for the conquest of Manila, carrying—in addition to a crew of more than five hundred sailors—1,500 soldiers who would prosecute any land operations. These shipboard fighting men were to be drawn from existing foot regiments and designated "marines."

But, continues Admiral Richmond:

"In an enterprise of this kind, swiftness of execution, secrecy and good organization are essential to full success. None of these was present. Discussed in October 1739, decided on in December, and ordered at the end of January 1740, the expedition did not sail till September 1740—exactly eleven months after the first proposals were made in the Council."

By this time, efficient French secret agents operating in London knew all about Anson's plans and had conveyed this information to Spanish Intelligence in Madrid. The Spanish were busily preparing a counterexpedition under the veteran Admiral Don José Alfonso Pizarro—a descendant of the famous conquistador—to intercept the Commodore. Thus, the element of surprise had been lost nearly a year before Anson left Spithead.

Unfortunately for Anson, in the months between October 1739 and the following September, other priorities had come to the fore. His expedition, now deemed of tertiary importance to the war effort had been drained of resources. All available manpower and naval supplies were now set aside for a massive armada, including transports bearing eight thousand troops, making ready to sail from the Isle of Wight to the West Indies under Admiral Chaloner Ogle and Major General Lord Charles Cathcart. Despite Vernon's repeated warnings against prosecuting a tropical land war, this massive force would assist him in joint-amphibious operations against the Spanish colonies, whether he liked it or not.

The Council of War had strongly suggested Havana as the prime target: "All our hearts are bent on Cuba," wrote Sir William Pulteney, one of Vernon's main supporters in Parliament; but Pulteney concluded that he would leave the ultimate decision up to the fighting Admiral.

2.

Meanwhile, Anson stood by helplessly as the Admiralty loaded his ships with sickly pensioners from the Royal Chelsea Hospital.

This institution, built by Christopher Wren, architect of St. Paul's, at the behest of Charles II in 1682, and still in use today, wasn't a hospital in the modern sense, but an "old soldier's home" where retired and invalid veterans of Britain's wars might live out their last days in peace. But the word "invalid" also had a different meaning in the eighteenth century; the Chelsea's aged or infirm residents were considered what we would today call "reservists." In time of need they might be drafted to fight again for their country. Most of the hospital's pensioners could barely walk; those that could quickly walked away when called upon to serve with Anson's expedition. The rest, too stupid or slow or maimed to flee were brought aboard his ship to fill out the required complement of men, according to the regulations. Some of the pensioners wept piteously as they were carried aboard; they knew they were sailing on a voyage from which they would never return.

Anson protested vigorously to the Council of War and the Admiralty concerning these unfortunates. But nothing could be done, given the lack of fit fighting men and supplies then plaguing England. The winter of 1739–40 had been hard, with crop failures, unseasonable rains, and an epidemic of typhus; much of the country was sick and half-starved. The Navy Victualing Board responsible for provisioning Anson's ships was hard pressed to find enough food for a long voyage. The invalids supplied to him in this time of dire shortages were in "deplorable condition," and would be worse than useless, Anson complained. Most wouldn't survive the voyage across the Atlantic, let alone the always terrible passage around Cape Horn.

"The more Anson learned about these veterans, the more his horror and indignation grew," writes Glyn Williams, the preeminent modern historian of Anson's expedition. "Out of the 2,000 out-pensioners at Chelsea Hospital, he claimed that the 500 selected were the oldest and weakest—this presumably on the grounds that whatever the method of selection, those chosen were being sent to almost certain death. As the authorized account put it, they were doomed to 'uselessly perish by lingering and painful diseases; and this too, after they had spent the activity and strength of their youth in their Country's service.'"

Anonymous in the official narrative (*Lord Anson's Voyage Round the World*, published London, 1748), recent scholarship offers us a clearer picture of the invalids sent with Anson: The average age of those hauled aboard the *Centurion* was fifty-five, with some over seventy; the majority had sustained disabling wounds in battles dating from Marlborough's time. A cursory list of the men and their injuries compiled from Admiralty records includes, according to official records:

Niel MacNiel, 56 years old, wounded in the Right Thigh at del Rey cut on the nose and in the forehead at Brihengel and on the left side of his belly also the left leg hurt by a bombshell at Saragossa; Denis Bryan, 54 years old, stabbed through the left hand by a boat hook, wounded in the right arm and in the right leg; John Bridgeman, 53 years old, dim-sighted and rheumatic; Charles Ross, 53 years old, convulsion fitts and hard of hearing; George Walker, 55 years old, rheumatic, weak in both legs, bruised at Gibraltar, worn out; Edward Butler, 70 years old, a Hurt in his back, worn out.

But Anson himself represents the best sort of officer the eighteenth-century Royal Navy had to offer—and would have been a credit to any navy in any century. He was handsome and well-liked, an elegant even dandyish gentleman who nonetheless often toiled alongside his men like a common sailor. His urbane manner concealed an iron will. As the youngest son of a minor country squire, he could expect to inherit nothing except his family's good name; another age might have found him a career in the church or in politics. Like Vernon, drawn to the sea, he joined the navy at a young age, made lieutenant at nineteen, and was appointed commander of the North Sea sloop

Weasel at twenty-five. Two years later, now captain of the South Carolina station ship *Scarborough*, Anson settled in Charles Town. There, he cut a dashing figure at the frequent balls and parties of what was then the largest American city south of New York.

"Mr Anson . . . is far from being an anchorite, though not what we would call a modern pretty fellow," commented a Charles Town matron, "because he is really so old-fashioned as to make some profession of religion: moreover, he never dances, nor swears, nor talks nonsense. As he greatly admires a fine woman, so he is passionately fond of music."

Unlike Vernon and Oglethorpe, Anson had nothing against a glass of rum punch, but his chief entertainment seems to have been gambling for high stakes. Frequently successful, his winnings allowed him to purchase large tracts of land in the Carolina backcountry. He might have ended his days as a prosperous rice planter, the owner of an in-town home on Charles Town's Battery, a country house, a wife, and a few hundred slaves, but that sort of life did not attract him. After a half-dozen years, the navy called him from his comfortable South Carolina routine.

Destiny and the Admiralty had cast him in a more heroic role as one of the Great Captains of the age.

3.

Anson and the Pacific Squadron left Spithead for the far side of the world on September 18, 1740. In addition to the invalids, his crews were padded with raw recruits—called "marines" for want of a better term, many of whom had never fired a musket. The invalids quickly began to fall sick and die; the new marines proved equally fragile "growing sick very fast . . . devoured by the Itch, Pox and other Distempers." The voyage began inauspiciously, with

Centurion and the other vessels in Anson's command pressed into service as escort for Admiral Ogle's invasion fleet. Now swollen to more than 150 sails—the largest armada ever to appear in those waters—it must have made a magnificent sight, running before the wind toward the setting sun.

Anson, however, found this duty frustrating. For him it only meant more delays; his squadron would now be rounding the Horn in a month usually plagued by many vicious storms. The voyage from the English Channel ports to the island of Madeira, a refreshment station for vessels on their way to South America, usually took two weeks. Anson, always plagued by bad weather, needed six to make this passage. By then, he had left convoy duty behind, separating from Ogle's armada in the mid-Atlantic to resume his course toward Brazil. Mortality in Anson's little squadron had not abated upon reaching open ocean, with sixty-five to seventy men dead per weeks aboard each ship from typhus and other maladies. At this rate, the expedition would not maintain sufficient strength to complete its mission. Rounding the Horn alone required a full complement of able-bodied seamen; once in the Pacific battles would be fought against unknown armies in distant lands. But the hardest fight, against disease and malnutrition lay just below deck.

In his famous novel *Roderick Random*, Tobias Smollett, now serving as a surgeon's mate with Ogle's armada, describes the foul conditions below decks that led to such a high death count aboard overcrowded Royal Navy vessels in the first half of the eighteenth century:

> Here I saw about fifty miserable distempered wretches suspended [in hammocks], so huddled one upon another, that not more than fourteen inches space was allotted for each with his bed and bedding; and deprived of the light of day, as well as of fresh air; breathing nothing but a noise-some atmosphere of the morbid steams exhaling from their

own excrement and diseased bodies, devoured with vermin hatched in the filth that surrounded them, and destitute of every convenience necessary.

Worse conditions cannot be imagined, except perhaps aboard a slave ship of the era, which these sad-sack sailors matched in everything but the chains.

Setting out from Madeira, Anson anxiously scanned the horizon for enemy sail. From Admiralty dispatches, he now knew he was being hunted; Pizarro's squadron might intercept him at any time. Anson's ships, wallowing and heavily laden, decks crowded with extra provisions for the long voyage, were in no condition to encounter an enemy at sea. In a fight, excess provisions would have to be jettisoned to make room for deployment of the cannons, putting an end to the expedition before it reached the Pacific.

And it is here, in the South Atlantic half way to Brazil, beneath a lowering sky, that we must leave him to pick up the main thread of this narrative: To Anson's misadventures rounding the Horn; to the famous wreck and subsequent mutiny of the *Wager*, so eloquently described in his narrative by Midshipman John "Foul Weather Jack" Byron, the poet's grandfather; to the mid-ocean attack on the Manila Galleon *Nuestra Señora de Covadonga* and Anson's subsequent circumnavigation, we shall return at the appropriate place.

4.

Admiral Vernon had repeatedly warned the Council of War in London against a land-based campaign in the West Indies. In yet another one of his hectoring letters to Secretary of State Newcastle in December 1739, he wrote:

The almost general disappointments of past expeditions in America . . . were principally owing to delays in order to gather more strength, by which they were weakened more in the force they brought out within that time than any additional forces they collected amounted to: and gave the enemy all they could desire to strengthen themselves against them. So that in my judgement, I should limit all expeditions to this country to be entered upon immediately on their arrival, and to be executed within the first six weeks, before their men would begin to fall sick.

Wise words from a veteran of tropical warfare. But by January 1740 it was already too late: the eight thousand troops called for had assembled on the Isle of Wight under the command of General Lord Cathcart, a highly regarded soldier and veteran of Marlborough's continental wars. Training and preparations for the army dragged on; victualing alone for the fleet under Chaloner Ogle took the better part of ten months. At last, on October 26, 1740 Ogle's armada sailed for the West Indies—escorted part of the way by Anson's squadron—and soon followed by Cathcart's army in the transports. Both halves of this invasion force reached the Caribbean island of Dominica within days of each other, after a relatively brief crossing. There, on that small island, a disaster befell the expedition of great consequence to the success of the war against Spain—and indeed, as some assert, the subsequent course of world history.

General Cathcart, forty-six years old and apparently healthy, suddenly died after an attack of the "bloody flux"—amoebic diarrhea—so violent that he literally shit his guts out in a matter of days. He was a veteran of Ramillies and Oudenaarde and Malplaquet; he had commanded the Scots Greys at Sheriffmuir in 1715, the battle that destroyed Jacobite hopes for a generation; he had survived cavalry charges and cannon bombardments and in the end was felled by a single-celled organism too small to see with the naked eye. They buried Cathcart on Dominica on the beach at Prince Rupert's Bay. An impressive monument later raised in his honor has long since weathered away, a plinth engraved with his titles and victories, yet another illustration of those melancholy lines from Grey's *Elegy*:

> *The boast of heraldry, the pomp of pow'r,*
> *And all that beauty, all that wealth e'er gave,*
> *Awaits alike th' inevitable hour.*
> *The paths of glory lead but to the grave.*

The course of history often turns on small events, relatively unremarkable at the time, but acknowledged by later generations as of supreme importance: The great Spanish historian Cesáreo Fernández Duro sees in the death of General Cathcart the fate of the entire Spanish dominion in the New World. An excellent and vigorous soldier, Cathcart was also an able diplomat, an unusual combination in a single individual. The diplomatic Cathcart and the irascible Vernon, both bold tacticians, working together—so Duro hypothesizes— would have made an unbeatable combination against Spain. England had long sought a permanent foothold in South America, a base from which to launch a conquest all of Spain's possessions on the continent. Voltaire guessed at these ambitions; Walpole's council of war tacitly fixed its overall strategy to this guiding star; Cathcart and Vernon, working together might have made it happen.

Vernon had meanwhile decided on the walled maritime city of Cartagena de Indias in what is now Colombia, one of the home ports of the Spanish Treasure Fleet, as the next objective in this campaign of English conquest:

"Had it been properly handled," Duro speculated, "the English could have driven Spain out of the West Indies and South America, and the whole of the New World would have fallen under Aglo-Saxon domination. . . . England alone could have achieved it, and she undoubtedly would have achieved it, had the expeditionary force of 1740 been commanded by a good general."

Unfortunately, Cathcart's successor was anything but a good general: Major General Thomas Wentworth, chosen by Cathcart as second in command, made a poor choice indeed. Timid, punctilious and, like many emotionally weak men, obstructively passive-aggressive, he had after twenty years' service in the army no battlefield command experience. Smollett, an eyewitness to the events of the campaign, described Wentworth as "an officer who had neither knowledge, weight, nor self-confidence sufficient to conduct an enterprise of such importance." Lord Hervey, the contemporary diarist, a sort of British Saint-Simon, commented that Wentworth's "chief merit consisted of being in favor with those in power."

Wentworth, however, was not entirely without military attributes—even if his knowledge of the battlefield came from textbooks. He excelled in his specialty, logistics. During the months of training on the Isle of Wight, his administrative and organizational abilities had made him the perfect complement to Cathcart, the seasoned war chief. Wentworth wasn't much of a soldier, but he did make a good acquisitions officer. Still, in hindsight, Cathcart had blundered in his decision to anoint Wentworth: an untried soldier would be commanding one of the largest military amphibious operations between the Spanish Armada and D-Day. Of course, no man can predict the hour of his death; had Cathcart known he would soon be relinquishing his earthly command, he might have chosen another as his successor.

"Lord Cathcart is dead," wrote a chagrined officer, "and General Wentworth commands the forces, which gives great concern as he was never yet in any service, but is certainly a very sensible man."

Sensibility in warfare is often exactly the wrong quality, as warfare is not an inherently sensible undertaking. A portrait of Wentworth shows a spit-and-polish officer, correctly dressed in a red army coat and buff waistcoat, kid gloves held lightly in one hand, a short military wig perched just-so on his oblong head. The expression on his face is one of diffident calm. Alas, an even temperament and a talent for logistics are not quite those qualities most needed for an assault on a major citadel, or, as it turned out, for dealing with as obstreperous and overbearing an officer as Admiral Vernon, who remained in charge of the naval arm of the expedition.

5.

Following Vernon's victory at Porto Bello, after all the celebratory bonfires had burned out, war planning stumbled. The council of war haggled endlessly over what to do next. England had been at peace for too long; the men in power seemed unsure of the necessary steps to achieve victory over Spain.

Vernon, given ultimate authority to plan his own next move soon lacked the resources for anything but the smallest undertaking. Still the drumbeat for a major attack on Havana grew louder in Walpole's council and in the London press; Vernon continued to insist on the inadvisability of such an attack. Havana was too well fortified, too populous, and well protected from the sea by rocky shoals and a sturdy *castillo*. For more than a year, Vernon's command languished on Jamaica, as the council debated and hatched various schemes only to discard them, and as the men fell daily to fever and the pernicious influence of the Jamaican "punch houses."

To Vernon's supporters in Parliament, it seemed Walpole's ministry had secretly determined to sabotage his efforts. Hadn't the first minister opposed the Spanish War and wrung his hands upon its declaration? Meanwhile, Vernon continued to write his usual vituperative letters—to Secretary Newcastle, to his major supporters in Parliament (Pulteney, Lords Bathurst, Carteret, and Chesterfield) and anonymously to the press, complaining of his lack of critical supplies. The war could not be prosecuted without tar, rope, and men. The longer he and his command loitered along the malarial coasts of the Spanish Main, the more his men rotted in the holds of his ships or succumbed to the effects of fever and demon rum.

At the Admiralty, Wager agreed with him and fretted: "You know as well as I," he wrote to Vernon in January 1740, "that whatever is determined to be put into execution must be immediately be proceeded upon; for soldiers, no more than other people, cannot do anything when they are dead, and that will be their fate if you stay too long in Jamaica."

Hosier's ghost loomed again.

Vernon would not sit idle for long. Keeping his own counsel, he had already rejected the ministry's suggestion of Havana as the war's next major campaign. Cartagena made the obvious choice; it was just as important an entrepot for Spanish silver as Havana and had been seized and sacked twice before, once by the immortal Drake in 1588 and once by the French soldier, Bernard Desjean, Baron de Pointis in 1697, leading an army of buccaneers. On that occasion the Frenchmen and his pirate crews carried off millions in gold and treasure. Though the city looked impregnable on Admiralty charts, it wasn't.

Accordingly, on February 25, 1740, Vernon set out on a reconnaissance mission to Cartagena with a small squadron of five ships—*Stanford, Princess Louisa, Windom, Norwich,* and *Greenwich.* The Admiral's pennant now unfurled from *Stanford*'s mainmast, his flagship *Burford,* having run aground a few months earlier, still under repair in Jamaica. Though in a state "too weak for any considerable enterprise," as Vernon later wrote to the Admiralty, he anchored on March 2 in the roadstead of Playa Grande within sight of Cartagena's walls and proceeded to test the defenses of the city. Spanish gunners offered only a tepid response, the antagonists were too far away from each other to do much damage, why waste shot and powder? Vernon wrote another hasty letter to the Admiralty: with three thousand men, he might easily take Cartagena in a few days. But this was idle boasting. A strong Spanish squadron consisting of five heavy ships of the line and five galleons had recently arrived from Santander, Spain, and lay safely within Cartagena's protected anchorage.

In command, unfortunately for Vernon, King Felipe V had appointed the pugnacious Basque Don Blas de Lezo y Olavarrieta, one of the greatest fighting admirals of the age. Known to his men as El Medio Hombre (Half Man) and *Patapalo* (Peg leg) Blas de Lezo y Olavarrieta had lost a substantial percentage of his body parts in the various wars of the Spanish Empire. Born in 1689 in the small town of Pasages in the Spanish Basque province of Guipúzcoa, of the same doughty stock as St. Ignatius Loyola, founder of the Jesuits, Don Blass—as the English came to call him—had entered the Spanish navy as a midshipman in 1701 at the age of twelve. He fought with distinction through the War of Spanish Succession, participating in the Battle of Malaga in 1704 against the same Anglo-Dutch fleet that had captured Gibraltar. Bloody but inconclusive, it was the largest naval engagement of the war.

During a particularly fierce cannonade in this battle, Don Blas's left leg was struck by a cannon ball. Cartilage and bone hung in shreds from the remains of his mangled knee; blood pooled on the deck. The ship's surgeon amputated in situ during the heat of battle. Don Blas was fifteen. Three years later, at Toulon, promoted to ensign and fighting alongside the French Navy, a splinter from the pulverized gun deck of his ship pierced his eye; the damaged orb was then removed with a surgical spoon. At Barcelona in 1714—the last major battle of the war, which pitted Spaniard against Spaniard, one side loyal to Felipe, the other to Charles of Austria—Don Blas, now a Captain, lost the use of his right arm, shattered by a rain of grapeshot. In this reduced condition, one-eyed, one-armed, one-legged, he nonetheless continued to serve the Spanish king with distinction: in the Pacific from 1720–28 and in the Mediterranean, commanding in 1732 a hard-fought campaign against the Barbary Pirates during which he seized Oran from its Ottoman-backed overlord, the dreaded Bey Abu Hasan Ali.

Don Blas bore all his battle scars proudly—refusing to cover his empty eye socket with a patch or fill it with a cold glass eye. Why hide honorable wounds, received in the service of His Majesty, King Felipe V? He sought, in the scarification of his body, to inspire others to similar sacrifice—though in March 1740, his greatest sacrifice and greatest victory over vastly superior odds still lay ahead of him. For years, Blas de Lezo's achievements on behalf of Spain lay unremembered, consigned to the dust bin of history—which is to say the back pages of books like this one. Calumnized by political enemies after his death, neglected in Spain because of his Basque roots, he remained a hero only in Cartagena where his peg-legged statue, raising a sword toward the sea, has defended the city for nearly seventy years. But not until 2014 was he so honored in his native Spain. A realistic statue showing all his amputations and injuries now stands in the Plaza de Colon, alongside the statue of the Great Navigator.

That Vernon found himself up against a greater adversary at Cartagena he had yet to realize. He began his bombardment on March 6, 1740, aiming his Protestant guns at the Jesuit College and the spires of the Roman Catholic Cathedral. He hoped, as had Oglethorpe before St. Augustine, to draw Spain's forces out into the open. But the mutilated Spanish admiral, veteran of so many fights with the English enemy, would not be tempted. From his position of strength in the Surgidero, Cartagena's naturally fortified harbor, ringed by a series of *castillos*, Don Blas remained untouchable. For the moment, he contented himself with a bit of eighteenth-century psy-ops, needling the irascible English Admiral with the same kind of "thunderers" the latter usually reserved for his superiors.

Vernon had recently captured a small boat containing several Spanish prisoners whom he now returned to Don Blas unscathed, with a polite letter and the king's compliments. Don Blas resenting this act of kindness, took it, perhaps rightly, as condescension. He fired off an outraged response implying Vernon's return of the prisoners had not sprung from any humanitarian impulse but had rather been guided by fear of Spanish imperial might. And that this same fear had led Vernon to destroy Porto Bello when he ought to have held it intact for his English king. Someday, Don Blas concluded, he would meet Vernon on the high seas and pay him back in person for the destruction of Spanish property he had wrought in Panama.

Vernon, at first amused by the Spanish Admiral's bellicose manner, at last counted himself insulted. He sent no reply to Don Blas, commenting instead in a letter to secretary Newcastle that such insolence was "best answered from the mouth of our mortars, which may instruct him where to find me, if he continues in this heroic disposition."

6.

The purpose of Vernon's first mission to Cartagena had been intelligence gathering. And in this, it had been a success. He had tested the city's resolve to fight and gauged its defenses, both natural and man-made. Also, for the price of an amnesty, he purchased a detailed map of the local coastline from an English pirate, Captain George Lowther who wanted to return home without the inconvenience of being strung up on Execution Dock. From Lowther he also learned that the *guarda costas* now made their home base at Chagres. Determined to strike a quick blow against these hated adversaries, Vernon weighed anchor and sailed for this small town on the Panamanian Coast.

With Porto Bello reduced to rubble, Chagres, situated on opposite banks of the river of the same name, had recently become a major transshipment port for the Spanish treasure fleets. The Chagres River ran dry for part of the year; during the rainy season it overflowed its banks with frothy brown water upon which rafts bearing treasure from the Pacific reached Chagres's stone warehouse—the only building of consequence in the town. Chagres few hundred citizens were protected by a small fort, the Castillo San Lorenzo, mounting twenty-three guns.

Vernon sailed into Chagres Bay with only two ships (*Windom* and *Greenwich*) on March 21, 1740 and anchored just beyond the reach of San Lorenzo's guns, though, as he soon discovered, only five of them remained operable. He began his bombardment on March 22 and proceeded in a leisurely fashion for two days. The commander of the Castillo San Lorenzo, Captain Juan Carlos Gutiérrez de Cevallos at the head of a garrison of thirty, could only reply with the occasional round shot. On March 23, Diamond, under the ubiquitous Captain Charles Knowles—the same competent officer who had supervised the destruction of Porto Bello's Iron Castle along with Captain Boscawen—sailed in to join the attack.

At last, at dawn on March 24, having satisfied the requirements of honor, Captain de Cevallos surrendered his sword to Captain Knowles. Admiral Vernon came ashore in a jolly boat later in the day to inspect the newest British territory in the New World. He looked around at the rough dwellings, piles of rubbish and half-starved dogs and deemed it unworthy of a second glance. The *castillo* he ordered destroyed after removing its few workable cannons. But the warehouse he found stuffed with a small fortune in trade goods, including barrels of cocoa, bales of Alpaca wool and a quantity of "Jesuit Bark," the papery dried sheath of the Andean cinchona tree whence quinine is derived. (Because of its salubrious anti-malarial effects, Jesuit Bark eventually enabled Europeans with no resistance to malaria to success-fully colonize Africa. Sebastian Bado, the renowned Italian physician, later declared the stuff "more precious to mankind than all the gold and silver of the Americas.")

A few days later, with Chagres thoroughly pillaged, Vernon sailed away after having sent a fast sloop bearing the news of this fresh victory to England. Predictably, he made much of the place and the battle for Castillo San Lorenzo in his dispatches, emphasizing the treasures of Chagres's warehouse and not the poverty of the town. The London press again fulsomely celebrated this latest exploit of the apparently unconquerable Admiral Vernon. Surely, as Voltaire feared, all of Spain's South American possessions would soon be gathered under the billow-ing folds of the Union Jack.

Vernon's exploratory squadron returned to Jamaica in early June. There, he immediately began busying himself on behalf of his men, designing a new type of land-based naval hospital to be built on the island, somewhere in the countryside: It would be open to the air and accessible through one tightly guarded entrance, this to prevent the sickly inmates from escaping to Port Royal where they could become "better acquainted with Captain Punch." Vernon's anti-rum prejudices, perhaps a bit of an obsession, were nonethe-less shared by many at the time:

"Rum punch is not improperly called Kill-devil," wrote a Jamaica correspondent to the London papers, "for thousands lose their lives by its means. When Newcomers use it to the least excess they expose themselves to imminent peril, for it heats the blood, and brings on fevers which in a few hours send them to their grave. The greatest moderation is necessary in using it, and could be avoided altogether, 'twere much better; at least till one be well seasoned to the place."

Unfortunately, Vernon's hospital was never built.

7.

In July, the Admiral made his last appeals to the council of war on the inadvisability of an extended land-based campaign in the tropics and was again ignored. He sent several letters marked "VERY PRIVATE" (the eighteenth-century equivalent of "Top Secret") to Secretary Newcastle, expressing his views in his usual forthright, undiplomatic manner. Newcastle neglected to share these final desperate appeals with the rest of the council. It was too late. Cathcart's army of eight thousand pallid and undernourished Englishmen had nearly completed training on the Isle of Wight.

The Council, however, did offer one concession to Vernon's tropical anxieties. "Unseasoned" troops from England would be augmented by a newly raised regiment of three thousand Anglo-Americans, to be recruited in the American colonies. These men, supposedly already inured to the extreme climate and unfamiliar diseases of the New World were considered "seasoned." Never mind that most of them would come from Virginia, Massachusetts, Maryland, and points north, hardly tropical regions. American troops had fought for Britain many times before—in Oglethorpe's South Carolina Regiment, for example—but only in their own locality, as militia units recruited and paid by local legislatures and fighting a local foe, usually Indians, most often in defense of their own homes and families. This would be something entirely new:

The American troops would be counted as regulars, paid and equipped "on the Establishment" and, like Oglethorpe's personal regiment, given a British regimental identity: the 43rd Regiment of

Foot. And they would be fighting far from home in an unfamiliar part of the world, becoming, in effect, America's first "Veterans of Foreign Wars." Also they would be risking their lives for something intangible: imperial policy, that is British hegemony over Spain and the right to free trade in the West Indies.

Like most undertakings of dubious merit, the effort to recruit American colonials for the war against Spain began with great fanfare and the highest hopes: On April 21, 1740, Governor Belcher of Massachusetts appeared on the balcony of the Council Chamber in Boston to read the declaration of a war that had already been officially declared on October 23 the previous year in London. By this time, news of Vernon's victory at Porto Bello had reached the Boston newspapers and the crowds were in a celebratory mood. The packed square below the governor's balcony resounded with huzzahs and the crack-crack of volleys fired by local militia, all echoed by the booming of cannon at Castle William, overlooking Boston Harbor in the distance.

The governor then made an unexpected announcement. The king had decided to enlist at least four battalions of *Americans* to fight alongside British regulars in the West Indies. Each volunteer ". . . would be supplied with arms and proper clothing and be paid by His Majesty, and have their share in any booty that shall be taken from the enemy, and be sent back to their respective habitations when the service shall be over, unless any of them shall desire to settle themselves elsewhere . . . and for the further encouragement of this affair, all volunteers that shall enlist and proceed in this service shall be exempt from all impress for three years after their return."

That is they would be free from the roving press gangs that scoured American port cities for much hated and often fatal service in the Royal Navy.

The governor went on to praise Vernon's recent victory, echoing breathlessly patriotic news reports; Vernon's "six ships only" must have been crewed with angels bearing flaming swords. Vernon had been able to "vindicate the Glory and retrieve the Honor of the British Flag," after so many years of unanswered "Spanish insults and depredations" at the hands of *guarda costa* ruffians.

Though fresh news to most Bostonians assembled that day, London's *Gentleman's Magazine* had already reported in February that

> Three Regiments of Foot, 1000 Men each, are raising with all speed in our American colonies, and will consist of Natives or those inured to the climate. The Colonels, Lieutenant Colonels, Majors and Subalterns are appointed by his Majesty, and their general rendezvous is to be New York, where the Royal Standard is set up. Their clothing is to be made up here, which is camblet coats, brown linen waistcoats, with two pairs of canvas trousers for each man.

Much about this statement was a hopeful fiction. Recruiting wouldn't begin for another couple of months and many of the men who joined up eventually received neither clothes nor arms and fought in the rags they wore when they volunteered, their only uniform in the end a burial shroud. They were, however, paid a traditional recruitment bonus—derisively called the "King's Shilling"—that usually added up to several pounds sterling, a substantial amount in those days. Many volunteered, took the bonus then deserted, a common occurrence. (One soldier later in the century took the bonus forty-seven times, deserting each time; this "professional deserter" was eventually caught and hanged.) But expectation of an easy victory is the delusion of many an army at the start of any war. Americans volunteered enthusiastically, enough to more than fill the king's quotas.

The idea of using American troops to support an expedition to the West Indies originated with the war council in 1739, before Vernon's victory at Porto Bello. From the beginning, Walpole believed only a major victory on land—as opposed to supremacy at sea—would win the war and save his now unpopular ministry from collapse. Colonel Martin Bladen, military and trade advisor to Secretary Newcastle, presented the use of American troops as a necessary evil. A major assault on Havana or Cartagena would not be possible without them, so he informed the secretary. The war council feared France might soon join the war on the side of their Spanish cousins (in fact, the 1733 Bourbon *Pacte de Famille* insisted on this point) and had necessarily reserved the bulk of the army to defend the homeland. Bladen also pointed out that Americans had served creditably alongside British regulars in the past: In 1690, for example, Colonel William Phipps of Massachusetts had seized Port Royal in Nova Scotia from the French.

The council approved Bladen's proposal and forwarded it to Parliament. On April 25, 1740, Parliament officially commissioned the 43rd Regiment of Foot, to be raised in America. It would be commanded by Colonel Alexander Spotswood, former lieutenant governor of Virginia, another veteran of Marlborough's wars. Spotswood had been wounded at the Battle of Blenheim and later served as Marlborough's quartermaster general. Known for his intelligence and initiative, in 1718, he had privately outfitted two sloops of war—*Jane* and *Ranger*—hired a crew of Royal Navy officers out of his own pocket, and sent them to capture the vicious pirate Edward Teach, known as Blackbeard. *Ranger*, captained by Lieutenant Robert Maynard, encountered Blackbeard's *Queen Anne's Revenge* off Ocracoke Island, North Carolina. During fierce hand-to-hand fighting, Maynard himself decapitated Teach whose headless body, thrown overboard, swam around the ship three times, so legend has it, before disappearing into the murky waters of Pamlico Sound.

Spotswood was well liked, both in Virginia and England, and had maintained strong connections in Virginia's House of Burgesses. Most considered him the ideal commander for the heterogenous and often cantankerous Americans who would hail from nine very different colonies ranging from New Hampshire to North Carolina. His sudden death from an illness at Annapolis, Maryland on June 7, 1740 perhaps foredoomed the American Regiment, as serious a blow to its success as Cathcart's to the expedition as a whole. Unfortunately, Spotswood's replacement was the obsequious Sir William Gooch, Virginia's current acting governor, after whom the regiment ultimately took its name. Gooch possessed none of his forebearer's talent or decisiveness; his greatest virtue, so he boasted, was an ability to ingratiate himself with his superiors. To the insecure and passive-aggressive General Wentworth, Gooch's commanding officer, he made his best attempt to appear the lesser man:

"The General hearing and finding I was better received at Jamaica than himself," Gooch later wrote, "and being proud and stingy, tried all ways he could think of to let the people know, that though I was a Governor, yet he was the greater man, and indeed some orders he made might have been spared, however, I submitted and was all obedience, resolving that if military subordination was carried to slavish subjection, he should not tire of me."

This made an unfortunate strategy for someone tasked with protecting the rights and welfare of men participating in an entirely new experiment in the British military.

8.

Surviving records—including the scrupulously kept Massachusetts Muster Rolls—indicate that "Gooch's American Regiment" eventually encompassed 3,700 men give or take; with each company of roughly one hundred men allowed two American officers of varying military experience and two veteran officers from the regular British

Army. Massachusetts raised five companies; Rhode Island two; Connecticut two; New York five; New Jersey three; Pennsylvania eight; Maryland three; Virginia, four.

What sort of soldiers were these Americans? According to overtly biased observers like Captain Charles Knowles, in his controversial pamphlet *An Account of the Expedition to Carthagena, with Explanatory Notes and Observations,* they presented a motley appearance indeed: the rank-and-file included white indentured servants who had joined up in violation of their service contracts; Irish "Papists"; debtors released from jail or one step ahead of the local sheriff; free blacks; slaves offered a release from bondage in exchange for military service and a number of Indian scouts; in short, all the diversity the continent had to offer. Including Indians in the regiment raised a few eyebrows among the English establishment, though Governor Belcher of Massachusetts in whose companies many of them served, defended their inclusion and insisted on equal treatment:

"They are the King's natural born subjects," he said of the Indians, "are good shotsmen, & their having black hair & tawny faces don't at all disable them from being good soldiers . . . it will contribute better to the service to have them mixed with English than to be in a body by themselves . . . I shall give the kind caution that . . . white men shall not insult or use them ill." Belcher had just proposed the first completely integrated American army, more than two hundred years before President Harry S. Truman signed Executive Order 9981 in 1948 and made integration law for the Korean War.

Gooch's American Regiment also reflected a cross section of the less skilled trades in the colonies; most volunteers were working class or landless men, without regular employment. Many deserted after taking the King's Shilling and it is from descriptions of these absconders—verbal "wanted posters"—to aid in their capture, that we are able to put together a mental picture of the average recruit:

There were Irishmen who spoke "pretty good English," reports historian Albert Harkness Jr. in his seminal essay "Americanism and Jenkins' Ear, . . . three white men who escaped by boat with another recruit who was a negro; a parolee who had been recently pardoned from a death sentence. One had 'a fallen nose'; another a 'sickly countenance.' They were a disheveled lot, clad variously in corduroy coats, striped jackets, leather breeches, flannel, coarse linens, and 'Kersey' jackets . . . the captains seemed to be more interested in filling their complements than in enlisting exclusively the mentally, morally, and physically fit.

The fierce English prejudice against Papists advocated even by the generally unbiased Oglethorpe, held firm in all colonies except Maryland which had been founded by two shiploads of English Catholic refugees aboard the *Ark* and *Dove* in 1634. Though the Maryland Assembly in Annapolis, dominated by Protestants since 1690, had passed an act restraining the entrance of 'too great a Number of Irish Papists' into the colony, Newcastle was informed by the Speaker of the House that there were no volunteers for the Cartagena Expedition 'to be expected from Virginia, Maryland, and North Carolina who are not Irish, Papists, or English convicts of whom we have but too many in these four battalions.'"

Allowing indentured servants to volunteer despite their contracts was also considered controversial. Pennsylvania, dominated by parsimonious and peaceable Quakers—according to their creed opposed to war—after much debate enlisted three hundred indentured servants, much to the outrage of the masters who had brought them over from England and elsewhere at great expense. Indeed, a few of these masters sued the government and were eventually compensated for the loss of their servants. In Virginia, debtors gave the most trouble: Though supposedly free from arrest upon enlistment, many were tracked down and dragged off transport ships by local constables. When recruiting officers pointed out to the sheriff of Hampton, Virginia, that these men were patriots fulfilling a greater debt to the king, he replied "God dam King George and all his souldiers!" and arrested them anyway.

9.

Gooch's American Regiment sailed for the West Indies in two separate flotillas in September 1740: half from Hampton, Virginia, under Gooch himself; half from New York under the command of Colonel William Blakeney, an experienced regular army veteran who had been dispatched from London to supervise training and recruitment. Blakeney had also brought blank officers' commissions signed by the king—these destined for American gentlemen of good family not necessarily experienced in military affairs. But experience didn't matter; it had been decided by the Council of War that American troops would more readily serve under their own officers.

Among the eager, young American officers leading the Virginia companies we find a certain Captain Lawrence Washington. The Washington family, not at this point as prominent as they later became, could by this time trace their roots back in Virginia nearly a hundred years. John Washington, the first to arrive on these shores in 1657, had signed on as first mate aboard a trading ketch, the *Sea Horse* of London, in whose profits he had purchased a share. He was twenty-five, the son of an earlier Lawrence Washington, an Anglican priest who had been educated at Brasenose College, Oxford. This Lawrence, defrocked and booted from his parish, by Puritan authorities stood accused of being "a frequenter of alehouses," and "oft drunk." Douglas Southall Freeman, biographer of the elder Lawrence Washington's great-great-grandson George, notes that these charges against Lawrence were "probably false."

False or not, Lawrence's son John Washington was driven to seek his fortune in the New World. There, "circumstances favored him," as Freeman puts it—oddly, when the *Sea Horse*, its belly full of a rich cargo of Virginia tobacco, ran aground on a shoal in the Potomac on its homeward voyage. John Washington labored alongside slaves and sailors to raise the vessel off the river bottom and render it seaworthy again. The process took months; the tobacco was ruined. By this time John had realized a fortune might be more readily made in Virginia which then offered millions of acres in rich undeveloped land and more-or-less friendly tribes of Indians. John married an heiress, beginning a Washington family tradition. His new wife was the daughter of a rich Marylander who owned parcels of land in Virginia. When the *Sea Horse* at last sailed for home, John Washington stayed.

But the vessel's Captain, a hard, superstitious man named Prescott, left owing John a tidy sum for his investment in the original voyage. Here, the Washingtons first showed their litigious side: John sued for the amount, lost, and was counter-sued, accruing a debt fortunately paid by his new father-in-law. Upon the *Sea Horse*'s return to Virginia a year later, John learned the obnoxious Prescott had hanged a female passenger for witchcraft during the course of the voyage. The Washingtons were even then practical people, more interested in business and politics than witches. John, who most likely didn't believe in witchcraft, still bore a grudge against Prescott for the previous lawsuit and now initiated murder proceedings against him—though the charges were later dropped when John failed to testify. He was too busy begetting children with his wealthy wife, acquiring more farmable acreage and rising in the colonial administrative class.

John Washington "sought and gained in succession an ascending order of profitable offices and court appointments," says Freeman. "As early as 1661, he was Coroner. Later, he was trustee of estates, guardian of children, and Justice of the County Court . . . His family increased with his honors and his acres."

Flash forward twenty years: The Washingtons now owned thousands of acres in Virginia's fertile "Northern Neck," all acquired legally, by purchase, marriage and patent. This last method involved surveying and laying claim, or "headrights" to untenanted lands and having those claims confirmed by the House of Burgesses. Some of the land thus acquired had been set aside for the Nanzatico Indians as a sort of reservation; the Washingtons agreed to forbear possession until and only if the Nanzaticos vacated, which they eventually did, drifting off for deeper woods.

Over the next decades, the family fortunes waxed and waned with the country, but generally waxed. Augustine Washington, Captain Lawrence's and George's father, known as "Gus," was a massive man, famously strong, more than six feet tall, a stature his youngest son George would eventually attain. The physically imposing and industrious Gus—planter, slave owner, iron smelter, entrepreneur—also possessed a forceful character and boundless energy and tended to suck the air out of any room he entered. By the early 1700s, he had acquired acreage "between Pope's and Bridges Creeks on the south bank of the Potomac," a property later called "Little Hunting Creek." Here a modest residence was built and rebuilt several times over the years and eventually acquired and renamed by Lawrence. His younger half-brother George, born February 22, 1732, would refer to this house as the "ancient mansion seat" of the family and in turn claim it as his own.

When war and the appeal for American volunteers came in 1740, Lawrence immediately sought one of the four captain's commissions offered to Virginians by Colonel Blakeney. An old saw has it that "Happy men don't volunteer" and it might be surmised that Lawrence found it hard to breathe in proximity to his forceful father, the gigantic Augustine. The former had been educated in England and perhaps felt more English than American, though this distinction had yet to solidify. Now he sought glory on behalf of king and empire and to get out from under his father's long shadow.

On June 17, 1740, Lieutenant Governor Gooch announced the winners of the four Virginia commissions: the very wealthy Richard Bushrod of Westmoreland County who had raised a full company of men at his own expense; Charles Walker; James Mercer, and the idealistic, young Lawrence Washington.

Five months later, the wet-behind-the-ears and poorly trained twenty-two-year-old Captain Washington sailed from Hampton, Virginia with the southern contingent of Gooch's American Regiment. All sought military adventure on foreign shores. Most expected to return heaped with glory and gold taken from the cowardly Spaniards at Cartagena.

10.

The trouble started long before the Americans reached the assembly point in Kingstown, Jamaica. Conditions aboard the transports worsened as they meandered down the coast toward the West Indies. The men hot and cramped below decks and allowed only a few minutes of exercise a day topside, grew mutinous. The colonies in which they had been recruited, obliged to provide transportation fees and upkeep until these expenses could be assumed by the British establishment in Jamaica had done a deplorable job: Provisions, substandard and already half-rotten, moldered in the holds of the ships.

"As a spirit of dissatisfaction is natural with men in affairs of this kind, I am afraid it will prevail with much reason to the dishonor and disgrace of our Country," wrote one of the Virginia officers. "The Expedition goes on with so much sloth and seems to be so ill concerted that I begin to be ambiguous whether it will go on or not. . . . We shall certainly be deficient in Provisions before we reach Jamaica having already expended about forty days and having about thirty yet to come. Some of our Assemblymen were pleased to tell me that the seventy days Provisions were to last ninety. I should be glad to have some of these Gentlemen on board at a pound of salt Beef for twenty-four hours."

The novelist Smollett puts it more colorfully in *Roderick Random*: an army like an infant, must be fed, clothed, and housed, but mostly fed. Unfortunately, according to Smollett, the rations provided for the men "consisted of putrid salt beef, to which the sailors gave the name of Irish horse; salt pork of New England, which though neither fish nor flesh, savored of both; bread from the same country, every biscuit whereof, like a piece of clockwork, moved by its own internal impulse, occasioned by the myriads of insects that dwelt within it; and butter . . . that tasted like train oil thickened with salt."

But even this disgusting fare was denied the Americans upon reaching Jamaica at last in December 1740. They had by this time eaten their way through their provisions and teetered on the brink of starvation. Colonel Blakeney, charged with purchasing fresh food for the regiment, found himself at odds with wary Jamaican victualers. They refused to provide him with the usual credit, insisting the Americans could not be maintained on the establishment until General Wentworth's army arrived from Dominica. Blakeney and other officers were then forced to purchase emergency supplies out of their own funds.

Malnourished, denied exercise and fresh air, the American volunteers, many still confined aboard the fetid transport ships even after reaching Jamaica, began to sicken and die in alarming numbers. A report dated January 11, 1741 lists 93 American dead and 351 sick; a brief hiatus ashore provided forty-five men the opportunity to desert, bringing the regiment's effective strength down to just over 3,100. The men appeared "quite broke up and torn to pieces," remarked an English observer; those who had survived "the fevers and fluxes of the voyage," had "succumbed to Sir Richard Rum."

Fearing more desertions, Gooch pushed most of his men out of their encampments and back into the transports which were then sent to secluded anchorages along the coast, away from the punch houses and temptations of Kingston. But more subtle tortures awaited both those few who remained ashore and those afloat. The British attitude toward the Americans as depicted in Knowles's *Account* quickly ripened from curiosity into total contempt:

"From the first Sight of the American troops, they were despised," he writes. "Raw, new-raised undisciplined men . . . mostly Irish, suspected Papists;" their officers worse: "Blacksmiths, Tailors, Barbers, Shoemakers, and all the Banditry the colonies afforded."

From contempt to mistreatment is only a step. The American volunteers, according to Colonel Blakeney, perhaps their only English champion, lacked the basic military supplies—weapons, uniforms, tents—provided to regular British regiments. He had brought from England three-thousand muskets, bayonets, and cartridge boxes; sixty drums; five hundred uniforms to use as patterns; for more and a hundred tents. Very little of this equipment, much of it commandeered by regular army regiments, actually reached the Americans. Meanwhile, Admiral Vernon, whose crews had already been decimated by the usual causes—disease and drink—broke up entire American companies to fill vacant billets in his ships. The Americans, originally recruited as land forces, to their disgust soon found themselves being used as sailors and marines aboard Vernon's ships; though for this reason at least one military historian, Lee G. Offen, bestows upon them the honorific "America's First Marines" and sees a straight line from Cartagena to Iwo Jima.

Certainly, we find here for the first time the beginning of a basic dichotomy: the division of the English-speaking peoples into *Americans* versus *Englishmen*. Albert Harkness, Jr. wrote:

> In these miserable surroundings the mutual feelings of the Americans and Europeans ripened into deep mistrust . . . the British began to refer to their northern colleagues as "Americans" and the term seemed to carry with it some disrespect. At best they were thought of as different and therefore less than natives of the mother country. Admiral Vernon wrote that a good many of the "Americans" were slothful. . . . The British made no attempt to hide their sentiments and the Americans keenly felt this scorn.

In this scorn, perhaps, and in the unequal and cruel treatment parceled out to the soldiers of Gooch's Regiment in 1741, lies the roots of the American Revolution a generation later.

11.

Meanwhile, heavy war clouds had drifted across the Atlantic to darken the skies of the European continent. No one in Walpole's ministry doubted France would soon join their Spanish cousins in the war against England. Their kings—Louis XV and Felipe V— were, after all, both grandsons of Louis XIV. But Cardinal Fleury, unofficial First Minister of France, held well-known pacifist views and was a surprisingly devout man for such a highly placed Catholic prelate. France didn't want war with England, he insisted and would not intervene in the quarrel between England and Spain in the West Indies. Unfortunately, Fleury was nearly ninety—born in 1653, he had been Louis XV's childhood tutor; his grip on politics had grown weak with the years. Now, Walpole's war council worried that a combined Franco-Spanish Caribbean fleet would outnumber even the substantial armada Britain had assembled there. Any plan to wrest Spain's American colonies from her palsied grasp must now take into consideration the possible involvement of muscular France. Suddenly, a World War loomed.

And while Fleury didn't want war, he wanted a South American continent dominated by England even less. Following Vernon's surprise victory at Porto Bello, the cardinal resolved to support Spain against England in everything short of an all-out conflict. Accordingly, in August 1740 he dispatched to the French island of Martinique a squadron of warships under Admiral Antoine-François de Pardaillan de Gondrin, Marquis d'Antin. d'Antin had been given orders of Jesuitical subtlety by Fleury: the Admiral should endeavor to "help protect" Spanish possessions in the West Indies, but should not engage in any hostilities against English ships unless attacked first. Exactly how Antin d'Antin was to walk this tightrope, the cardinal didn't say.

News of d'Antin's squadron reached Vernon in Jamaica in October 1740—along with the uncertain intelligence that the French admiral had united with his Spanish counterpart, Admiral de Torres, in the mid-Atlantic. Supposedly a massive Franco-Spanish invasion fleet was even then grouping for the conquest of Jamaica. In diplomatic dispatches to Secretary Newcastle, Fleury denied everything. Yes, he admitted, a squadron had been sent to the West Indies but only to protect French interests there. Vernon immediately doubted these protestations of innocence and wrote to Secretary Newcastle that Antin d'Antin's squadron had certainly not sailed across the Atlantic just to "take the air," but for more sinister purposes.

Vernon now sent the fast sloop *Wolf*—captained by a Virginian named William Dandridge, whose niece Martha would later marry George Washington—to gather more accurate intelligence regarding d'Antin's squadron. Dandridge sailed to the French island of Hispaniola, where the French fleet supposedly lay at anchor. Arriving off the port of St. Louis on January 30, 1741, he observed according to his ship's log:

> nineteen sail of ships, one whereof had a large white flag at her maintopmast head, another with a white broad (admiral's) pennant; their colors were all hoisted, etc. awnings spread, at the same time the flag on the fort and that on the look-out were hoisted. It being very hazy under the land, that we might better view them, hauled the mainsail up and backed the maintopsail; judging ourselves about five miles from Port Louis Castle, and being much embayed, at 2 P.M. out reefs and worked to windward.

In other words, Dandridge saw what he thought he saw from a safe distance—many French warships in the harbor at Port Louis—and hightailed it out of there. He sailed directly to Admiral Vernon to impart this disquieting news. Vernon called a council of war and in consultation with his captains and Governor Trelawny of Jamaica, decided to attack d'Antin's fleet no matter its strength. He had no doubts that he would prevail in such an encounter: "The whole question lay in whether French or British should take the initiative," wrote Admiral Richmond, in his *The Navy in the War of 1739–48*. "The council . . . decided that it should be the British."

Vernon sent another fast sloop, the *Spence*, under Captain Richard Lawes to gather further information, and began preparations to meet d'Antin for a decisive battle at sea. Lawes returned with intelligence that supported Dandridge's observations. At least sixteen

French men of war lay at anchor within St. Louis's protected harbor, he said. But Vernon had meanwhile received conflicting reports from small trading vessels that had passed closer to Hispaniola than either Lawes or Dandridge dared. He dispatched Lawes to get a second look. This time Lawes returned with the truth: both he and Dandridge had been mistaken, tricked by marine haze and distance. No French fleet lay at Port Louis. Only a few unarmed merchant vessels and a single frigate. The maintop masthead of the latter, lying in a line with the white gable-end of a house had looked like an admiral's pennant and thus suggested the presence of an entire fleet.

"In hazy weather," Admiral Richmond adds, "[Lawes] had made his examination from about five miles from the Castle, inside which the squadron would be lying, a distance in such circumstances that was too great to ascertain the particulars of the ships with the exactitude which a reconnaissance demands."

Both Dandridge and Lawes had been tricked by a mirage. By their joint mistake, they delayed the sailing of the Vernon/Wentworth/Ogle Cartagena expedition by at least a month—thus placing the British expedition's arrival beneath that city's sea walls closer to the pestilential rainy season beginning in May.

The delay would prove fatal.

But where was the French fleet? Where had it gone? Was it lurking just around some nearby cape, ready to pounce? Vernon, exasperated, now sent Captain Knowles aboard *Diamond* to make contact with Port Louis's governor, M. de Larnage. Hoping to avoid attracting any more English warships to his little harbor, Larnage offered the truth: d'Antin's squadron had been there but had sailed back to France a month earlier. Its departure from the West Indies, had in fact, caused consternation in Spain. Queen Isabela, Spain's de facto ruler, had nearly dissolved the *Pacte de Famille* over this incident.

According to that treaty, France was bound to support Spain against Britain in the West Indies; d'Antin's withdrawal seemed to annul this pledge of mutual support. But the French admiral's orders had been superseded by more practical considerations. Lingering at Port Louis and elsewhere, awaiting the call to action, the fleet's French sailors had succumbed to the heat and disease and deadly lassitude prevalent in the tropics.

"Half dead, half roasted and half starved," as Admiral Wager later put it, they had sailed back to France in desperate circumstances and barely made it home. Admiral d'Antin had lost nearly three thousand men to disease in two months in the tropics, almost as many as Admiral Hosier in similar circumstances a decade earlier. d'Antin's homeward voyage had been a close run thing, his ships manned by what were literally skeleton crews, reduced "to an allowance of three ounces of bread a day for a man, and that half worms and dirt." d'Antin himself, like Hosier before him had succumbed to yellow fever and died a few days after arriving at Brest. He was just thirty-two. A talented officer, he had been one of the great hopes of the French Navy.

12.

Meanwhile, the only encounter between English and French warships during the War of Jenkins' Ear had already occurred: On January 7, 1741, lead vessels in the Ogle/Wentworth expeditionary force—at last on its way from Dominica to rendezvous with Vernon in Jamaica—sighted a small squadron of four unidentified ships sailing near the western end of Hispaniola. Ogle detached six of his warships under the command of Lord Aubrey Beauclerk to investigate; with him went Captain Knowles now aboard *Weymouth*. The strange ships flew no colors. Were they pirates? Spanish? French? At about 3 P.M., pursued closely by Beauclerk's squadron, the ships at lasted hoisted the fleur-de-lis bedecked royal flag of France. But these were the days of "false flag" operations (the original meaning of this now over-used term); French colors offered no real assurance of their true identity. Lord Beauclerk sent Knowles in *Weymouth* to make contact.

Knowles closed to within "a pistol shot" of the nearest vessel and hailed her in several languages:

"What ship are you?"

An officer aboard replied in French with the same question.

"We are an English man-of-war," Knowles responded.

"And we are a French man-of-war, what is it you want?"

Knowles persisted: He wanted to talk to the captain.

The officer hesitated: "Has war been declared between England and France?"

"Not yet," Knowles replied, "at least not at the time our fleet left England."

"Then go in peace."

Satisfied, Knowles sheered away to rejoin the squadron, but the hotheaded Lord Beauclerk had already started shooting, sure the ships were Spanish. He put a shot across the bow of another French ship, then a second shot a little closer and the latter replied with a full broadside. This exchange begat a sharp little running battle, lasting throughout the night until 4:30 A.M. when Knowles was finally able to convince Beauclerk that the ships did not belong to the Spanish enemy; also, as far as anyone could tell, hostilities had not commenced with France! Fortunately, there had been no casualties, only damage to the ships.

As dawn brightened the sky, Knowles hailed the nearest French ship under a flag of truce. Apologies and "restrained mutual compliments" exchanged, the two squadrons separated, ending what might now be termed an "unfortunate diplomatic incident," between two nations who were not quite at war but wanted to be.

Upon reaching Jamaica, in advance of Ogle's flotilla, Beauclerk and Knowles felt the keen edge of Vernon's famous anger. The fighting admiral viewed the episode with the French ships as an unfortunate blunder. Shortly thereafter, Ogle's arrival with eight thousand troops and nearly two hundred ships filled Vernon with "chagrin and dismay." He had hoped to meet up with Ogle at sea and proceed directly to Cartagena. The expeditionary force's arrival at Jamaica would sorely tax the resources of the island and lead to the deaths of scores more men from disease and rum. To his mind, the Cartagena expedition—first step in the conquest of South America—had just gotten off to a terrible start.

13.

Cartagena de Indias (the qualifier to distinguish it from its namesake port in the Murcia region of Southwest Spain) was founded by the famously combative conquistador Pedro de Heredia in 1533. Heredia, veteran of many a lopsided fight, had an eye for a good defensive position: Once, beset by six would-be assassins in Madrid, Heredia lured them into an alley and, back against the wall, successfully fought them off. On that occasion one of Heredia's assailants lost a piece of his nose, another an eye, before they all ran off. The future conquistador later hunted them down and killed three, forcing his flight to the Americas. Once there, he ambled about the region that later became New Granada (encompassing modern-day Columbia, Venezuela, and bits of Ecuador) conquering Indian villages and looting the tombs of their ancestors. From one of them he took a solid gold porcupine weighing 132 pounds, the single heaviest gold object looted during the Spanish Conquest.

Cartagena, carefully sited by Heredia and built on the bones of a Turbaco Indian village named Calamari stood along the sandy spit of an inner bay—later called the Surgidero—with its back toward a wilderness of rocky shoals along an inaccessible stretch of the Caribbean coast. The city's outer bay was protected by an island called Tierra Bomba which guarded the only channel passable to deep-draft vessels, Boca Chica or "Little Mouth." A recent hurricane had washed through another entrance, Boca Grande, "Big Mouth." Shallow and sandy, it remained impassible to all but the shallowest launch.

Cartagena prospered. It became the largest Spanish city on the South American mainland and the second largest in the Caribbean, after Havana, with whom it shared the galleon trade. In 1740, it boasted a population of roughly twenty thousand, a cathedral, a college, a library, and numerous domiciles. And over the two centuries since the city's founding by Heredia, the Spanish, indefatigable fort-builders, had added greatly to its natural defenses.

Tall and imposing walls punctuated by bastions had risen up, looming over what had once been a scraggly village. A marine obstruction of cement and heavy logs had been added to the city's seaward side, and nearly a dozen forts and batteries had been built guarding all approaches: The closest fort to Cartagena was San Felipe de Barajas. Atop a hill called Mount San Lázaro, its guns overlooked the city and guarded the western shore of the inner bay, including the outlying districts of La Quinta and Texar de Gracias. The Surgidero's entrance was itself guarded by two more forts, the *castillos* Cruz Grande and Manzanillo.

The real trouble, from Vernon's perspective, lay with Boca Chica: His huge expeditionary force must pass through this little mouth, wide enough to accept only one ship at a time, into the outer bay. Only then might the expeditionary force's troops be landed for an assault on the city which much to Vernon's sorrow could not be taken by sea power alone. The assault on Cartagena would have to be an amphibious operation, requiring close cooperation between the British Army and Navy.

Boca Chica was itself guarded by an imposing array of forts: Fort Santiago and Fort San Fernando guarded the Caribbean shore of the Tierra Bomba just to the north of the mouth; Fort San Luis faced inward toward the bay; tiny Fort San Jose ingeniously built on a sandbar in the middle of the channel aimed twelve cannons at incoming vessels. In addition to these structures, five other batteries had been entrenched on Tierra Bomba and on the southern side of Boca Chica, on a spit of land called Albanicos. Here the Spaniards had also installed a fascine (fortified battery) boasting fourteen guns; some distance behind it lay another such battery called Baradero with four more guns.

All these structures had recently been reinforced and rebuilt by a furiously active Don Blas de Lezo, stumping around on his peg-leg, hauling bricks and logs like the lowest *grumete*—cabin boy—working against time and the obstructive actions of his immediate superior, the young, newly appointed viceroy Sebastián de Eslava, just twenty-five years old. Eslava, a native of the Pyrenean province of Navarre had a few years before graduated from the new *Academia Militar de Matemáticas* in Barcelona. Following the recent death of Cartagena's former governor, Pedro Fidalgo, Eslava had been assigned to Cartagena's defense with a good deal of book learning but little practical experience. He had arrived in Cartagena from Spain on April 23, 1740, knowing nothing about the place. Portraits show a thin, elegant, fox-faced man, wearing a tightly rolled wig falling to the shoulders of a velvet coat adorned with almost unimaginably ornate gold trim.

Between the young, foppish Eslava and Don Blas, grizzled mutilated veteran of a hundred fights, sprang up an instant antipathy. Eslava, insecure and jealous of his authority, refused to allow the admiral a free hand in the defense of the city, countermanding his orders and diverting much needed supplies for his personal use. The young viceroy's attitude in the face of an existential threat to the city under his protection can be described as one of aristocratic diffidence.

Don Blas later wrote an angry letter to minister La Quadra in Madrid complaining of Eslava's lack of serious preparations for the siege:

"It seems hardly possible," Don Blas fumed, "that a city threatened by the enemy and given anticipatory notice by the king for its preservation, as well as being ordered to create a six-months' stock of provisions, should have such a scarcity of stores that D. Sebastian de Eslava should be under the necessity of taking what I had for the crews of my ships."

Still, despite the "lethargic indifference" of the Viceroy, Don Blas somehow managed to ready the city as best he could for a major assault. He stretched a boom of logs and cables across the narrowest point of Boca Chica between Fort San Luis and Fort San Jose; he strengthened all forts to the limits available military stores would allow and took charge of all Cartagena's land forces: Some historians say the city's defenders consisted of "1,100 regular troops, two companies of negroes and 600 Indian *flecheros* [archers]" Other sources—most notably the historian Charles E. Nowell in his authoritative monograph *The Defense of Cartagena*—place the land-based strength of the Spanish defenders at roughly 5,000 men—including veterans from the regiments of Aragon, Espana, Toledo, and Navarra—Cartagena colonials and five companies of local militias. The difference in these estimates, while not negligible is more-or-less academic: the first has the Spaniards defending Cartagena outnumbered at about five-to-one; the second at three-to-one.

Finally, Don Blas anchored his small fleet of warships—*Galicia*, *San Felipe*, *El Africa*, *San Carlos*, *El Conquistador*, and *El Dragon*, all third-rate or less—just inside the Boca Chica, with their guns facing the sea. And then he settled down to wait for the coming attack.

14.

On the morning of March 5, 1741, the British Fleet anchored off Cartagena in the Bay of Canoas, up the coast slightly to the north of the walled city. Its total strength consisted of roughly 27,000 military personnel, including over 8,000 regulars, marines, and militia, 3,000 Americans, 500 "negroes" from Jamaica, and 15,000 sailors, all aboard, respectively, twenty-nine ships of the line, twenty-two frigates, 135 transport ships and sundry other vessels. It was "by far the most powerful armament that had ever been seen in that part of the world." Cartagena's anxious defenders must have peered over the battlements of their forts and quailed at the sight of blue water covered with English sail. Surely, no city, no matter how strongly defended could resist such a force.

Recalling the abuses perpetrated on the population by de Pointis's buccaneers in times past, the matrons of the city now made hasty arrangements for their daughters to visit relatives in the countryside while the *pater familias* hid the family silver down wells and under floorboards and carefully oiled their ancient matchlocks. Only Don Blas de Lezo, perhaps, regarded the invasion force with something like equanimity. Of Don Blas it might be said—as it was later of Napoleon—that his presence on the battlefield was worth 40,000 men.

Vernon, aboard his flagship—now the *Princess Carolina*—dispatched Dandridge in *Wolf* to England with news that the assault on Cartagena was about to begin. On March 6, the Admiral sent his most trusted officers—Knowles, Renton, and Lawes—to reconnoiter the Spanish forts guarding Boca Chica one last time. Then he called a meeting of his captains to explain the plan of attack—outlined in a typically meticulous memorandum. As always, he stressed his "Additional Fighting Instructions" and his expectation of personal initiative.

Having thus informed and instructed you according to the best intelligence I have received, and furnished you with pilots of the best abilities and experience I could procure, I rely on your judgement and resolution for the due execution of my orders giving such additional orders as you shall find to be necessary from the motions and dispositions of the enemy and other events that may arise in the vigorous execution of these orders.

Overall strategy had already been discussed and roughed out by the top brass. These worthies included Admirals Vernon and Ogle, General Wentworth, and Brigadier General Guise, "a stout old soldier" who had recently arrived from Scotland, in conjunction with Governor Trelawney of Jamaica. This conclave had occurred at the gubernatorial mansion in Spanish Town on January 10, with Vernon's views on how the war should be prosecuted given a full airing.

Considering Vernon's famously dominant personality, a great anxiety had recently blossomed in the minds of the war council in London regarding the expedition. They worried about the potential for friction between the admiral and the army commander which might easily doom a joint amphibious operation of this kind. The flexible and capable Cathcart had been sent; Cathcart died. A by-the-book soldier about whom little was known had assumed command. How would General Wentworth get along with the notorious Fighting Admiral? The success of the war against Spain depended on close cooperation between the two most important branches of the service. The ministry fretted—at this stage, pointlessly, as no action had yet occurred.

In an effort to calm these fears, Vernon sent a letter from Jamaica to Secretary Newcastle shortly after the meeting in Spanish Town insisting that a "complete harmony" existed between himself and General Wentworth. Together, the Admiral insisted, they would free an entire continent from the Spanish yoke.

Boca Chica was the key to Cartagena, as it had always been.

Only through this "Little Mouth" could Vernon and Ogle intrude their warships and transports into the Outer Bay for an all-out assault on the city. The Frenchman de Pointis had managed to take Boca Chica in 1697 in a day, landing his buccaneers in a secluded cove on Tierra Bomba and quick-marching overland to overwhelm Spanish defenses. Vernon believed a similar tactic might work again, but Boca Chica was far better protected than in de Pointis's time. Many guns had since been mounted in carefully considered batteries; strong forts had been built, dominating the channel. The strongest of these was Fort San Luis, garrisoned by more than five hundred men, bristling with cannons, and commanded by a talented Franco-Spanish military engineer, Don Carlos Desnaux. But the weather was the enemy asset to be feared the most: tropical humidity and blazing sun. The pestilential rainy season approached; it usually began in the first week or so of May. Cartagena must be in British hands by then. If not, ceaseless sheets of rain and murderous mosquitos would render all military operations impossible. That left about eight weeks to achieve a victory over one of the best defended cities in South America.

At first, Vernon contemplated a purely naval assault on Boca Chica's defenses. But, as Admiral Richmond put it: "prevailing winds being east by north to east-north-easterly, the passage could not be rushed by ships under sail so long as the shore forts and castles covering it were in the hands of the enemy. Besides these forts, a boom was in place across the channel, covered by the guns of four Spanish ships of the line."

Troops must be put ashore on the Tierra Bomba and the castles taken by a land-based assault before the navy could get close enough to Cartagena to batter its walls. All now looked to General Wentworth and the army.

15.

At 11 A.M. on March 9, 1741, the attack began.

Five ships of the line—*Norfolk, Princess Amelia, Shrewsbury, Lichfield,* and *Russell,* with Admiral Ogle's pennant flying from the latter—sailed in to blast the Spanish batteries on the Caribbean shore of Tierra Bomba. Thick white smoke filled the morning air as these formidable vessels opened up with all three tiers of guns. Two bomb ketches, *Alderney* and *Terrible*, followed the battleships into the fight. Bomb ketches, much used in eighteenth-century naval warfare were small, sturdy, shallow-draft vessels with reinforced decks, one mast removed to make room for a single heavy mortar. Commanded by Royal Artillery officers, these floating gun platforms could throw huge balls great distances; hence their target—Fort Luis on the far side of the Boca Chica peninsula.

Norfolk, *Shrewsbury*, and *Russell* opened the attack on Forts San Felipe and Santiago—confusingly transcribed as St. Jago in British accounts of the campaign. *Princess Amelia* and *Lichfield* concentrated their fire on an elusive battery called Chamba, which faulty intelligence had caused Vernon to count as a deadly obstacle. Though Don Blas had raised the place to take a dozen guns, he had run out of time and resources to mount a single cannon or garrison the place with a single soldier. Unmanned and unarmed, in fact deserted, Chamba quickly surrendered. Forts Santiago and San Felipe gave up later that afternoon; exactly when remains uncertain. Captain Lorenzo Alderete, in command of the *San Felipe*, evacuated his eighty-man garrison, spiked the few guns still in operation and retreated across the peninsula to find refuge behind the stronger walls of Fort San Luis.

From this point on, controversy and confusion regarding the campaign for Cartagena bedevils the modern historian. Where to lay the blame for the outrageous debacle that followed? What to make of contradictory accounts of certain actions taken by British forces during the next two weeks? Both Vernon and Wentworth have their partisans, with the modern revisionist school (seeking to exonerate the incompetent Wentworth) led by British military historian Richard Harding. Unfortunately, Admiral Vernon, prone to exaggeration and self-puffery in his dispatches to Newcastle and others on the War Council did not help his case for posterity. Vernon claimed, for example, that on March 9, "in less than an hour, the ships shattered the forts sufficiently and drove every soul out of them, so as to enable us the same evening to make good a Descent with the grenadiers."

Actually, the silencing of the shore batteries took the better part of the day, Spanish gunners returning a vigorous fire, sometimes with deadly accuracy. Right off, a shot fired from Fort Santiago severed *Shrewsbury*'s anchor cable. A strong current bore her inexorably into the maw of the Little Mouth, studded with guns like sharp teeth. Drifting in the narrow channel, *Shrewsbury* took relentless fire from three forts, a couple of heavy batteries and Don Blas's carefully positioned warships, anchored just inside the Outer Bay. Soon Boca Chica became a shooting gallery with *Shrewsbury* as the clay pigeon. Her commanding officer, Captain Isaac Townsend refused to retreat, his ship absorbing round after round from Spanish cannons and returning fire as best she could. Ships couldn't exactly "reverse gear" and "back up" during the age of fighting sail. To exit the Little Mouth would have required attaching cables and lowering tow boats, thus exposing the oarsmen to almost certain destruction.

Outgunned and afflicted by contrary winds, Townsend chose to stand and fight. He endured the fury of the enemy's cannons for seven brutal hours; *Shrewsbury* took 250 shots to her hull, sustaining twenty killed and forty wounded, a relatively high casualty rate for an eighteenth-century naval engagement. At last, with a green tropical dusk falling, Vernon ordered the obstinate Townsend to withdraw. Under cover of darkness several boats came forward and *Shrewsbury*, damaged beyond repair, was towed out at last into open water. She was the first major loss sustained by the navy during the campaign.

Several accounts agree that the first wave of troops to land—perhaps 300 grenadiers under General Wentworth and Lt. Colonel

Cochrane—disgorged from the transports into long boats and hit the beach on Tierra Bomba some time in the late afternoon or early evening, between 5:00 and 7 P.M. Knowles in his opinionated and spirited eyewitness *Account of the Expedition to Carthagena, With Explanatory Notes and Observations* brings the opening charge of incompetence against Wentworth with this very first landing of troops on an enemy shore.

According to Knowles, not 300 but 800 grenadiers hit the beach at 5:00 P.M. But the cautious Wentworth, spooked and fearing a Spanish counterattack, immediately re-embarked them into the boats. The grenadiers then wallowed in the swells twenty yards offshore for the next two hours, dangerously exposed to enemy fire, until reinforcements arrived. Where does caution turn into cowardice; skittishness into incompetence? Wentworth, as demonstrated here, one source asserts, was "nervous as a kitten," during the entire campaign. Not a great quality in a commanding general.

Knowles further claims that only the cravenness of Tierra Bomba's Spanish defenders prevented the grenadiers from being blasted out of the water. One imagines them packed into their landing craft, ears straining for the first enemy shot, the only sound a few half-suppressed coughs and the water lapping at the sides of the boats as light fades over an alien shore. At last, only their cross-belts are visible in the gloom, and the whites of their eyes staring out at the pale ribbon of beach and the rim of dark forest beyond. Other sources record however that at most 400 troops—about six companies of grenadiers—landed that night. Once ashore, however many of them there were, they dug into the beach to wait for dawn.

Disembarkation of the entire army of approximately 8,000 men followed slowly over the next two days. Only the Americans of Gooch's American Regiment remained at sea. Vernon and others believed the Americans, slovenly and mutinous, would desert to the Spaniards the minute they hit shore. Recruited as a regiment of foot, they were now assigned both less dangerous and more onerous duties. Many, pressed into the navy, were were kept imprisoned and festering in the foul holds of the transports. Others, dispersed widely among Vernon's ships, filled out his allotment of marines. All this, contrary to promises made by recruiters in the colonies. Denied fresh air and proper food, the Americans cooped up aboard ship, began to die by the score.

Captain Lawrence Washington escaped this grim fate through a lucky chance: Fate had assigned him to Vernon's flagship, *Princess Carolina*. The Fighting Admiral, famous for his pugnaciousness, was equally famous for his cleanliness: He kept one of the cleanest vessels in the British Navy, regularly ordering the lower decks of his flagship scrubbed down with vinegar. It was a precaution that undoubtedly kept bacteria levels down and saved many lives. Still, Vernon had lost far too many of his sailors to disease. He needed the Americans to help sail his ships, now critically undermanned. These poorly trained and disciplined colonial troops made the obvious choice for this duty; their absence from the ranks wouldn't overly detract from the fighting strength of the land forces. But, in truth, the bulk of Wentworth's army of regulars weren't much more impressive than Gooch's unmilitary Americans.

That the whole body of the Troops that came from England were raw, new-raised, undisciplined Men, is a fact known to every one," Knowles wrote bitterly in his *Account*, "and the greatest Part of the Officers commanding them, either young Gentlemen whose quality or Interest entitled them to Preferment, or abandoned Wretches of the Town, whose Prostitution had made them useful on some dirty Occasion, and by Way of Reward were provided for in the Army; but both these sorts of Gentlemen had never seen any Services, consequently, knew not properly how to act, or command;

so that the worthy old experienced Officers, who had served long and well, underwent a continual Hardship, in teaching and disciplining a young, raw Army, at a Time when they were on Service, and every one ought to have been Masters of their Trade, instead of having it to learn; and thus, by more frequently exposing themselves, most of the veterans were knocked on the Head."

By which Knowles meant that many battle-hardened veterans, critical to the success of the army, were soon killed or wounded by Spanish fire.

Before he died, General Cathcart had made equally critical observations, remarking on the youth of the average recruits, most of whom were "only boys." "They may be useful a year hence," he wrote in one of his last dispatches, "but at present they have not strength to handle their arms."

With such unpromising human clay, the council of war had hoped to mold an army capable of storming a major Spanish citadel.

16.

On March 11, almost all the troops ashore, Wentworth made his next major misstep. He began constructing an elaborate, European-style encampment for the army, complete with defensive trenches and palisades on an open stretch of sandy ground about a mile from Fort San Luis. Unfortunately, Wentworth's largely incompetent junior engineers sited the camp in the full blast of the tropical sun rather than in the shade beneath a nearby canopy of trees; they also put it directly behind the heavy battery of twenty-four pounders the General had ordered raised to bombard Fort San Luis. (In time, Spanish cannon balls, attempting to destroy the British guns, would overshoot them and land among the soldiers' tents in the camp. More than a hundred men were killed in this manner in the opening day's bombardment alone.)

Wentworth aimed to blast a breach in the fort's walls large enough to admit an assault by his grenadiers—this was what the books said to do. His chief engineer, a frightened man named Jonas Moore, had to be driven from his ship to attend matters in the field. He suffered from an attack of nerves the moment he stepped ashore—or, some say, felt a presentiment of his own death. He was killed just days into the campaign.

Construction crews, mainly composed of American troops drafted from the ships, got busy building Wentworth's fortified camp and raising his battery. They also began clearing a military road through the jungle to the other side of the island. All the while the tropical sun blazed down and malarial mosquitos took their pints of blood. Their numbers were soon halved by heat stroke and disease. Men passed out over their shovels, faces beet red, dying for lack of potable water. Work battalions composed of Jamaican slaves, tasked with bringing up construction materials, dropped their loads and ran for the woods at every stray shot from a Spanish gun. Construction thus proceeded at a leaden pace. Days passed with men dying hourly of disease. Yellow fever, dreaded and deadly, made its appearance. It seemed the Americans weren't digging to build a battery or a road but a graveyard.

Vernon watched these dilatory proceedings aghast from the quarterdeck of his flagship. He had expected an immediate assault on Fort San Luis. General Wentworth seemed to be preparing for a major siege operation, an assault on one of the great capitals of Europe like Belgrade or Vienna, not as Vernon later wrote, the reduction "of a paltry fort." Speed was the thing, as he kept reminding Wentworth in an endless series of angry letters sent from ship to camp. From his experience at Porto Bello, Vernon believed any Spanish fort could be taken in a sudden rush. The Spaniards always crumbled and ran. Meanwhile, General Wentworth ignored Vernon's continual entreaties for speed and action and instead "sulked in his tent."

Determined to show the lethargic general and the army how things should be done, on March 18, Vernon ordered an overland assault by naval officers and marines on the Abanicos Battery located on the southern jaw of Boca Chica. A contingent commanded by Captains Watson and Boscawen set out on the night of March 19 to destroy the battery's guns; with them went a company of American marines led by Captain Lawrence Washington of Virginia. This little force of less than a hundred men landed on the narrow peninsula of Baru beneath a moon half-hidden by scudding clouds and struck up the dunes through the brush to attack the battery which mounted fourteen guns. In the process they stumbled across the smaller supporting battery at Baradera, bearing its four additional guns.

At the first crackle of British musket fire, Spanish gunners ran for the safety of a resupply ship anchored close by in the Outer Bay. Ordered only to destroy the guns, the raiding party went about burning gun carriages and spiking the barrels of the cannons and did not pursue. Work done, they withdrew to the beach and re-embarked—though as it turned out they would return in a few days to take care of four guns that had not been properly put out of commission. Later, Captain Washington received a commendation for bravery during these actions from Admiral Vernon himself. It was the first time but not the last that a Washington would distinguish himself fighting alongside—or against—British troops.

This assault on the batteries had been conceived to serve two purposes: 1) To shame the recalcitrant Wentworth into making his attack on Fort San Luis and 2) to show that, properly led, the Americans of Gooch's Regiment made good soldiers, capable of initiative and bravery. However, on both of these counts it failed. Wentworth continued to dither, digging and chopping and refusing to attack; the treatment of Americans by British commanders didn't improve in any discernible way.

With no progress made ashore, a council of captains convened aboard Vernon's flagship on March 22. During this contentious meeting, the assembled navy officers proposed a purely naval attempt to reduce the Boca Chica forts. Vernon and Ogle, initially opposed the idea; the besieging of fortifications was the army's job. But at last they reluctantly agreed. Anything to push operations forward before the advent of the rainy season. The next day, as Wentworth's heavy guns finally opened the bombardment of Fort San Luis, Vernon sent a reserve squadron of five ships of the line into the Little Mouth.

These—*Boyne, Prince Frederick, Hampton Court, Tilbury,* and *Suffolk*—were under the command of Commodore Richard Lestock. Until now, Lestock's squadron had been wasted on a ruse at La Boquilla, a shallow entry point into the Ciénaga de Tesca lagoon a few miles north of the city. Vernon had hoped to fool Cartagena's defenders into thinking the expedition planned to establish its beachhead at this location. But Don Blas knew local conditions made La Boquilla a poor choice and the feint fooled no one. No precious Spanish troops were diverted from the city's defenses to protect this impracticable channel.

Lestock's squadron moved into Boca Chica in the morning, sailing past the line of the assembled fleet to cheering from all ships, their bands blaring out "Britons, Strike Home." Almost immediately upon entering the channel Lestock was under heavy fire. He anchored his ships as close as possible to Fort San Luis and let loose with all tiers. But the Boca Chica channel, deep at the center, shallowed near the shore and did not allow any deep-draft warship to approach any closer than seven hundred yards. At this distance ships' guns were relatively ineffective, while exposing themselves to damaging land-based enemy fire. Admiral Lord Elibank who later wrote an account of the Cartagena Expedition explains it this way:

Tis most certain that where a ship can come within musket-shot of a fort there is no withstanding her. The constant fire from three tiers of guns, joined to that of the small arms from the poop and tops, make it impossible for an enemy to stand to their guns, and indeed such a fire is irresistible. But it is quite otherwise where a ship attacks at a distance; for besides that it is impossible to take aim from a ship so well as from a battery, every shot that hits any part of a ship has its effect. The sides of a ship are so far from covering the men that the splinters do more execution than the ball itself, and every man on board is more exposed than if he had nothing to cover him.

Nevertheless, Lestock's squadron kept up their pointless broadsides until their ammunition ran out two days later. With *Boyne*, *Prince Frederick*, and *Hampton Court* now blasted beyond repair and many sailors, gunners, and officers dead, Vernon at last ordered the cessation of an operation about which he'd had misgivings from the beginning. Among the officers killed was Lord Aubrey Beauclerk, captain of *Prince Frederick*. Lord Beauclerk, a grandson of Charles II, had died in a fashion not out of keeping with the deeds of his royal ancestors: Both of his legs severed by Spanish chain shot, he continued to give orders in a calm voice as his life's blood reddened the decks. With his last breath he ordered his men to fight on to the bitter end. Beauclerk's heroic death recalls the similar fate of the legendary Admiral Benbow fighting in nearby waters against the French nearly fifty years before. Benbow, also de-legged by chain shot had given a similar order for which he was immortalized in a famous sea shanty, still part of the standard repertoire of English folk singers:

Brave Benbow lost his legs
by chainshot by chainshot,
Benbow lost his legs by chainshot

And on his stumps he begs
"Fight on my English lads,
tis our lot, tis our lot . . .

Let a cradle now in haste
on the quarter deck be placed
that the enemy I might face
till I die, till I die . . .

17.

At last, on March 25, Admiral Vernon, by now beside himself with rage and frustration, fired off one of his thunderers to Wentworth, cosigned by Admiral Ogle and Commodore Lestock:

Diffidence of troops we fear tends only to discourage them; and in our opinion you have numbers sufficient for finishing the attack of such a paltry fort with vigor, that has no outworks. . . . As we are best acquainted with this intemperate climate, we think it our duty to advise your pursuing more vigorous measures as most conducible to the preservation of your men's lives from the ravaging sickness.

Perhaps galled by this letter, copies of which were sent to Secretary Newcastle in London, Wentworth at last ordered his grenadiers to attack the Castillo San Luis that very evening. It would be a momentous night—the high watermark of British efforts to take Cartagena from Spain and establish a firm foothold on the South American continent. Vernon, overjoyed at the news of the impending attack, offered all the support his navy could give. He called in the bomb ketches to soften up the fort from the sea in support of the British assault.

But the night before, unbeknownst to General Wentworth, Don Blas de Lezo in a meeting aboard his flagship *Galicia* with the Viceroy had decided to abandon the fort, now severely damaged by British bombardments from both land and sea. During this meeting, a British cannon ball crashed through *Galicia*'s poop deck in a shower of splinters, wounding Don Blas in his only remaining serviceable hand and Viceroy Eslava in the thigh. Following their orders, Don Carlos Desnaux evacuated all but a couple dozen of the fort's five hundred defenders in the morning, withdrawing them for the defense of Cartagena itself. Most of these soldiers now awaited rescue ships in an abandoned stone quarry on the Boca Grande side of the island.

At 5 P.M., on March 25, 1741, fifteen hundred British grenadiers, commanded by General Guise, advanced steadily up the new military road through the parrot-green twilight toward San Luis. The fort's defenders immediately put out a white flag. Presently, a lone drummer emerged, beating the "chamade" a military tattoo that signified a "request to parley," in other words, the Spanish officer left in charge wanted to discuss terms of surrender. But Guise's grenadiers misunderstood this signal as a call to arms; expecting a momentary sortie from the fort they fired on the drummer and killed him. The remainder of the garrison, now fearing no quarter and a general slaughter scrambled over the rear walls and ran pell-mell through the jungle toward Don Blas's squadron still anchored at the inner gullet of the Boca Chica.

The peg-legged Admiral had planned to scuttle his ships there to impede the entry of Vernon's flotilla into the Outer Bay. Holes had been drilled and temporarily plugged below the waterline of all the

Spanish ships. At a signal, plugs pulled, they would sink in unison, blocking the channel and buying time for Cartagena's defenders. It had all been carefully planned by Don Blas, his ships kept afloat by skeleton crews until the final moments. But now, the terrified garrison of San Luis had reached the shore of Boca Chica, gesturing wildly for rescue. Their panic communicated itself to the remaining crews; Spanish sailors jumped over the sides into the water or pulled away in the long boats. No one rescued anyone else.

Somehow during the confusion, the *San Carlos* caught fire. Sixty barrels of gunpowder stored in her hold ignited, setting off a terrific explosion. Burning debris fell on the *San Felipe* and *El Africa* like a rain of flaming stars; these exploded in their turn, scuttling themselves without the help of their hapless, fleeing crews. Night fell swiftly, the black night of the tropics, now red with the glow of burning ships. Taking possession of Fort San Luis at last, an officer of grenadiers expressed his surprise at its poor condition. It wasn't so much a fort as a heap of rubble and would have fallen to a breath of air, let alone a massed assault by British troops. "It was surprising," he later wrote, "to reflect upon their having kept this place for so long, for besides the breach in the walls the embrasures were all knockt down and of 90 cannon, only two remained fit for service, with one iron mortar of vast diameter."

Fort San Luis's dilapidated condition seems to vindicate Vernon's initial impulse that it could have been taken in a rush upon landing weeks before.

Meanwhile, Captain Knowles, acting according to the spirit of the Additional Fighting Instructions, took advantage of the darkness and landed with a small force at Baradera. From the vantage of the captured battery, he observed the blazing Spanish ships in the Boca Chica below and could just make out the Union flag now flying above Fort San Luis's crumbled battlements by the light of the flames. Naval debris still burning lit the dark water of the bay. Quickly re-embarking his forces, Knowles pulled his long boats around the point, intent on capturing San Luis's sister fort, San Jose, on the opposing jaw of Boca Chica. San Jose's Spanish garrison fired a few haphazard shots at Knowles and his men in the gloom, then turned and ran, leaving one unfortunate engineer behind to blow up the fort. The engineer had been drinking to steel his nerves. Presently very drunk he bungled his task; Knowles took the fort and the drunk engineer without a shot fired.

Knowles left half his force behind to garrison San Jose, re-embarked once again and rowed out to the *Galicia*. This proud vessel, still relatively undamaged and flying Don Blas's forty-foot-long pennant, lay beside the burning hulks of the *San Felipe* and *El Africa*. Sixty men, including the *Galicia*'s captain had been left aboard. The reminder of the crew had rowed away in the boats as Fort San Felipe fell. The captain awaited rescue and had failed to scuttle the ship. He now surrendered to a small English boarding party led by Knowles. But this energetic English officer didn't rest here; after securing the *Galicia*, he returned his men to the boats and rowed out to break the nine-foot-deep Spanish boom blocking the narrow end of the channel. It had been a *vesperum mirabilis* for Knowles. In one night he had taken a Spanish fort, an admiral's flagship, and severed the boom that had frustrated Vernon's entry into Cartagena's outer bay for weeks.

18.

Captain Knowles—later Sir Charles Knowles, 1st baronet, a highly competent, controversial naval officer, engineer, royal governor, author of strenuously worded pamphlets, scientist, and inventor was reputedly the illegitimate son of an earl. Born in 1704, he died seventy years later, as the American colonies fought for their freedom—a struggle Knowles himself had helped precipitate by his brutal impressment policies, setting off the so-called "Knowles Riots" in Boston in 1747. These riots, the most serious revolt against British authority in the colonies before the Boston Tea Party of 1773, were supported by John Adams who praised the rioters for defending their "natural rights." On that occasion, Knowles impressed forty-six random locals for service aboard navy ships; working-class Bostonians objected, rampaging through the streets and capturing several British naval officers and the Deputy Sheriff to hold as hostages for their compatriot's return.

Appointed governor of the Louisbourg Fortress on Cap Breton Island, after that impressive citadel's capture by American colonial forces in 1745, and governor of Jamaica from 1752 to 1756, Knowles also proved himself a talented administrator. In Jamaica, he reformed the legal system and moved the capital from Spanish Town to Kingston, where it remains to this day. But the Royal Navy benefitted most from Knowles's energy and expertise over the course of her eighteenth-century imperial wars: He had been present at the Battle of Cape Passaro as a young lieutenant in 1718 and ended his career as vice admiral of the Red, achieving the honorific of rear admiral of Great Britain in 1765. After his resignation from the service in 1770, he accepted the post of admiral in the Imperial Russian Navy of Catherine the Great. For that energetic monarch, he rebuilt the Black Sea Squadron, commissioned five new ships of the line and designed modern dry dock facilities for St. Petersburg.

Among his contemporaries, Knowles's strong personality, frantic energy, and brilliant, caustic mind inspired either love or hate—with his enemies ever ready to pounce. Few remained neutral in his presence. Some of his military decisions, however, though strategically sound, fell short on execution, especially the failed bombardment of Rochefort in 1757 during the Seven Years' War. Over the course of his long career, Knowles faced court-martial at least twice and participated in several duels and libel suits—one of the latter successfully against the novelist Smollett, who had written a critical account of Knowles's actions at Rochefort.

In his spare time, Knowles married twice, fathered four children, and translated scientific texts from French into English, notably La Croix's *Abstract on the Mechanisms of the Motions of Floating Bodies*, whose theories he tested through careful experimentation. He also invented practical devices for use aboard ship—including one for measuring the pressure and velocity of wind.

Knowles was a figure of the Great Enlightenment. The world has produced few soldier-scientist-inventor-governors since his day. The compartmentalization of modern life, the handing over of personal sovereignty to accredited experts would seem to make his varied achievements impossible for any contemporary Englishman.

19.

Dawn on March 26, 1741 broke with the smoke of an English victory hanging in the air above Cartagena de Indias like the bad dreams of its inhabitants. Finally, after weeks of frustrating delay, Boca Chica had been forced and the way made clear for the invasion fleet. The city, tucked away at the far end of the Surgidero, was protected by another half-dozen forts and batteries but Vernon now regarded these as minor obstacles and Cartagena as good as taken. The Fighting Admiral awoke that morning feeling elated, sure of impending victory. Without a second thought he fired off another one of his bombastic letters to Secretary of State Newcastle, predicting the imminent fall of Cartagena.

"Tho' the Bully Don must be said very well to know how to make a disposition, he is very far from convincing me he knows how to make the best defense with it afterwards," he wrote. "The wonderful success of this evening and night is so astonishing that one can't but cry out with the Psalmist—'it is the Lord's doing and seems marvelous in our eyes.'" Vernon neglected to say that the price for this hour of elation had been high: more than a thousand men dead in Wentworth's camp and aboard his own ships, almost all from disease.

The historian Charles E. Nowell suggests that, at the very least, Vernon "exaggerated his opponents' discouragement" with his hasty dispatch and points out that Don Blas was just then busy shoring up the defenses of Cartagena, bulking out the garrison with a few final levies from the countryside and preparing the city for a long last-stand siege. He had personally supervised the rescue of San Luis's garrison troops from their lonely hiding place in the stone quarry on the Boca Grande side of the island and their reassignment to the walls of the city. And Viceroy Eslava had ordered the obstruction of the Surgidero by sinking merchant ships in the Manzanillo channel, the only entry point into the Inner Bay, loomed over by its opposing forts, Cruz Grande and Manzanillo on opposite mandibles of yet another "mouth."

Later that morning, Vernon began moving his fleet into the safety of the outer bay. The weather had darkened since the arrival of the fleet in the Bay of Canoas three weeks before. Many ships' cables had been cut on the unexpectedly rocky bottom and the spring winds were beginning to blow. The burned-out wrecks of the *San Carlos* and *El Africa* still lay scuttled on the bottom of the Boca Chica; these had to be pulled off to make way for Vernon's ships which could now only proceed up the narrow channel by the painfully slow process of warping. More than two days would pass before all the expedition's ships and transports attained the safe anchorage.

Characteristically, once his ships had assembled there, the anxious and energetic Vernon sailed to make an immediate attack on Cartagena itself. Just beyond *castillos* Cruz Grande and Manzanillo, lay the walled and fortified suburb of Jesemani on an island connected to the city by a footbridge; beyond this to the west lay the open terrain of Texar de Gracias. Straight, easy roads led from there to the city about three miles distant, but two strong points guarded this access: the Castillo San Felipe atop San Lazaro and the convent of Nuestra Señora de la Candelaria de la Popa atop another, higher hill a mile or so to the northwest. Troops must be landed and these hills taken before the city could be approached by troops from the landward side.

Now, *Burford* and *Orford* sailed to within a cannon shot of the Castillo Cruz Grande and began a bombardment. Their guns were very effective at this range. The captured *Galicia* had been turned into a floating gun platform and this too was brought to bear on the *castillo's* walls. It must have galled Don Blas, watching from one of Cartagena's bastions, to see his own flagship used against him. But the Castillo Cruz Grande itself had already been abandoned as had Manzanillo across the channel, their garrisons withdrawn to Cartagena proper. English landing parties soon took possession of both forts.

Meanwhile, Vernon, exulting in the latest turn of events, sent Captain Lawes in a fast sloop to London carrying yet another crowing dispatch detailing the capture of Tierra Bomba and the Surgidero *castillos* and the impending fall of Cartagena. It was only a matter of time, a few days, a week, before the Spanish city fell into English hands. Admiral Richmond wrote:

Vernon felt justified, as well he might do, in writing a trium-phant dispatch which he sent home at once. The ease with which the Baradera battery, Fort San Luis and particularly Fort San Jose had fallen, and the abandonment by the Spaniards of four ships of the line without an attempt to defend them, gave him confidence that the enemy would not stand if they were pressed vigorously. The capture of the town should therefore follow quickly.

Lawes arrived in London with this exciting news on May 17, 1741, after a swift Atlantic passage of just over six weeks. With him came spoils of war: two Spanish officers taken prisoner aboard *Galicia* by Knowles along with Admiral Lezo's enormous pennant. Cartagena's supposed fall, which surely must have been achieved by now, engendered a near hysterical outburst of national pride in England, exceeding even that exhibited after Vernon's capture of Porto Bello in 1739. Church bells rang out for days. Bonfires blazed from every hill and crossroads; fireworks illuminated the night skies. Triumphal arches depicting Vernon's victories arose in London and elaborate pageants were staged. Vernon's health, drunk equally in common taverns and aristocratic houses across the land led to more roadside inns bearing his name. And the makers of cheap, collectible medals quickly cranked out a bewildering array of new examples.

Some showed Don Blas wearing an odd fez-like hat—similar to the unfortunate *chapeau* worn by the young Charles Bovary as described by Flaubert in *Madame Bovary*. Resembling a circus clown on his knees, he offered his sword to Admiral Vernon. Others showed Vernon's tidy ships blasting Cartagena's crenelated walls. Still others showed Vernon and Ogle embracing; none showed Wentworth, who apparently hadn't caught the public's fancy. He just wasn't collectible. All bore bombastic legends like TRUE BRITISH HEROES TOOK CARTAGENA or THE SPANISH PRIDE PULLED DOWN BY ADMIRAL VERNON. In the Tower menagerie zoo, a lioness gave birth to two cubs immediately christened Vernon and Ogle by the zookeeper. Even Walpole joined in the fun—at a society wedding, when asked to give the toast, he grinned and with a wink at the virginal groom, offered:

"Why, drink to the Admiral in the straits of Boca Chica!" The guests responded with gasps and titters of laughter, the young couple blushed. The First Minister, known for his ribald sense of humor, had just dropped another off-color witticism.

But in Europe, busily arming itself for yet another major war over the succession of the young Maria-Theresa of Austria to the ancient throne of the Holy Roman Emperors, news of Cartagena's assumed fall was regarded with decidedly mixed emotions: "Rejoicing" in Vienna, St. Petersburg, Turin, and the Hague, and "acute depression," in Paris and Madrid. This is where the battle lines would be drawn: The Bourbon powers against the rest. A British victory at Cartagena meant that all Spanish South America would soon fall into her hands. To France's peaceable Cardinal Fleury, this meant sixty-million livres in lost revenue from trade and perhaps world domination by Protestants.

François de Chambrier, counselor to Frederick the Great of Prussia dissected the significance of the Siege of Cartagena for his royal master. This wasn't just a city falling but an age of peace giving way to an age of war.

"Fleury has the unhappiness of seeing that the conquest which the English have just made, places them in a condition to become masters of the American trade and to carry further weight in the great affairs of Europe," Chambrier wrote, "and that if he wishes to oppose her in it, he must come to a general war, which he greatly dreads."

Fort St. Lazare

SEVEN

Disaster

"While Vernon sate all glorious. From the Spaniards late defeat. And his crews with shouts victorious. Drank success to England's fleet."

1.

Though this verse, written by an anonymous newspaper poet to celebrate Vernon's successful campaign against Porto Bello in 1739, when Lawes reached London with the Admiral's overly optimistic dispatches in May 1741, the sentiments might have just as easily been applied to Cartagena's putative fall. But, as Lawes sailed off for England aboard the *Spence*, the task facing Vernon and Wentworth remained far more precarious than the dispatches allowed. Don Blas still held all territory beyond the Surgidero including the city itself. Meanwhile thousands of British soldiers and sailors had been felled by disease, chiefly yellow fever; the rainy season drawing ever nearer would only increase these mortalities. The change in weather could almost be heard coming, beating at the humid air above Tierra Bomba like the wings of a great black bird.

Again, Vernon urged the utmost speed in the conduct of operations ashore through a series of strongly worded letters: "As every day's experience has shewn the Spaniards are an enemy that cannot stand being vigorously pushed," the Admiral wrote to Wentworth, "we cannot but advise you against slow proceedings"; and in another: "As we are best acquainted with this intemperate climate, we think it our duty . . . to advise your pursuing more vigorous measures as most conducible to the preservation of your men's lives from the ravaging sickness."

Still, the transfer of the expeditionary force to the head of the Outer Bay took a week; a slow progress which Vernon blamed on the laziness of soldiers commanded by an overly cautious general.

On March 30, another council of war was held aboard Vernon's flagship with Admirals Vernon and Ogle, Captain Knowles, Generals Wentworth and Guise, Colonels Blakeney, Wynyard, Wolfe, and Grant in attendance. By this time, relations between army and navy command had deteriorated to the point where the navy men could barely stand to be in General Wentworth's presence. Other officers observed that Vernon and Ogle treated General Wentworth like a child, explaining obvious points in a condescending manner and leaving him out of discussions of overall strategy. Nonetheless, a plan of attack gradually solidified, in conjunction with General Guise and guided by a Scottish engineer off the *Sandwich* named Alexander MacPherson who claimed an intimate knowledge of Cartagena and its suburbs.

Castillo San Felipe, called San Lazar by the British for the hill it surmounted, was the last major bastion defending the city remaining in Spanish hands. Should it be taken by the expeditionary force, its guns could be turned against Cartagena's inhabitants; capitulation of the city would not long follow San Lazar's fall. McPherson suggested landing a substantial body of men at Texar de Gracias, just northeast of Fort Manzanilla, already garrisoned by Knowles's men. From here, roads led to La Quinta, the large country estate of one of Cartagena's leading citizens, to Fort San Lazar on its hill, and on to the walled suburb of Jesemani. Troops must be landed without delay and Fort San Lazar taken immediately by assault for the British to be in possession of the city before the start of the rains.

General Wentworth reluctantly acquiesced to this plan, with one caveat: he requested the release of all remaining troops from the transports, about 5,000 men. Though Vernon and Ogle believed the general already had at his disposal sufficient forces for the conquest of San Lazar, they agreed reluctantly to his request. Anything to get the man moving forward.

On April 5, 1741, an advance force of about 1,400 grenadiers commanded by Colonel William Grant and Colonel Blakeney landed on the beach at Texar de Gracias and struck inland. They were supposed to be accompanied by a battalion of Gooch's Americans with entrenching tools to act as work crews and "Jamaican negroes to reconnoiter the woods" but these contingents did not join the invasion force at the time of disembarkation. The unsupported grenadiers advanced smartly up the narrow road toward San Lazar, eventually forced by difficult terrain (a lagoon on one side and thick woods on the other) to march one platoon abreast at a time. This was enemy country; they marched in silence, except for the clank of equipment and the loud chirruping of insects from the thick tropical vegetation.

Halfway to the fort, the grenadiers encountered a force of seven hundred Spanish soldiers blocking the path. This marked the first time during the campaign that a substantial body of Spanish troops had met an English army in the open. Now, eager for combat, the leading grenadier platoon knelt and fired off a quick volley, then wheeled off into the woods for a reload as a second platoon stepped forward to deliver a second volley, and so on.

The Spanish troops crumbled beneath this disciplined fusillade and fell back at a run, clearing the way to the fort. Meanwhile, the Americans had at last joined the fight. They were ordered to execute a flanking maneuver to root out any Spanish soldiers still firing from the cover of the woods. The Americans fell to this task with gusto; here at last was the work they'd signed up for back home: They had until now been unfairly judged a bunch of disloyal "Irish papists," and mostly confined to the ships to prevent desertion. According to Lord Elibank, Americans were only of use to the army as "cutters of wood and drawers of water." But the terrible attrition rate of the British army from disease had made the Americans' employment in other capacities a necessity. Vernon had at last ordered "all the Americans that can be trusted" placed at Wentworth's disposal.

Their fight in the woods was brief. The Battle of Texar de Gracias only lasted about twenty minutes. In its aftermath, joined by the "Jamaican negroes," the Americans were again put to work cutting fascine and digging trenches in the hot sun. The ever-cautious Wentworth, having by now landed necessary equipment and supplies fell back on regulation tactics with his "usual leaden deliberation." Disembarking, he ordered the construction of another elaborate fortified encampment and another raised battery with which to pummel San Lazar. It was Fort San Luis all over again—though San Lazar apparently presented much less of an obstacle: this fort wasn't much of a fort, rather "a small, square building mounting six guns on each face," its walls barely twenty feet high.

At the moment, however, the Spanish regulars were on the run. Military instinct honed by centuries of experience dictated a fleeing enemy must be pursued: "the Spaniards gave way and retreated pell mell for the town," says Admiral Richmond. "Now was the moment to dash! The enemy, wholly demoralized . . . the road was open to the city gates and there were those present who though a rapid pursuit would have carried the British troops into the city with the fleeing Spaniards." Lord Elibank, with the van of the army that day supports this judgement. "Twas the opinion of most of the generals that had we pursued the enemy in their retreat," he said, as quoted in Lord Hervey's voluminous *Journals* "we should have with very little trouble at least have gained San Lazar."

But General Wentworth, advancing from the beach, called off Colonel Grant's pursuit and settled down determined to build his camp and battery. As the books said, a breach must be made in the walls of any fort before an assault could be attempted—never mind that San Lazar at that moment might have lain open and unoccupied. Wentworth's decision, widely seen as a major tactical error in his own day, has its apologists in our own. Harding in his revisionist *Amphibious Warfare in the Eighteenth Century* insists Wentworth made the right decision in not pressing an immediate attack on the fort:

> There is much to be said in Wentworth's defense. The army was straggling over two miles of unknown territory and the advance body cannot have consisted of much more than the 1,400 that landed with Blakeney. These troops had to push on another mile to reach Jesemani and had to pass directly under the guns of San Lazar. The Spaniards might have abandoned the fort, but this is by no means certain. The defense of San Luis demonstrated that the enemy was capable of stout resistance when not faced by overwhelming

firepower. Spanish losses in the little battle that morning were not heavy, possibly seven dead and thirty wounded, and although panic is conditioned by psychological as much as physical factors, there is no reason to believe the garrison of San Lazar would not have steadied the broken ranks of the advanced force. Also, if the British had got into Jesemani, an orderly surrender would have been impossible. The troops would have had to fight through the streets, over the dyke and into Cartagena itself, against an enemy which might expect no quarter after the unfortunate killing of the drummer at San Luis. The risks were very high.

In response to this statement, it can only be said that Harding writes from the comfortable vantage of more than two hundred years. He wasn't there that day. Those that were felt Fort San Lazar, and perhaps Cartagena itself, might have fallen with a simple push.

2.

Admiral Vernon, now beside himself with frustration certainly thought the fort was ripe for a fall. He fired off a series of blunt letters at Wentworth dallying in the midst of his new camp for "two whole days, during which the General neither advanced to seize the fort by assault nor took steps to raise a battery."

Presently, the recalcitrant general held a council of war with his officers to decide how best to capture the convent of Nuestra Señora de la Candelaria de la Popa located on an adjacent and higher hill. From this eminence, San Lazar might be bombarded into submission by a nicely placed battery. Elaborate plans were considered; but while the officers talked, a platoon of "marauding American soldiers," acting on their own initiative climbed the hill and finding the convent deserted, occupied it without a fight.

Wentworth's reaction to this bold action is not known. He probably viewed it as a dangerous breach of military discipline. The Americans had taken La Popa without orders, something all the books he read regarded as fatal to military discipline. In any case, Wentworth, typically, failed to follow up on this advantage. He did not immediately order any cannon dragged up La Popa, nor up a closer hill about three hundred yards distant from San Lazar. "A battery mounted on this hill," says Admiral Richmond, "would have knocked the fort to pieces in a few hours."

In truth, Wentworth's weakening army, devastated by disease, would have found even this project a difficult task. Rather, the general requested sailors and marines from Vernon's ships be released to build and man the battery. The Admiral refused this request, though he did allow naval engineers to visit Wentworth's camp in an advisory capacity, including Captain Knowles. Vernon now characteristically demanded an immediate assault on San Lazar, pointing out that de Pointis (a Frenchman!) had taken the fort by storm in 1697, surmounting the walls with ladders and a thousand buccaneers. Wentworth, Vernon insisted, ought not to be raising more batteries but, in emulation of de Pointis should assault the place "sword in hand." The general, again hesitating, asked that the navy first bombard the fort from the Inner Bay off Texar de Gracias. This was an impossible suggestion, given the shallow water and the distance involved.

Another day passed. Another party of engineers came out, this time under Colonel Thomas Armstrong, to assess the feasibility of raising a battery on La Popa or the nameless nearby hill. The distance between La Popa and San Lazar would have challenged the range of available guns, they decided. Any battery raised should be sited on the other hill, its elevation steep but not impossibly so. But, as Admiral Richmond puts it, "the mosquitos were already at work" on

Wentworth's men. Armstrong, perhaps supported by Knowles, now concurred with Admiral Vernon and decided that San Lazar could after all best be taken by assault.

A military council met on April 8 to discuss the matter further. Debate grew heated, with Colonel Blakeney and Colonel James Wolfe both arguing against an assault, asserting that the army had already waited too long. The Spaniards, they said, had taken advantage of Wentworth's hesitation and strengthened the outer works of the fort with trenches three rows deep and had dug a deep ditch around the perimeter of the walls. These now presented greater obstacles than the fort itself. Somehow Armstrong's engineers had missed these developments—though, as Admiral Richmond says, "from what point they made their reconnaissance cannot be said." They had also overlooked the location of the fort vis-à-vis the guns of Cartagena less than a mile distant.

In truth, perhaps the moment for an all-out assault à la de Pointis had passed. Fort San Lazar rose more than seventy feet above the bosky plain below. Its eastern face presented assault troops with a steep incline which they would be required to scale on hands and knees; the southern face offered a gentler incline—a better place for scaling ladders. Wentworth, realizing only too late that vigorous action must be pursued, or the campaign fail altogether, decided to attack the fort the very next morning, April 9, 1741. In this uncharacteristically bold decision, he overruled his now cautious subordinate officers.

General Guise in overall command of the battle chose San Lazar's southern face as the main point of attack. Here, marines under Colonel Wynyard, a force of about a thousand men, would throw themselves at the walls, followed by about 1,100 Americans carrying the scaling ladders, burdened by heavy wool packs and armed only with grenades. Colonel Grant, leading a smaller force would assault the northern face simultaneously. This secondary attack was designed as a feint to divert Spanish defenders; de Pointis had taken the fort by attacking exactly here in 1697. General Wentworth, whose personal bravery had been in doubt, would head his own regiment in support of the northern column. This decision to participate "sword in hand" in the battle has been criticized; in so doing, he absented himself from overall control.

"His major error," Harding says "was to accompany the diversionary attack. He was not it the right position to respond to unexpected events in the decisive area to the south. His presence would not have altered the result, but might have saved some lives and consequently preserved the strength of his best units."

3.

At 4 A.M. on April 9, 1741, "the air speaking of tragedy . . . close and still," the attack began with Wynyard's column, followed by the Americans, filing off silently into the thick tropical darkness. Groping toward the southern face, and perhaps misled by two untrustworthy Spanish deserters acting as guides, they failed to wheel far enough to the south and ended up at San Lazar's steep eastern face. Here, they encountered the three rows of trenches and the deep ditch, now filled with water, that would render the American's scaling ladders too short by ten feet. As dawn broke, Colonel Wynyard and his men reached the summit of the hill, only to face an unexpected Spanish volley from a mere thirty yards distant. The trenches were held by elements of the Aragon and Espada regiments, fortified with 250 of de Lezo's crack marines. Wynyard's men had hit the wrong face, whether because of the guides' misdirection or the darkness, and lost the element of surprise. Then, as dawn broke, they came under fire from the ramparts of Cartagena.

Colonel Burrard, serving with Wynyard that morning, describes the ensuing chaos in one of his letters:

We received a continual fire of their cannon from the town and fort and their batteries, which swept off many of our men, being quite exposed to their shot, and when we drew near enough for them to make use of their muskets, their fort and batteries seemed one continuous light. Our men behaved with the utmost resolution but 'twas our misfortune to attempt an impossibility. 'Tis true we got up to their breastworks and drove them from their trenches but what could we do when we came up to the fort, we found it surrounded by a very deep trench and the walls of the fort too high by ten feet for our ladders, and we in return firing against stone walls.

The Americans, called forward with the ladders, abandoned them when they reached the ditch around the fort and, according to a *Boston Evening Post* account of November 9, 1741, deserted, or as the *Post* put it, "retired to their camp." Other sources, notably Smollett, praised the American's bravery and reported that the unarmed soldiers, realizing their ladders were useless, threw them down and grabbed up the muskets of their fallen British comrades and "with characteristic pioneer individualism" returned Spanish fire.

Captain John Lloyd of Maryland, in the mix with the other Americans of Gooch's Regiment wrote another account of the bitter fighting around Fort San Lazar in his journal:

Ye enemy kept an incessant fire on us while we advanced & at 4 we got under ye walls & began our fire which we continued till 8 of ye clock when we found it impracticable to continue any longer & was obliged to retreat with great precipitation while our enemy kept firing at us, we had killed or wounded near 700 men but ye greatest part kill'd dead on ye spot we was so near ye walls that we could hear our enemies say in English words God Damn you, why don't you lower ye muzzles of ye guns lower ye muzzles & fire away I am sorry that some of our Subjects Eyes are not yet open.

It does appear from other accounts that a few British troops managed to gain the ramparts of the fort but were thrown back by a shower of grenades, rockets, and stones. Colonel Wynyard's marines then managed to work around to the southern face—their original target—around dawn, but now found San Lazar's Spanish defenders "as thick as they could conveniently stand all along the entrenchment," and backed away. At about 7:30 A.M., the fort's emboldened commander threw about two hundred men, bayonets fixed, out the sally port for a downhill counterattack. These encountered Wentworth's column preparing to march up the northern face and drove them back.

The growing daylight revealed an unfolding British defeat. The attack on San Lazar had been repulsed on all sides. After two-and-a-half hours of fighting, according to Harding, British losses stood at 200 killed, 377 wounded. According to Admiral Richmond 600 dead, not including 43 officers, while about 500 men lay in camp "tossing and raving with yellow fever" helpless and waiting to die. Among the officers killed on the field lay Colonel Grant, whose last words condemned the treacherous Spanish guides no less than his incompetent commander: "The general ought to hang the guides," he gasped, "and the King ought to hang the general." Then he turned his face from the world.

General Wentworth, admitting defeat, called off the attempt to wrest Fort San Lazar from Spanish hands at 8:30 A.M. It had been botched from beginning to end, a bloody chaos on an alien hill.

4.

Recriminations quickly followed the end of the battle.

Lord Elibank blamed both Vernon and Wentworth, citing the general's cautious tactics, but also the admiral's refusal to help build the requested battery and his all-around intransigence. Captain Knowles blamed Wentworth exclusively in his famous *Account*. Harding blames Vernon's refusal to cooperate with the army in what was supposed to be a joint amphibious operation, and the Admiral's inclination to save his ships and his own ass. There may indeed be enough blame for everyone involved, but there is no denying Vernon's repeated warnings about making war in the tropics, where speed of operations must trump all other considerations.

"The failure of the Cartagena expedition was very largely due to General Wentworth's lack of enterprise," says Vernon's chief modern biographer.

His dilatory methods, his inability to adapt to unfamiliar conditions and his unwillingness to listen to the advice of men who knew all about West Indian warfare. . . . That Vernon was right in proffering a good deal of this advice, even unasked is scarcely open to question. In the first place, Vernon out of his great experience had repeatedly advised against the taking of such expeditions at all, and had represented all the dangers inherent in the treacherous climate and the swift toll that tropical disease would take among the troops . . . a successful expedition had to be undertaken immediately.

But perhaps a more serious criticism than any of those above might be laid at the Admiral's feet. He had committed a mortal military sin in underestimating the enemy he faced—the indomitable Don Blas de Lezo, who in the end might be called the better soldier.

Vernon's experience over the previous decades fighting Spanish troops, prone to break and run when pushed, had only solidified his contempt for them. Their behavior on this campaign up to the defense of San Lazar had done nothing to change this opinion. The Spanish had failed to make a convincing stand at San Felipe, San Jago, San Luis, the Abanicos and Baradera batteries, Castillo Cruz Grande, Fort Manzanillo, and on the Cartagena road. Why would they now stand firm against a massed British assault on San Lazar?

Certainly, Vernon failed to understand Don Blas's strategy of "tactical retreat." The peg-legged old sea dog knew his Spanish troops, vastly outnumbered, wouldn't long stand against disciplined British regulars in the field. Also, like General Kutzov during Napoleon's disastrous 1812 Russian campaign, Don Blas knew the climate for his greatest military asset. The trick lay in keeping the British Army occupied just long enough; defend each strong point, then fall back. Delay the enemy long enough and moisture and mosquitos would wreak a carnage beyond the firepower of Spanish guns.

Admiral Vernon, no less than General Wentworth, had been beaten by a superior tactician.

The day after the battle passed in disarray and confusion and in counting the dead. The army ashore had been reduced by losses and disease to 3,569 man, out of which perhaps 1,000 remained fit for duty. Wentworth and his officers, meeting at La Quinta in the afternoon, finally decided San Lazar could only be taken following a heavy bombardment; that a battery must be built atop the nearby hill for this purpose and that the navy must immediately supply the men to both build the battery and man the cannons. The army at its current strength could not manage this task, they said. Then they requested a general council of war aboard Vernon's flagship, to be attended by officers of both services. If the battery could not be built and manned as suggested, they concluded, the attack on San Lazar must be called off and probably the entire expedition against Cartagena.

Meanwhile, General Guise asked San Lazar's commandant for a cease fire to allow the English to bury their dead and collect any wounded who remained alive on the field. The commandant, his garrison exhausted from the fight, readily agreed to this request. The gates of San Lazar swung open at last as English officers in charge of burial parties moved among the stiffening corpses. Under a flag of truce, Spanish officers emerged to meet their English counterparts—enemies, but gentlemen all, engaged in the honorable profession of arms. In another war, in another age, they might have exchanged cigarettes and regimental patches. Now they shook hands and conversed politely in French—literally the *lingua franca* of the educated eighteenth-century elite. The Spanish officers expressed universal amazement that Wentworth's superior army had failed in its assault on the fort. Had the English attacked a few days earlier, just after the Battle of Texar de Gracias, they might have taken all in a quick rush—exactly as Vernon had suggested. But General Wentworth's plodding tactics had given the fort's defenders enough time to reinforce the place, build breastworks and trenches and dig the ditch that foiled the scaling ladders.

This assertion made a bitter intelligence for the English officers; no less bitter for Admiral Vernon who came ashore on April 11 to inspect the smallish fort that had broken the army. It seemed, as he had thought, a paltry place that might have been easily taken by a properly executed and correctly timed assault. He fired this opinion and many others at Wentworth over the course of an uncomfortable breakfast in the general's tent. The two commanders parted, following tea and sea biscuits, barely on speaking terms. They met again at the council of war aboard *Princess Carolina* on April 14. At this contentious meeting, Vernon whose hold on his explosive temper had ever been slight, could hold it no longer. He swore at the tight-lipped Wentworth whom he blamed entirely for the failure at Fort San Lazar: "His fury and disillusionment so great, that he could not trust himself to say more."

Vernon slammed out of his admiral's quarters and strode about the outside gallery, calming himself. Eventually he rejoined the shocked officers. A quieter discussion followed; no use to lay blame now, plenty of time for that later in a flurry of pamphlets and eyewitness accounts. Time now rather to decide what to do next. All reluctantly agreed the taking of Cartagena from Spain no longer lay within reach, given the depleted state of both army and navy. As Smollett wrote in *Roderick Random*, drawing from his experiences as a surgeon's mate, shipboard conditions had become critical:

> The sick and wounded were squeezed into certain vessels, which thence obtained the name of hospital-ships, though methinks they scarce deserved such a creditable title. . . . Such was the economy in some ships, that rather than be at the trouble of interring the dead, their commanders ordered their men to throw their bodies overboard, many without either ballast or winding-sheet; so that numbers of human carcasses floated in the harbor, until they were devoured by sharks and carrion crows, which afforded no agreeable spectacle to those who survived.

At last a vote was taken and the decision to abandon the expedition reached. Overwhelmed with emotion, Vernon gave a moving speech to his men:

"'Tis well known that in a season for action, I don't use to express myself in words," he said, his voice cracking. "But that season is now over, and the impotence of talking all the comfort that remains in our power." The army and navy was now "surrounded with the toils of death; before them threatens a fierce, vindictive enemy, flushed with unexpected success, and, in the midst of them, rage diseases, yet more dreadful and destructive. While I yet speak, the infection gains strength, and numbers die, with their last breath cursing the sluggishness to which principally they owe their bane."

All Spanish forts remaining in British hands would be destroyed and all forces would be re-embarked for Jamaica. Vernon would then ask for a recall to England where he could explain the failure of the expedition in person to the king. He blamed it all on Wentworth's torpid strategy, but in his heart knew the truth: he too had failed. He did not, however, include his subordinates in the navy, his captains and sailors when apportioning blame for the defeat. A notable measure of the man.

"The report I shall make of your merit and importance I flatter myself, will not be to your disadvantage," he continued. "I am not without hope to see the day when Court as well as Country, Ministers as well as Patriots, shall be obliged to acknowledge that you are the only natural strength of Great Britain."

5.

The following day, however, as re-embarkation commenced, the admiral pursued a final action that has remained controversial. He sent the *Galicia*, now a floating gun platform, in close to the walls of Cartagena to bombard the city. Sailors and officers aboard her, all volunteers, were paid double for this hazardous duty with special compensations for wounds received. The *Galicia* stayed at her post from 5 A.M. until noon, taking heavy fire, with six men killed and seventeen wounded.

Vernon's motivations for ordering this attack have remained cloudy. Smollett says the admiral had intended to "demonstrate the impracticability of taking the place with ships only." In other words, to show that the failure of the expedition must be laid at the feet of the army. Admiral Richmond shrugs his shoulders and merely says Vernon's motivations here are "not easy to understand." Vernon himself said he did it "for the satisfying of gainsayers," which supports Smollett's explanation. As it was, the *Galicia*'s bombardment had little effect on Cartagena's stout walls and the ship was warped out of the Surgidero, riddled with Spanish shot.

The *Galicia* incident occurred on April 15, 1741. On that day, Wentworth's remaining troops were put aboard the transports. Wentworth himself, as if again seeking to prove his personal courage, was the last man to leave—perhaps with a sour look back at the proud battlements of the undefeated city he had failed to take.

Ten more days elapsed, however, before the flotilla finally weighed anchor for Jamaica. During this time the Boca Chica forts were blown up by Knowles, who had perfected the technique at Porto Bello—though the heavy rains of the season had set in, making it difficult to keep the requisite barrels of powder dry. During this period of inactivity, the death rate from disease shipboard continued to grow.

Military historians have since asked why Vernon hadn't garrisoned the Boca Chica forts and kept them under British control. This occupation would have secured dominance of the coast; the city might then be starved into submission by a future expedition. But the expedition could no longer spare the men to mount an effective defense of a single square foot of Spanish property, let alone a couple of half-destroyed forts.

Vernon limped into Port Royal, Jamaica, on May 19. The admiral was "a deeply disappointed man . . . heartily sick of conjunct expeditions with the army." The expedition to take Cartagena had been one of England's greatest military debacles to date, a disaster equal to the defeat at Yorktown forty years later. Of the Cartagena expedition's nearly 30,000 participants, roughly 13,000 died, most from disease, besting the death rate of Hosier's 1727 expedition by a factor of three. They had also experienced heavy losses on the material side.

Seventeen ships of the line severely damaged and six sunk; also four frigates, twenty-seven transports and 1,500 cannons gone. Spanish losses were comparatively light. Only 800 dead, with six ships of the line scuttled, five forts reduced, and three batteries spiked.

The greatest loss to Spain, however, cannot be counted in ships or regiments, but in the death of a single man. The peg-legged Admiral, *Patapalo, el Mediohombre,* Don Blas de Lezo. He died in September 1741, a few months after Vernon's departure—some say from sepsis caused by the splinter wounds sustained aboard the *Galicia* on March 24; others from typhus. His valiant and sustained defense of Cartagena had saved an entire continent for Spain: "If the English had made themselves masters of this place," commented Duro, the Spanish historian, "all the Indies on the mainland would now be in their possession."

Today, Spain regards Don Blas's defense of Cartagena as one of the greatest episodes in her long military history, of equal note with Cortez's 1519 Conquest of Mexico and Don John of Austria's defeat of the Muslim fleet at Lepanto in 1571. Ironically, at the time of Don Blas's death, he had been recalled to face charges of incompetence brought by Viceroy Eslava over the scuttling of the Spanish fleet at Boca Chica. Time has at least righted this injustice. Today, Don Blas's statue in the Plaza de Colón in Madrid never lacks an evergreen wreath of victory laid at its base.

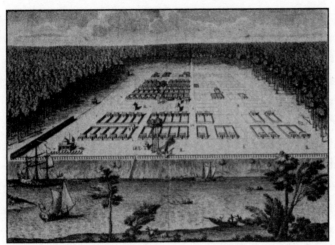

Peter Gordon's view of river bluff GA

EIGHT

The Invasion of Georgia

1.

When news of Admiral Vernon's failure to take Cartagena reached the Spanish capital at last in early June 1741, the bells of Madrid rang out peals of victory for three days. Sermons boomed from the pulpits of churches across Spain. Almighty God had shielded the faithful from the violence of the English heretics. Masses of thanksgiving were offered from Santander to Cádiz. Even King Felipe V raised himself from his depressive stupor at the glad news. He took off his wife's nightgown, bathed, put on royal regalia, and temporarily gave up screeching out Farinelli tunes at dinner. In full kingly mode he attended balls and levees smiling like an idiot at the side of his florid Italian queen.

It seemed for a moment Spanish glory had undergone a renaissance; the great days of Isabela and Ferdinand and Christopher Columbus would surely come round again. King Felipe's chief military strategists—War Office Commissioner Ustaritz, Marine Secretary Quintana, and President of the Council of the Indies Montijo—made immediate plans to follow up the unexpected victory at Cartagena over the most powerful navy in the world. The British, staggering beneath this blow, disoriented and weakened by disease, were more vulnerable than they'd been at any time since Marlborough's great victories during the War of Spanish Succession. Now was the moment to strike!

Illegal British occupation of the Spanish province formerly known as Guale still rankled, the Debatable Land now renamed Georgia by that monster of egotism Don Diego Ogletorp. Treaties broken and ignored had long established the Florida frontier at Port Royal/Beaufort, South Carolina, not far from the former site of Santa Elena, the ancient Spanish colonial capital. Spain now aimed to reassert her authority to this line and seize Charles Town itself and perhaps English territory as far north as Virginia. But first, Oglethorpe must be driven from Georgia.

Meanwhile, shock and incredulity settled like a cloud of soot over England. King George II initially sought to suppress all news of the defeat, censoring newspapers and other outlets, but reports of such a major disaster could not stay buried for long. The public dissection of events, the writing of pamphlets, the publication of journals and accounts defending or accusing either Wentworth or Vernon would soon begin. The makers of collectible medals portraying the fictional English victory at Cartagena melted down their unsold stock; collectors tossed them with disgust into the bottom of drawers. Two-and-a-half centuries later, one of these made it to an antique dealer's case at the flea market in the Washington, DC, neighborhood of Georgetown, so designated after the monarch who had been England's king during the War of Jenkins' Ear.

In England, some of the roadside taverns recently renamed in honor of Admiral Vernon were again renamed, this time in honor of someone else. Though Pulteney, Vernon's most ardent supporter in Parliament assured the Admiral he remained the "most popular and best loved man in England," this was no longer true. To Horace Walpole, one of Vernon's great detractors, he was nothing more than a "simple noisy creature," a parliamentary irritant worthy only of being ignored.

Writing to Secretary Newcastle from Jamaica, the Admiral sought recall to England to explain himself to the war council and to blame the failure of the Cartagena expedition on General Wentworth. But he was not recalled, not yet. Work remained to be done in the West Indies; the war was far from over there, and Walpole needed a victory, something to redeem the deaths of all those Englishmen on the battlefield in the stifling, fever-ridden holds of warships and transports in the torrid zone. Walpole's ministry now stood in danger of falling; his grasp on English politics, dominated by him since 1721, was suddenly precarious.

On May 26, 1741, the in-theater council of war again met at the gubernatorial mansion in Spanish Town, Jamaica, this time to assess the condition of the army and navy and to decide on the next campaign. Panama was suggested—a favorite obsession of Governor Trelawny's—and rejected. Cuba remained the target of choice, though British forces in the West Indies were no longer of sufficient strength to attack Havana itself. A squadron of twelve Spanish ships of the line under the command of Admiral Don Rodrigo de Torres had recently anchored in the harbor beneath the guns of Moro Castle.

Vernon wisely hesitated to attack the Cuban capital. Death rates in the army and navy had only increased since the evacuation of British forces from Cartagena; in the previous three weeks, 1,100 more men had died, including 100 officers. Also, Vernon worried a combined Franco-Spanish fleet might soon attempt to land an invasion force on the English coast. This possibility compelled him to send his best ships under Commodore Lestock to protect the homeland: *Princess Carolina, Russell, Shrewsbury, Norfolk, Princess Amelia, Torbay, Chichester, Hampton Court, Burford, Windsor, Falmouth,* and five frigates were already under sail for Spithead.

After several days' discussion, the council of war in Jamaica decided on a relatively minor target—Santiago, Cuba. This decision has been much criticized by generations of historians; at the time it made sense: Santiago, a hotbed of *guarda costa* activity commanded the straits between Cuba and Haiti and might serve as a base for combined Bourbon military operations should France officially join the war. Also, should the place fall to Vernon, his much-depleted expeditionary force might rest there to refresh and await reinforcements for an attempt on the entire island.

But even this relatively minor expedition would take weeks of preparation to execute. Exhausted troops must regain their energy; sailors lying sick with yellow fever must either die or recuperate; fresh victuals must be purchased and loaded aboard Vernon's remaining ships for the next attack.

2.

As the council of war debated in Jamaica, Spain moved forward with a plan to reconquer Georgia and capture or kill Oglethorpe whose "restless spirit" had so vexed them. Since the general's defeat before the walls of St. Augustine in 1740, Governor Montiano had been itching to strike a counterblow.

Bad blood had arisen between Georgia and South Carolina, brought about by Oglethorpe's botched siege—so Montiano had been informed by English deserters. The Georgians and the South Carolina planter elite were now at odds. South Carolina's Lieutenant Governor William Bull, once Oglethorpe's friend and supporter, blamed the general's high-handed tactics and undeniable ego for the botched Florida invasion. Also, as a major slave owner, Bull resented Oglethorpe's anti-slavery and anti-rum dictums. Was there anything finer in this life, after all, than a cooling rum-punch brought with gentle deference on a silver tray by one's own personal body slave?

Encouraged by the British disaster at Cartagena, Governor Montiano and his Cuban counterpart, Governor Juan Francisco de Güemes y Horcasitas of Havana, began to assemble an army for the invasion of Georgia. In October 1741, English prisoners held in Havana escaped, making the six-hundred-mile voyage across the Florida Straits and up the coast to Savannah in a stolen boat to report on frantic preparations for war in the Cuban capital. Newly built shallow-draft warships, capable of in-shore maneuvers and fitted with an impressive number of cannons crowded the Havana shipyards; *guarda costa* captains, now licensed privateers, had been set free by Cuba's governor to pursue the piratical trade in which they already engaged. These would-be buccaneers soon captured many English ships, some right off the South Carolina coast. "The English must be asleep," one of the *guarda costa* captains commented, "otherwise they'd not have let us take their vessels even on the bar of Charles Town."

In truth, a kind of deadly somnolence had descended upon the inhabitants of South Carolina. Sunk in subtropical torpor beneath their Spanish moss, they refused to take seriously the threat of a Spanish invasion. Lt. Governor Bull drowsed on the gallery of his plantation house at Waspee Neck, not far from Beaufort, a glass of rum-punch dangling from his hand, oblivious to the juggernaut headed his way. But Oglethorpe, ensconced with the 42nd Foot at Fort Frederica on St. Simons Island remained very much awake—his eyes fixed on the horizon in the direction of Florida. Fortunately for South Carolina, he had regained his health and famous energy after a long period of recuperation. To many it seemed the old vigorous Oglethorpe of pre–St. Augustine days had returned for his second act.

Montiano was bent on revenge for the 1740 attack on his city— of this Oglethorpe had no doubt. Vigilant at Frederica, the general awaited the Spanish governor's counterblow. In a series of alarmist letters addressed to the South Carolina legislature, to the Georgia Trustees in England and to Secretary Newcastle, Oglethorpe now outlined what he described as a nefarious Spanish strategy. Some of its details came from deserters, some from his own best guesses and knowledge of the enemy: Montiano and Güemes planned to retake Guale and conquer South Carolina and all English territory as far north as Maryland; they would use a combination of Spanish regulars, Florida militiamen, and an eighteenth-century "nuclear option," the dreaded implement of slave uprisings. This possibility seemed incredible to everyone at the time, an example of Oglethorpian hot air. But he was neither alarmist nor wrong in his reading of a precarious situation. As Governor Montiano had recently written to Güemes in Cuba, the new year of 1742 would see an aggressive campaign to "destroy the plantations and settlements of the English interlopers."

For such an ambitions campaign, however, Spain would require the help of more than just her own soldiers and sailors. Güemes had lately recruited a regiment of free Cubano-African *agents provocateurs*: These "negroes . . . of all languages" would be sent into the hinterlands of the Carolinas and into Virginia with the usual, electrifying offer from King Felipe of Spain: any slave of the English who agreed to convert to Catholicism and fight for the Spanish flag would receive freedom and land in Florida. The offer was, in the end, a cynical one. South Carolina's Stono Uprising of 1739 had ended in slaughter and savagery and black heads on pikes for miles along the Stono Road. Güemes and Montiano hoped to inspire many more like it, never mind the fate of the slaves involved. Amid such bloody chaos, Spanish troops might sweep north to topple British rule in the Americas.

Lt. Governor Bull and others in South Carolina laughed off Oglethorpe's dire predictions. They had listened to him in 1740, with the result of an expensive debacle at St. Augustine. They would not listen again. The London-based Georgia Trustees, too far away from the scene, couldn't offer much help. Now only Oglethorpe and his personal regiment of about 600 men augmented by 200 or so Indian auxiliaries—Creek, Choctaw, and Yamacraw—stood in the way of renewed Spanish imperial ambitions in North America.

3.

Spain's feverish preparations for the Georgia War continued through the last months of 1741 and into early 1742. Governor—now General—Montiano had appointed himself to lead the invasion and officially asked Güemes for sixty ships and 5,000 Spanish regulars to which he would add 500 men from the garrison of St. Augustine. But Güemes offered only 1,300 men and thirty ships—a puny force, Montiano retorted, for the conquest of a continent.

Now began a Havana–St. Augustine pas de deux, the mirror reflection of the same dance for men and supplies Oglethorpe had endured with the South Carolina legislature in 1740. In the midst of this frustrating number, reinforcements arrived unexpectedly from Spain. These fresh troops brought Montiano's fighting strength up to roughly 3,000 men, still an overwhelming force in that backwater theater of war. But estimates vary: some historians say Montiano in the end commanded the 5,000 troops he had asked for—a claim the venerable Oglethorpian Phinizy Spalding calls "preposterous";

others say Montiano led as few as 2,000, but most agree on the figure of 3,000, loaded aboard thirty-six ships. No matter how modern historians tabulate these numbers, most agree Oglethorpe now found himself outnumbered by at least three-to-one. Of course, Don Blas de Lezo had just faced down worse odds at Cartagena.

On June 10, 1742, Spain made her first attack on a British outpost in Georgia. They landed an advance force on Cumberland Island, where Oglethorpe had built a battery he called Fort St. Andrew. Now he began a series of strategic retreats that would have made Don Blas proud. Oglethorpe reached Fort St. Andrew from Frederica after riding a night and a day; he quickly spiked its guns and shepherded the garrison to the safety of St. Simons Island, called "Gualquini" by the Spanish. Here in Forts St. Simons and Frederica he had concentrated his forces—a meager army augmented at the last minute by a company of Highland warriors from the Scottish settlement at Darien, a dozen or so Georgia rangers called in from outlying posts and about a hundred Yamacraw Indians dispatched by Mary Musgrove, the Georgia Sacagawea. Among these was Tooonahowi, nephew of Tomochichi, Oglethorpe's great friend.

The invasion of Georgia had begun, Cumberland Island had fallen, but the legislature in South Carolina somehow still did not take the threat seriously. Oglethorpe's letters begging for military aid, turned from entreaties to threats. "If there's any trifling in this and an accident thereupon should happen," Oglethorpe wrote to Lt. Governor Bull, "you may depend on it you are answerable." Despite the odds, he said, he planned to make "a considerable stand" at Fort Frederica. But Bull and the rest of the colony had sunk further into their "curious lethargy." Oglethorpe now faced a situation so desperate as to be irretrievable; his decision to stand and fight was considered suicidal by many South Carolinians.

Bull himself had already given up on the Georgia Colony. From the illusory safety of his plantation house at Waspee Neck he wrote to Secretary Newcastle that it was "not expected that Oglethorpe can long hold out against so great a force as Spain has dispatched." And indeed, the situation looked gloomy for the impetuous general. "Everything tends directly to the catastrophe," as Horace Walpole later wrote his peculiar Gothic masterpiece, *The Castle of Ontranto*. Gloom on the part of the English had its flip side among the Spanish in St. Augustine and Havana. Montiano, in expectation of a successful campaign had embarked a company of horseless dragoons. They brought only their saddles; the horses they would take from the English in Georgia after an easy victory.

But all of them had reckoned the future without the redoubtable Oglethorpe. He had lately rediscovered the brightness and energy that had astonished the Creeks and Chickasaws in 1738. Here was the brave young cadet who had mounted the trenches at Belgrade in 1717; the commander who had single-handedly put down the murderous mutiny of his own regiment. Here was the soldier as ever "stimulated by the odds against him." He would stand or fall for the cause and on the ground, he had chosen and nowhere else.

As Oglethorpe made last-ditch preparations to resist Montiano's Spanish armada, the South Carolina legislature at last ambled to his aid.

On July 3, after a long series of windy debates, they voted to fund a relief force commanded by Oglethorpe's old second-in-command, Colonel Vander Dussen, though the latter proved a controversial choice. Many in South Carolina still associated Vander Dussen with the St. Augustine defeat; more hours of debate would pass before final confirmation of his appointment. But it was all just another waste of time. Such an expedition would take weeks to mount and Montiano's armada of nearly forty ships and 3,000 men now stood off the St. Simons bar. They had arrived on June 28; only a lucky week of wind and heavy rain had prevented their landing on the island.

Now the weather had cleared. The invasion was imminent.

4.

July 5, 1742 dawned calm and sunny over the St. Simons Sound. The Spanish flotilla began its stately progress through the maze of channels and shoals toward a landing place on the island, near Gascoigne Bluff which overlooks the Frederica River. Oglethorpe had previously established batteries here on the point and a sturdy log fort named after the island. These opened up with all guns on the slowly advancing Spanish ships. For several hours both sides exchanged "hot" fire, but the Spanish fleet managed to wend its way through the complicated channels without too much difficulty; Montiano had purchased the excellent piloting services of a traitor from South Carolina named Alexander Parris who knew these waters intimately—and the entire armada had anchored in the Sound by sundown.

Fort St. Simons now stood in danger of being flanked and overwhelmed. Oglethorpe made the difficult decision to abandon the place; he ordered its cannons spiked and at midnight by dark of moon lowered the British flag from the pole on the ramparts. With the fort's garrison at his back, he retreated up the Military Road to Fort Frederica. This rustic thoroughfare, little more than a dirt track and wide enough for only one wagon to pass, had on Oglethorpe's orders been cut through the heavily vegetated heart of the island, connecting the forts at its southern and northernmost points. But Fort Frederica itself was more than just a fort. Rather more of a military *urbs* in the making, built according to ancient Roman principles. Its walls, only half-finished, enclosed a planned settlement complete with barracks, baths, arsenals, storehouses, and military housing for married soldiers. According to Spanish sources, 200 women had arrived on a separate ship with Oglethorpe's regiment from England in 1738 "the purpose being to compel the soldiers to marry them," wrote a cynical Spanish commentator. The new settlement now included a couple dozen children from these arrangements.

Steam rose from the subtropical marshes and dense palmetto thickets of St. Simons on the humid morning of July 6. Oglethorpe's prospects looked grim. A powerful Spanish army under Manuel de Montiano had landed less than ten miles away and now occupied the island's secondary fort. Montiano was even now preparing to launch a full-scale assault on the Fort Frederica settlement.

At about 10 A.M., Oglethorpe's Yamacraw scouts reported a large Spanish war party on the move; not yet Montiano's full weight, but a "reconnaissance in force" up the Military Road of about 125 men, commanded by the veteran Captain Sebastian Sanchez. Rather than await the enemy in a defensive posture, Oglethorpe "leaped on the first horse" assembled about sixty regulars, the Darien Highlanders and a few of his Indians and rode out to meet his fate. He hoped to stop this first wave of Spanish troops before they left the cover of the marshy woods at the center of the island and reached the open ground fronting Fort Frederica. Here, they might dig in and await the rest of their army backed by artillery for the final assault.

The opposing forces ran straight into each other in the woods about a mile-and-a-half south of Fort Frederica. The fighting, hand-to-hand and fierce, lasted about an hour as the war whoops of the Indians echoed horribly beneath the dome of trees. Oglethorpe himself "took two Spaniards with his own hands" during the fight. Captain Sanchez, wounded in the arm, was captured; his second-in-command, Captain Nicholas Hernandes, killed. With their chief officers down and many more taken prisoner, Spanish troops broke and ran back down the Military Road toward Montiano's main encampment, closely pursued by Oglethorpe.

A small creek ran near the site of the skirmish; this innocuous rivulet gave its name to the first phase of the struggle for St. Simons Island that day, later dignified to history as the Battle of Gully Hole Creek. The Spanish lost perhaps thirty-six men; Oglethorpe described his own losses as "light."

The hour advanced; heat rose; brief, heavy showers now dampened the ground. Another engagement between Oglethorpe and Montiano awaited. At the remove of nearly 280 years, important details of this second and more decisive battle grow faint. No one is exactly sure what happened; conflicting narratives exist, romantic extrapolations. An accurate picture of events eludes the modern historian, but a rough outline can still be sketched in: After the action at Gully Hole Creek, Oglethorpe continued to pursue the fleeing Spanish troops for about three more miles. Then he stopped, halting his men along the Military Road at what looked like a good place for a fight, Indian-style: "a clearing surrounded on three sides by dense woods" bordering a marsh.

This location remained unfound until 1912. That year, a vacationing party of US Army officers visited St. Simons Island, guided by a recent translation of Montiano's post-battle letters to Güemes made by a West Point professor of military science. Comparing British and Spanish accounts and walking the terrain, they determined that "the memorable battle was fought at a point upon the margin of the marsh, about two miles from the south end of the island, and about one mile from the hotel, where the road from Gascoigne's Bluff enters the road to Frederica. This spot agrees perfectly with the account of Captain Thomas Spalding"—one of Oglethorpe's officers—"which . . . is by far the clearest and most trustworthy." (Whether or not the spot is indeed the right one, it is certain no one in Oglethorpe's day booked a vacation stay at "the hotel.")

Oglethorpe deployed his men in the woods here, hiding them behind trees and in clumps of palmetto. This vantage allowed him to dominate the Military Road, which curved around the marsh in a semicircle and over a narrow brush and log causeway. He now questioned a few of the Spanish prisoners captured at Gully Hole Creek. These men revealed Montiano had that morning sent a squadron of his ships from Gascoigne's Bluff to attack Fort Frederica from the waterside. Had the "reconnaissance in force" under Sanchez been a feint to divert attention from the real attack? Worried, Oglethorpe now left his men with his second-in-command, Captain Sunderland, and hurried back to Fort Frederica to command his forces there. But finding all quiet at Frederica, with no Spanish vessels yet in sight, Oglethorpe quickly gathered some reinforcements and raced back toward his position athwart the marsh.

It was now about three in the afternoon.

News of the skirmish at Gully Hole Creek had reached Montiano two hours earlier, and what he heard prompted him to action: Captain Sanchez's men, survivors reported, were just then being beaten by Oglethorpe in the deep woods. To extricate Sanchez from this unfortunate encounter, Montiano now sent a major force up the Military Road, including a veteran grenadier company led by Captain Antonio Barba. Reaching the clearing by the marsh and unaware of Oglethorpe's troops hidden behind the trees, the Spanish, by some accounts decided to stop for a late lunch. As the Highlanders watched in astonishment from the cover of the underbrush, Spanish troops stacked arms, broke out their cookpots and began to prepare their food—a hearty paella, one would like to think, rich with the shellfish plentiful in the shallow, warm waters off sunny St. Simons.

But Montiano, no less than Oglethorpe, also employed Indian scouts. One of these, according to the official Spanish account of the battle now noticed "something new on the road, a felled tree and part of the branches like a breastwork on some sides where it was not before. Barba halted to reconnoiter it, and at the same time they [the English] began to fire on him from right and left, without his seeing more than the flare of the powder flashes."

The battle had begun, with Oglethorpe's Native allies and the Darien Highlanders blasting away at the lunching Spaniards from behind every tree. This was not a European-style fight, with neat opposing armies drawn up in even ranks and polite salutations between the officers, but a vicious American-style ambush. Volley after volley crashed into the disorganized Spanish troops.

Barba valiantly attempted to rally his men and a few grenadiers managed to return fire, but they couldn't see what they were firing at. A bloody chaos ensued; black powder smoke billowed with the screams of dying men into the air. According to some sources, two hundred Spanish troops fell to British muskets or Yamacraw war clubs in a matter of minutes. In any case, the Spanish panicked and soon abandoned their cookpots and their dead and scattered at a dead run back down the road and into the woods toward Montiano's camp, pursued by Oglethorpe's Indians. So many Spanish soldiers lay dead and bleeding on the forest floor and on the reedy loam that—as legend has it—the marsh turned red with their blood, giving the encounter its name: the Battle of Bloody Marsh.

5.

By the time Oglethorpe reached the site of the battle with his reinforcements from Frederica, the fighting had ended and the controversy begun. Future generations of historians regard this encounter either as a minor skirmish with major ramifications or a bona fide battle that decided the fate of Georgia. Spanish and English accounts do not seem to coincide; some sources have Barba killed during the fighting, others not. Two of his grenadiers, however, reached Montiano's lines at Fort St. Simon at 4:30 in the afternoon to report on the fate of their comrades to the increasingly disheartened governor.

But the battle had not been entirely one-sided. Apparently two companies of Barba's grenadiers had penetrated British lines around the perimeter of the marsh and driven off several of Oglethorpe's platoons of regulars. Oglethorpe later wrote in a report to the Trustees of his encounter with these retreating soldiers on the Military Road. They reported all had been "quite beaten" by the Spaniards at the marsh and that Captain Sunderland had been killed. Whether or not Oglethorpe believed this hysterical nonsense, he refused to be discouraged and spurred his horse toward the sound of the fighting, certain that his "appearance on the field might preserve" the fighting spirit of the men who remained. As it turned out, Captain Sunderland—who remained alive—and his men had no need of Oglethorpe's inspiring presence. The Spaniards had already been "intirely routed." In Oglethorpe's absence, the battle had already been fought and won.

Propaganda from both sides soon followed the action. Montiano claimed in his official report to Güemes that he had lost a mere handful of men in the Bloody Marsh fight; Oglethorpe claimed to the Georgia Trustees that hundreds of Spaniards had been killed. No doubt the actual number of dead lies somewhere between the two. But the significance of the battle cannot be exaggerated. With his few men Oglethorpe had made a successful stand against Montiano's invasion force of thousands—recalling Blas de Lezo's feat at Cartagena. Oglethorpe had risked his life again and again over the course of the day's actions, displaying an almost suicidal bravery. Still, Montiano was not yet beaten. It would take something more than a smallish military encounter in a Georgia palmetto-pinewood to turn back his invasion force.

6.

Hoping to follow-up on the sharp, unexpected success at Bloody Marsh, Oglethorpe gathered his forces and double-timed down the Military Road toward Montiano's camp beneath the walls of St. Simons. Nearly there, he paused and sent a company of Indian scouts ahead to ascertain the strength of the enemy's defenses. The

Indians quickly reported back distressing news: Montiano's army was too numerous, his position too strongly dug-in to attempt an assault "with so small a number" as Oglethorpe possessed.

Darkness fell; the noisy silence of the woods enveloped Oglethorpe's men. The glimmer of many Spanish cookfires could be glimpsed between the trees. The General paused, then reluctantly wheeled and marched his army back up the Military Road to Fort Frederica which they reached before first light. The next day, July 8, 1742, he began to prepare its defenses for the expected Spanish attack.

Hot rain came down all through the afternoon. Montiano brooded in his tent as Oglethorpe had done before the walls of the Castillo de San Marco in St. Augustine exactly two years before. Montiano had been instructed by Güemes not to risk the precious Spanish army in fruitless sieges on strongly held fortified positions— perhaps Fort Frederica was such a place. In any case, Güemes had urged caution. Montiano's men would be soon needed for the defense of Cuba should Admiral Vernon attack the island. Caution generally assures the defeat of an offensive operation. Victory is beyond price in either treasure or blood; to win, a commander must be prepared to sacrifice all. Montiano possessed imperfect intelligence; he did not know Oglethorpe's strength—perhaps Frederica was indeed impregnable, garrisoned by thousands of English troops. Why waste the lives of his men on such a citadel?

That afternoon, the governor sent out a dozen men in a boat to get the lay of the land and find a source of fresh drinking water for his army. These unfortunates were later found adrift on the Sound, their boat awash in blood, their bodies hacked to pieces. They had encountered a war party of Oglethorpe-allied Indians. Montiano, both enraged and enervated by this massacre, fell prey to a sense of "impending doom." Another day passed, with water rations growing short. A military council of his officers couldn't agree on an offensive strategy. Montiano, now decided to send out another reconnaissance in force—this time by boat via the Frederica River—to discover whether the Fort might be better assaulted from the water side.

This small Spanish flotilla set out on the morning of July 9. Oglethorpe, informed by his Indian scouts of the approaching enemy vessels, moved all available cannons to Frederica's waterside walls. He watched as the Spanish ships slowly approached up the green-brown Frederica, waiting for the exact right moment. At a signal his gunners opened up and "fired at them with the few guns we had, so warmly they retreated."

Stymied again and now riven with doubt, Montiano once more retired to his tent to brood. Three days of Spanish inaction followed. On July 12, Oglethorpe, eager for another battle gathered a raiding party of several hundred men for a guerilla-style sortie on the Spanish camp. His force crept through the woods to a point barely two miles from Fort St. Simon, now garrisoned by Montiano's men. Though the Spanish Governor commanded superior numbers, they might be routed by a smaller force in a surprise attack; surprise being the key. But suddenly, one of Oglethorpe's troopers, a Frenchman, fired off his musket to warn the Spanish of the British approach. He then threw down his gun and made a fast dash for Spanish lines. Had he been driven to this treachery out of discontent with the imperious Oglethorpe, or had he insinuated himself in the general's army as a Spanish spy? We will never know.

Oglethorpe quickly realized the danger inherent in the man's defection. This damnable French deserter would surely reveal the small size of his army and the vulnerable state of Frederica's defenses, still only half-finished. Bolstered by this intelligence, Montiano would undoubtedly attack with his entire invasion force and overwhelm the fort. But Oglethorpe found himself in a more immediate predicament. His raiding party was in danger of being chased down and destroyed, with himself killed or captured. Thinking fast, he divided his drummers and sent them off in opposite directions, "all beating the *Grenadier's March* for about a half an hour." With this ruse, he hoped to convince Montiano that his position was surrounded not by a single, undersized British army but several. The trick worked. Montiano refused to stir from behind his breastworks, allowing Oglethorpe time to complete a successful withdrawal to the safety of Frederica to prepare his next stratagem. In war, sometimes trickery will make up for the absence of decisively superior forces. The Greeks at Troy were not the only ones to prove the worth of this military dictum.

Oglethorpe now devised a neat little trap. A Spanish prisoner held at Frederica was promised his freedom if he would deliver a letter in secret to the Frenchman who had deserted the day before to Montiano's camp. The prisoner swore a sacred oath that he would deliver this letter and was released. He immediately broke his word and went to one of Montiano's officers instead. The letter, ostensibly addressed to the French deserter, contained a masterstroke of disinformation. Keep telling Don Manuel de Montiano that the British are weak and that Fort Frederica might be easily taken, the letter instructed. Encourage the governor to attack quickly so Oglethorpe might defeat him with his superior forces. It was a double-psyche and clearly transparent, but Montiano fell hard for this particular Trojan horse. The French deserter was immediately executed as a spy on the governor's orders.

Still, Montiano hesitated. Could Don Diego Oglethorpe be having him on? No, the truth of the letter had already been confirmed by the Frenchman's blood. But later that afternoon came another sign from heaven. Spanish lookouts sighted five British ships on the horizon to the north, toward South Carolina. Were these the advance guard of a major flotilla sent from Charles Town for Oglethorpe's relief? They weren't but Montiano now crumbled entirely. He'd been on edge since Bloody Marsh, further unnerved by the slaughter of his water-finding party, and perhaps longed for the certitude of the Castillo de San Marco's encircling coquina walls. The conquest of Gualquini would have to wait for another day. He impulsively ordered the evacuation of all Spanish forces from St. Simons, beginning the next morning, July 14, 1742.

7.

The first Spanish troops left for Cuba aboard the transports just before dawn. Montiano himself remained until July 20. Then he breathed a sigh of relief and sailed away. The invasion of Georgia by Spain had ended in a retreat more ignominious than the English defeat at St. Augustine in 1740. Spanish plans for the destruction of England's Southern colonies had been thwarted by the redoubtable Oglethorpe. It was, according to historian Phinizy Spalding "the high-watermark of his career" and "the last act of Spanish Florida in the drama of the War of Jenkins' Ear."

Ettinger puts it this way in his great biography of Georgia's founding father, praising his quick-thinking actions at Gully Hole Creek and Bloody Marsh:

> It may perchance be asserted that, had the battle of Bloody Marsh not been fought—and won, no matter how fortu-itously—by Oglethorpe, the Carolinas or even Virginia would later have been the scene of the decisive Anglo-Spanish struggle for American continental supremacy. But that is fatuous. *This* was the decisive battle, as decisive for Spain as two decades later the Plains of Abraham proved for France, or Yorktown two decades later yet for Britain.

Thus, a few hundred Spaniards lost on a hot day in a marsh on St. Simons Island in July 1742 had decided the fate of a continent.

General Wentworth

NINE

Santiago, Panama & Ruatan

1.

On July 25, 1741—as Oglethorpe began his preparations for the defense of Georgia—a detachment of a hundred American troops from Gooch's Regiment and a hundred Jamaican Black soldiers advanced for an attack on the village of La Catalina on the island of Cuba. This small, racially integrated force, much afflicted by heat and mosquitoes, fought under the partial command of Captain Lawrence Washington of Virginia. They moved cautiously, muskets unslung and ready, up the Santiago Road, little more than a sandy track between dunes and high brush.

Captain Washington's detachment, the first American soldiers to serve in this part of Cuba, would not be the last. Admiral Vernon's fleet, consisting of eight ships of the line (his pennant now flying from the *Boyne*) and a variety of transports and tenders lay at anchor in the nearby bay in what Vernon called "the finest harbor in the West Indies." Then known on English maps as Walthenam Harbour, it was immediately renamed Cumberland by the Admiral in honor of King George's son, William Augustus, Duke of Cumberland, the victor at Culloden. But this taxonomy would not long survive his expedition. The thousands of American sailors and marines stationed there today still know it by its Spanish name: Guantánamo.

The small action against La Catalina in which Lawrence Washington participated ended in a snappy success. A mounted party of Cuban cavalry sent out to protect the village turned tail and galloped off upon catching sight of the advancing Americans—so fast they left their reserve mounts behind. Also, as Vernon wrote in a dispatch to Secretary Newcastle three days later, "some of their ammunition and a good deal of jerked beef."

General Wentworth quickly occupied the place. It became his first base of operations against the city of Santiago, the expedition's ultimate goal, as he began the slow construction of his usual fortified compound. This base, surrounded by the customary ditches and palisades on a bluff overlooking the Guantánamo River, he dubbed George-Stadt. Vernon visited Wentworth at the new encampment on July 29, and for once approved of the site, on "an open rising ground, by fresh water river side, as beautiful a situation for a town as this country can afford." Being in a renaming mood, he promptly renamed the Guantánamo River below the bluff the "Augusta," after the Prince of Wales's German wife, Augusta of Saxe-Gotha. Vernon was then briefed on the military composure of Washington's Americans during their advance toward La Catalina a few days earlier.

"Though mostly composed of Irishmen, and some of them convicts," Vernon later wrote, "yet by the report of Capt. Washington, their Captain, they all went on service with great cheerfulness, and are all returned according to . . . orders, without a man deserting."

Vernon took the prompt seizure of the insignificant Cuban village—an action at which Wentworth had initially balked—as a change of heart on the general's part. Surely by now General Wentworth had learned the hard lessons of Cartagena! And would soon advance from George-Stadt's ditches and tents in even rows the sixty-odd miles through the bush to take Santiago. This plan of attack had been worked out in advance at a Council of War aboard the *Boyne* on July 18. Captain James Renton of the *Oxford*, Vernon's chief reconnaissance officer, had made a preliminary investigation of Santiago's seaward defenses from the deck of his ship a few weeks earlier: Cuba's "second city" could not be taken by the navy alone, Rentone had reported, "its high land, the failing breezes inshore and the strong forts covering the narrow entrance made a sea-attack impossible."

Here was Boca Chica redux. Here, once again the Spanish had demonstrated their genius for selecting positions of great natural strength, and their talent for improving on nature's art with *castillos* and other fortifications. The council of war, taking Rentone's observations to heart, decided that Santiago must therefore be taken by Wentworth's army from behind, which is to say the landward side, while Vernon's squadron subjected the city to a fierce bombardment from just offshore—a by now familiar and heretofore unsuccessful formula. Admiral Vernon expected the army's advance to Santiago would begin within hours of disembarkation, which had been accomplished with no opposition on July 20. One observer asserted that the march from Guantánamo Bay to Santiago could be accomplished easily in three days. Here was tropical warfare as it should be done. As quickly as possible, before the climate began its work of death.

2.

No doubt Vernon again emphasized the necessity for speed in his meeting with Wentworth at George-Stadt on July 29. Surely the Americans' swift advance on La Catalina betokened an equally swift advance on Santiago. But subsequent events would prove this assumption tragically mistaken. General Wentworth remained the same hysterically cautious commander he'd been at Cartagena. Vernon now returned to his flagship to wait for the General's next move according to the battle plan. He meanwhile made the necessary dispositions of his ships for the expected siege. He divided the squadron, sending several vessels to take up positions outside Santiago Harbor—thus blockading the city—and several more to watch Havana down the coast. These would sail off to warn him should Governor Güemes send reinforcements to Santiago by sea.

August began with the highest hopes on Vernon's part: He had received intelligence that Santiago itself was poorly garrisoned (her commander Carlos Riva-Agüero had only 350 regulars and 600 local militia at his disposal) and that the inhabitants, terrified at the approach of the English heretics, did little more for the defense of their city than offer masses for its deliverance in the basilica of Nuestra Señora de la Asunción. And also that Governor Güemes in Havana had refused to send any aid or reinforcements. No soldiers could be spared from those guarding the capital, the governor had sadly reported to Riva-Agüero. Santiago was a citadel made of paper. The mere appearance of an English army beneath its walls, Vernon believed, would result in an immediate capitulation.

True to form, Wentworth refused to see things Vernon's way. Instead, he saw Cubans armed to the teeth lurking behind every palm tree on the road to Santiago. Again "eschewing all enterprise" he failed to advance a single foot beyond the miserable village of La Catalina and found new fault with the battle plan. It could not be accomplished, he now insisted, using available forces. The sixty-mile march—closer to eighty on modern maps—through unknown jungle terrain would expose the army to Spanish hit-and-run guerrilla tactics. Also the general had reports that no potable water could be found along the march, though conflicting intelligence cited water as plentiful. Meanwhile, the council of war in London had expanded the expedition's mission on Cuba. They had decided to establish a permanent British base at Guantánamo; for this reason, reinforcements of about 4,000 men were on their way from England. Why not hunker down and wait for the fresh meat to arrive before besieging Santiago?

Days passed. The rainy season had arrived with the full force of its torrents. Nothing happened except for the rain now pouring down and the quiet dying of the sick. More angry letters blasted back and forth between Vernon's flagship and Wentworth's HQ at George-Stadt. The Admiral was in despair. He had seen this all before, at Cartagena. It was like the return of a nightmare. Days turned to weeks and weeks to months with more men dying each day from disease. The Cubans wisely sat back and allowed their climate to do the work of killing Englishmen who posed no threat the mosquitos couldn't eliminate. Spanish sources later translated suggest they were indeed prepared, as Wentworth feared, to defend the Santiago Road. But this is the face of war; occasionally there is a fight and soldiers die. Better to die with a musket in hand than on a pallet befouled with dysentery.

Increasingly desperate, Vernon now reconsidered whether or not the navy could proceed against Santiago without the help of the army. He transferred himself to a fast ship, the *Orford*, and sailed off to reconnoitre the city on his own. Perhaps Captain Rentone had been mistaken and it might be successfully assaulted from the sea—but his observations only confirmed Rentone's report. The admiral sailed back to Cumberland Bay hoping to find that Wentworth had at last moved up the Santiago Road with his dwindling army. In this hope he was again disappointed. Vernon's return marked the nadir of his relationship with General Wentworth and also of joint British army–navy amphibious operations in the War of Jenkins' Ear. Unable to trust his own volatile temper in the man's presence the admiral would no longer consent to meet with Wentworth in person.

Perhaps to construct a careful record of the general's fatal inaction, Admiral Vernon now insisted any further communication occur on paper only. The vitriolic letter-writing campaign that followed continued unabated for the next few weeks. It was certainly the most active campaign of the war so far. On October 5, Wentworth sent a letter to Vernon stating that not only could the army not advance on Santiago, it could also no longer afford to remain in George-Stadt. Attrition from disease had withered it to under one thousand effectives, certainly not a force capable of attacking a city. Only one action remained possible: evacuation to Jamaica before everyone died. Two days later, Wentworth's officers wrote a second letter to the admiral, seconding their general's views.

Vernon could do nothing against this monster of irresolution. General Wentworth and the army had malingered in Cuba for more than three months, when three days might have sufficed for the march on Santiago. Evacuation had now become a necessity. The tenacious Vernon still held out a vain hope the attack on Santiago might yet proceed but, as comments the admiral's biographer, he "cannot have considered this a very promising plan, for Santiago would still remain just as far away from Cumberland Bay, and the distance between the two places had been one of Wentworth's main objections."

Horace Walpole, as ever one of Vernon's worst critics and a Wentworth partisan, sought to excuse the general's inactivity by blaming Cuba itself. General Wentworth had been ordered to march on Santiago by the navy, Walpole wrote, "eighty miles through a mountainous unknown country, full of defiles where not two men could march abreast; and they have but four thousand five hundred men and twenty-four horses." Horace Walpole overstated the forces at hand and, needless to say, had never been to Cuba; the terrain between Guantánamo and Santiago is largely alluvial, jungled, and flat.

3.

Finally, by the last days of October 1741, it became apparent to everyone, even the obstinate Vernon, that the campaign to take Santiago had been lost—once again with hardly a shot fired. The rainy season, which the army had just endured at damp, mosquito-ridden George-Stadt, had come and gone with no decrease in the rate of sickness and death. On November 3, Wentworth informed Vernon that the passage of just a few more days would leave him with insufficient men even to garrison his fortified encampment. The ongoing misery of life at George-Stadt at this time can hardly be imagined. Work parties barely maintained enough strength to bury the dead:

"We have suffered and still suffer," wrote Wentworth's usually stoic officers in a joint letter to their commander, "but that our stay in this place has already brought us into great difficulties and are of the opinion that unless a speedy resolution be taken to extricate us it will be out of our power to retreat from hence."

Four days later, General Wentworth resolved to abandon Cuba and return immediately to Jamaica with what remained of his command. This time, Admiral Vernon did not object. Exhausted by Wentworth's endless objections against doing what he'd been sent to do, Vernon wrote another passionate letter to Secretary Newcastle, asking to be recalled: "I desire no longer to be conjoined to a gentleman whose opinions I have experienced to be more changeable than the moon," he wrote. He suggested the able Chaloner Ogle might assume command of the naval half of the expedition in his place. This would give the admiral time to go home to present his case. A thorough investigation of the conduct of the army, Vernon believed, would exculpate him from all blame.

The naturally choleric Vernon was by now, in Admiral Richmond's phrase, "bursting with rage." But it was a rage of the impotent sort; the expedition's divided command structure had allotted him only an advisory role in the conduct of land-based operations. He could not actually compel Wentworth to do anything. As November crawled into its third week, nearly 2,500 Englishmen and Americans on Cuba were dead or dying from fever; any sort of attack on Santiago, even the lightest reconnaissance, was now clearly impossible. Had Wentworth only ordered an advance directly upon landing back in July, rough terrain or not, water or no water, his men might then have carried enough water on their backs for such a march and taken Santiago by storm.

The re-embarkation of the remnants of Wentworth's army began on November 20, 1741. Proceeding at the usual leaden pace, this final operation took more than a week. Of the 2,158 Americans who had landed at Guantánamo, only 300 remained fit for service, Lawrence Washington among them—though the captain from Virginia had developed a worrying cough that would not seem to go away. He had written a letter from Jamaica to his father Augustine back in May, following the Cartagena disaster; it is one of the very few we have in his own hand:

> The enemy killed of ours about six hundred and some wounded, the climate killed us in greater numbers. Vast changes we have in each regiment; some are so weak as to be reduced to a third of their Men; a great Quantity of Officers amongst the rest are dead. . . . We are all tired of the heat & wish for a cold Season to refresh our blood. War is horrid in fact, but much more so in imagination.

These words were not lost on his little brother, George who more than fifty years later urged the new nation he had a hand in founding to "avoid foreign entanglements"—of the sort that had brought the American volunteers to grief at Cartagena and Santiago.

4.

On November 26, Admiral Vernon watched from aboard his flagship as the rear guard of Wentworth's army set fire to the fortifications of George-Stadt. "All cannon, baggage, provisions and sick men, being embarked . . . we discerned the huts of the camp to be on fire," he wrote to Newcastle, "Mr. Wentworth having that morning marched down with his remaining well men and embarked himself."

Vernon set sail later that day, but not for Jamaica. Instead he went cruising, hoping to intercept the reinforcements still on their way from England before they disembarked and fell victim to Jamaica's fevers and punch houses. But the transports had just left Cork, Ireland on November 5 and Vernon could not find them. He soon returned to Port Royal where dispatches awaited him denying his latest request for a recall.

"I am sensible how much fatigue and trouble you have to go through," wrote his friend Admiral Wager, from his seat at the Admiralty, "and that you would be glad to be relieved but I do not see how that can be yet." Though Wager goes on to offer some small comfort by placing blame for the military disasters in the West Indies where most believed they belonged—squarely on Wentworth's shoulders. "I have not yet seen General Wentworth's letters to the Duke of Newcastle," Wager concluded, "but I suppose he gives some reason why, with 4,000 men, he does not venture to look upon Santiago."

The English public and the London press also blamed Wentworth, criticizing the general's "lack of skill and resolution," and his "cautious inactivity." Despite the Cartagena disaster and the recent failure on Cuba, Vernon still remained the "Hero of Porto Bello" back home. The nation had once again celebrated his birthday on November 12. "It is Admiral Vernon's birthday," Horace Walpole wrote with undisguised disdain, "and the city shops are full of favors, the streets of marrowbones and cleavers, and the night will be full of mobbing, bonfires and lights."

But knowledge of the public's enthusiasm for his person would have given the Admiral little comfort. Vernon may have loved himself overmuch, as some of his contemporaries insisted, but he loved his country more. Britain had not only squandered thousands of lives and hundreds of thousands in treasure in a fruitless attempt to dislodge the Spanish from their strong places in the West Indies, it had squandered an opportunity history would not again afford—to plant an English seed on the rich soil of the South American continent.

5.

The slow-motion defeat of the Santiago campaign, with the re-embarkation of the dregs of General Wentworth's army on November 26, 1741, marked the end of major British offensive operations in the War of Jenkins' Ear.

But one war bleeds into the next, particularly in the bellicose eighteenth century. Thus, the wider European conflict of the War of Austrian Succession would soon sweep all combatants into its maw: Spain, France, and Great Britain, along with Prussia, Austria, Saxony, and Savoy. History may be, as the great historian Arnold Toynbee once supposedly said, "One damn thing after another"— but historians generally love discrete chapters as much as any novelist. Thus, the War of Jenkins' Ear. The struggle between Britain and Spain in the West Indies and in Georgia is considered to have occurred between 1739 and 1742. Its cause, generally, competition over trade in the Americas and the particulars of the *Asiento*—that tricky contract to supply Spain's colonies with slaves that brought about so much smuggling after the Treaty of Utrecht awarded it to Great Britain in 1715. Not to mention the lopped-off ear of an unfortunate Welsh mariner named Captain Robert Jenkins that gave the war its belated, but memorable moniker.

Still, as Admiral Vernon sailed disconsolate back to Jamaica in December 1741, a couple of minor acts in the miserable drama remained to be played out. The reinforcements sent from England intended for the invasion of Cuba might arrive at any moment. Since Cuba had been evacuated, what work could be found for them now?

6.

Another council of war met at Governor Trelawny's mansion in Spanish Town on January 19, 1742 to decide this question. In attendance, besides the usual cast of characters, the ex-pirate George Lowther, now a Lieutenant in the Royal Navy, serving with Vernon's fleet. Lowther proposed an attack on Panama as the expedition's next target. His intimate knowledge of local waters—he'd raided towns and taken ships up and down the Spanish Main since the 1720s—gave his plan an authoritative ring:

Artillery and supplies would be ferried on rafts up the River Chagres, running high after heavy rains, to a place called Cruzes. From Cruzes, good roads cut through easy terrain to the walls of Panama. Here a heavy battery might be raised. At the same time, Wentworth would land the freshly reinforced army at Porto Bello, lightly armed and with only what they could carry. (The city had remained open and undefended since Vernon's victory of 1739, its forts still in rubble.) From Porto Bello, the army would move quickly up narrow tracks across the isthmus to Panama, then join the artillery and assault the place after a prolonged bombardment. It was a pirate's plan, flexible and cunning. And had the ex-pirate Lowther been in charge of the army instead of Wentworth from the beginning, the siege of Cartagena and the invasion of Cuba might have had happier outcomes for the English.

After a minimum of debate, Lowther's plan was adopted by the council. Its target pleased Trelawny; he'd long supported this enterprise—control the isthmus and you severed the link between Spain's colonies in North and South America. Its proposed speed of execution agreed with Vernon's ideas of how warfare ought to be conducted in the torrid zone—faster than the mosquitos could kill the men involved. "Delay has been found to be the most dangerous enemy in these parts," he wrote to Newcastle at this time, sounding his characteristic bass note. As for Wentworth, no one knew exactly what he was thinking.

The reinforcements from England arrived at Port Royal at last on January 15, 1742. These consisted of the 1st Royal Scots Regiment and the 6th and 27th Regiments of Foot—about 2,000 men, a couple grand shy of the number expected. On January 20, the council met again to firm up Lowther's Panama plan. At this meeting, Wentworth agreed to all its particulars, but at a second meeting two days later, he expressed doubts. The injection of fresh troops brought his forces up to about 3,000—though with at least fifteen men dying daily, this number dwindled rapidly. Wentworth now worried he would not possess enough troops to take Panama. This time, the council took a firm stand against the recalcitrant general. Anyway, Lowther had already gone off aboard the *Triton*, a fast sloop, to prepare the way. He would return with fresh intelligence in a week or so and the army must be ready to embark, that recurrent deadline, the rainy season, looming yet again.

But upon Lowther's return, nothing had been done to move the campaign forward. Disputes with Jamaica's planters over obtaining an adequate number of slaves to move the cannon and heavy baggage up the Chagres had complicated the preparations. Also, they had experienced difficulties in purchasing the necessary supplies and finding enough sailors to man the ships—this last a perennial problem for Vernon and others. Not until March 25, 1742 was the expedition at last ready to sail. It consisted of eight ships of the line, forty transports, two hospital ships, and about 2,500 men, with Governor Trelawny aboard, now acting as colonel of the Jamaican forces.

After a calm three days' sail, the fleet passed the Bastimentos. Spanish lookouts stationed here warned Porto Bello's governor who decided to withdraw immediately to the hills, evacuating every soldier in the place (three companies of Spanish regulars and two of mulatto militia) and leaving the residents of the town to fend for themselves. Porto Bellians began to run for the woods in a panic, possessions on their back, children in tow, until Vernon sent a delegation ashore to assure them they would not be abused. When he had taken the town in 1739, they had not been abused; this time they could count on the same generous treatment. He asked only that they sell him their mules for transport purposes and their cattle to feed his men. For these he would pay the going rate. Then, he issued an order to all his officers "inviolably to preserve the clergy, magistracy, and inhabitants of the town of Porto Bello, in the quiet and peaceable enjoyment of their persons and properties."

All forces were now poised for the invasion of Panama. Vernon accounted the number of men at hand sufficient for the task. In 1671, the pirate Henry Morgan had scaled the walls and thoroughly sacked the place with only 500 lightly armed buccaneers. Surely several thousand British regulars could accomplish a task achieved by half a thousand pirates. But the next day, Governor Trelawny approached the admiral with an unexpected request. He asked for a fast ship back to Jamaica so he might attend the opening of the island's legislature.

Vernon, surprised, asked why the governor had suddenly decided to abandon the army on the eve of invasion. Trelawny's answer sent the admiral reeling in shock. Since the expedition had been canceled, the governor replied, he could better serve his duty back in Jamaica. At first Vernon took this for a joke. Everything was ready; they were about to land! But further investigation revealed the truth. In the middle of the night, General Wentworth, seized with his usual misgivings had withdrawn his support from Lowther's plan and his army from the Panama expedition. This decision had been seconded by a meeting of his officers that very morning. "The projected attempt was not consistent with his Majesty's service and should therefore be laid aside," they had written in a report explaining their actions. This decision had been arrived at after consideration of the following: "The season was now too far advanced . . . the number of troops available had been seriously diminished both by sickness and by the failure of some of the transports to arrive, and it was now known the garrison of Panama had been strongly reinforced."

Vernon's reaction to the army's latest about-face is not recorded. He should have expected as much from Wentworth. But in a piece of circular reasoning, Harding suggests in his *Amphibious Warfare in the Eighteenth Century* that Vernon was secretly pleased by the cancellation of the Panama expedition. Harding posits the admiral had intended to sabotage the landing all along over concerns for his warships, now dangerously undermanned. Vernon had hoped to fill critical gaps in his usual complement of sailors with impressed soldiers from Wentworth's army, but the general had objected. The expedition had very nearly stalled in Jamaica over this point. Only Governor Trelawny's intervention had allowed it to sail at all. Calling things off was the only possible decision, though "probably the most tragic of all the enterprises attempted by this expedition," Harding says. "After all the planning . . . and the death of over 200 troops, the operation was deliberately destroyed within a matter of hours."

Not by a recalcitrant Wentworth, Harding insists, but by a belligerent Vernon who valued his reputation and the navy more than the best interests of king and empire. This opinion is hard to swallow. Admiral Richmond offers a more palatable interpretation:

The reasons for this surprising decision were twofold. It was said that this weakly garrisoned place [Panama] could not be taken with less than 3,000 men, and owing to sickness on the voyage, the force now amounted to only 2,032, and that as the rainy season was so close it would be undesirable to make the attempt. . . . In any case, the reasons for abandoning the attack were of a kind which, even had they been sound, should—and could—have been advanced sooner. It was too late to make these discoveries only at the moment when, after three months preparation, the expedition arrived at the port of disembarkation.

In other words, Wentworth got cold feet. Admiral Wager at the Admiralty labored under no illusions regarding Wentworth's culpability in the matter: "The army seems to me to have lost so much time before they embarked that the rains were sufficient to lay aside that enterprise to which there did not seem any strong inclination."

The last chance for the British to achieve anything further in the War of Jenkins' Ear in the West Indies had passed with a whimper.

The Panama expeditionary force crawled back to Port Royal in April 1742. That it was now "in no condition for further large-scale amphibious operations," as Harding says, is an understatement of nearly comedic impact. On the return voyage, Vernon fired off another letter asking for recall and that his union with Wentworth, "such a yoke fellow," as he put it, be mercifully dissolved. All his plans, he wrote, had been undermined by the general's "Inexperience, Injudiciousness and Unsteadiness."

This, however, was not quite the end of the end of British blundering in this war. One small operation remained, the fruit of Vernon's determination to show the nation some small return for its vast investment of blood and treasure in the West Indies since 1739.

7.

The tiny Caribbean island of Ruatan, thirty-five miles off the coast of Honduras, now home to several exclusive resorts and much scuba diving, was in the eighteenth century ideally situated to protect settlements of English log-cutters along Honduras's "Mosquito Shore." These interlopers had long worked this valuable commodity in defiance of Spain's titular control of the area, though the fierce Mosquito Indians who inhabited the region had never submitted to Spanish rule.

In mid-July 1742, Vernon asked for two hundred American volunteers for a mini-expedition: They would seize Ruatan, fortify it, and maintain a garrison there under the command of Robert Hodgson, a British official who had been given the grand title of "Superintendent of the Mosquito Shore." Much to Vernon's surprise, only twenty-two volunteers assembled in Port Royal on embarkation day. Somehow, the Admiral had received the mistaken impression that most Americans had joined the Cartagena expedition hoping to be resettled on free land in the Caribbean. Vernon had now offered them this land in the form of Ruatan and only twenty-two had stepped forward to take advantage of his generosity. It hadn't occurred to him, after all the mistreatment and hardships Gooch's Americans had endured in the last two years, they just wanted to go home.

But Admiral Vernon was not one to let go of an idée fixe once it had lodged itself in his brain; unreasonably disgusted with the Americans' lack of enterprise, he rounded up the remaining 188 requested "volunteers" at bayonet point. Herded aboard the transports for Ruatan beneath the watchful eyes of Colonel Wolfe's marines, they had the air of convicts on their way to a terrible prison from which they'd never return.

Once on Ruatan, a miserable, primitive little island, trouble broke out. A mutiny led by long-mistrusted "papist" elements in the regiment nearly succeeded. Details remain obscure, but it must be assumed that the ringleader, an obstreperous Irishman, met his death by hanging. Two crude log forts, George and Frederic were built and garrisoned. But they didn't stand for long, decomposing in the moist tropical heat. And the island itself, abandoned by the Americans in 1749, after the end of the War of Austrian Succession, eventually returned to the state of wild nature in which they'd found it. Like nearly every other British enterprise associated with the War of Jenkins' Ear, the settlement of Ruatan by the Americans of Gooch's regiment ended in failure.

8.

On September 23, 1742, dispatches arrived from London aboard the frigate *Gibraltar*, Captain Fowke commanding. These contained letters from Secretary Newcastle ordering both Admiral Vernon and General Wentworth home at last. They would relinquish their commands and answer for the defeat of British arms in the war against Spain in the West Indies.

Vernon sailed aboard his flagship the *Boyne* on October 19. General Wentworth followed a few days later, escorted by *Defiance* and *Worcester* bearing the sad remainder of his army. The return of these commanders to England marked the end of the War of Jenkins' Ear as reckoned by most historians (1739–1742) and the subsuming of this conflict into the ongoing War of Austrian Succession (1740–1748). In other words, the war continued, but metamorphosed into a different beast altogether. Its major theater of operations shifted away from the New World to Europe—and eventually spanned the globe, with battles fought from the North Sea to the Malabar Coast of India. Its chief causes were no longer trade and mercantilism in the West Indies but the fate of dynasties— specifically whether or not a woman, Maria Theresa of Austria could succeed to her father's imperial throne.

In Flanders, the Malplaquet-style Battle of Fontenoy on May 11, 1745 would once again sicken observers with its toll of over 15,000 dead. During this sanguinary encounter, the French army, led by one of France's greatest marshals, Maurice de Saxe, bested the British under George II's son, the Duke of Cumberland. At one point during the battle, it seemed the British and their Dutch allies of the "Pragmatic Alliance" had won the day; the frivolous but not entirely unlikable Louis XV, King of France, present on the field, had been urged by his retinue to flee to safety. Only Saxe's ardent appeal to the king's courage, prevented the flight that would have demoralized his army:

"It is necessary, your majesty, to either conquer or die," de Saxe told Louis. The king stayed; the French prevailed though the victory was costly. But we get ahead of ourselves, looking toward different battles, different wars.

For the British, the War of Jenkins' Ear, begun with such high hopes in 1739, ended with the hand-wringing Robert Walpole had predicted on the night the bells tolled in London. Put simply, the British had lost, the Spanish had won—everywhere but in Georgia, by the grace of Oglethorpe. Its mortality rate still astounds. By 1742, nine out of every ten men who had served under Vernon and Wentworth had died, about 20,000 all told—almost all these deaths from disease. The much-abused volunteers of Gooch's American Regiment were hit particularly hard. Exact numbers are uncertain, but of the roughly 4,000 men who signed on with enthusiasm in 1740, less than three hundred lived to see their homes again.

First Lord of the Admiralty George Anson

TEN

Around the World

1.

We now rejoin Commodore George Anson and the voyage that "must always" in Admiral Richmond's memorable phrase "rank as one of the most wonderful exhibitions of dogged resolution of all time," on June 9, 1741, in the Pacific Ocean. His flagship *Centurion*, crab-sided and wallowing, its crew wracked with scurvy, the rest of his squadron apparently lost in a season of monstrous storms rounding the Horn, Anson made the only safe harbor in yet another Cumberland Bay, on Juan Fernández Island off the coast of Chile at 34.47 S. 360 miles west on nautical charts. It was late afternoon, the light golden and long on the water to the west.

The adventures of Anson's Pacific squadron, its horrible tribulations and singular triumph cannot be treated here in any great detail. They are the subject of a dozen volumes (including Anson's own best-selling account, *A Voyage Round the World in the Years MDCCXL, I, II, III, IV*, published in London in 1748) and only comprise a footnote in the overall conduct of the military struggle against Spain begun in 1739. "As an operation of war," as Admiral Richmond admits, "its effect was negligible."

Before attempting to round the Horn with his six ships and their complement of scurvy-weakened sailors, invalids, and untrained marines, Anson assembled his captains for a council of war at their first refueling stop in the Western Hemisphere, Ilha de Santa Catarina, then part of the Portuguese Empire, now a Brazilian dependency. At this meeting, the commodore established three rendezvous points in the Pacific should the squadron become separated by the Horn's notorious storms: these were Socorro (now Guamblin) Island at 45 degrees S., Valdivia on the Chilean coast, and Juan Fernández Island, furthest north, isolated in the Pacific about 500 miles southwest of Chile's Valparaíso Region, and 1,800 miles east of Easter Island.

Santa Catarina, a Portuguese colony, was a supposed ally of England, but her governor secretly alerted his Spanish Catholic counterpart in Buenos Aires regarding the arrival of Anson's squadron and their mission in the Pacific. The Spanish admiral Don José Alfonso Pizarro, resupplying there, had been hunting Anson since a near miss at Madeira. He immediately set out around the Horn with his own squadron of five ships of the line—*Hermoina*; *San Estevan*; *Esperanza*; *Guipuscoa*; and his flagship, *Asia*. All met with terrible fates. *Hermoina* probably went down somewhere in the frigid waters off Tierra del Fuego, in any case, she was never heard from again. The largest, *Guipuscoa*, split her sides open in heavy seas, lost all her masts and 500 of her complement of 700 men to scurvy. Forced back from the Cape into the South Atlantic, *Guipuscoa*'s crew mutinied and ran her aground at last at the River Plate. Only Pizarro's flagship

Asia made it into the Pacific at last, though months after Anson had attained Juan Fernández.

At one point, the dueling squadrons came within visual range and nearly within cannon-shot, but soon found a greater enemy to fight than each other: A season of once-in-a-hundred-year storms struck the Horn, smashing English and Spanish ships alike; crushing them beneath pelting hail and freezing rain, burying them in the troughs of mountainous waves. The going got so tough that Lt. Philip Saumarez, one of Anson's best officers, despaired. "Life is not worth pursuing," he confided to his journal "at the expense of such hardships."

Anson's passage around the Horn in a torturous zigzag fighting the winds and contrary currents took more than three months. The Captains of *Severn* and *Pearl* gave up and turned their vessels back to England. *Wager*, with Midshipman Jack Byron, the poet's grandfather serving aboard, wrecked on the rocks at an unnamed deserted island—now called Wager Island—in an uncharted archipelago off the storm-riven South Chilean Coast. Through expert seamanship and good luck Anson and *Centurion*, separated from the rest, reached Juan Fernández only to find a desolate harbor. The commodore thought he had lost his entire squadron to the "blind Horn's hate," then the tiny *Tryal* appeared on the horizon. More than half her crew dead from scurvy, only *Tryal*'s second-in-command and three seamen remained fit enough to guide her into Cumberland Bay. *Centurion*'s crew had suffered similar fatalities.

Of the three great afflictions of eighteenth-century mariners—typhus, dysentery, and scurvy—the last was by far the greatest scourge. Not for another fifty years would medical science recognize the cause of this killer of sailors as a deficiency of fresh fruits and vegetables, specifically the indispensable nutrient they carried, vitamin C, or ascorbic acid. The addition of lime juice to every British sailor's daily rations early in the next century earned them their famously derisive nickname and eventually saved thousands of lives.

But in 1741, medical experts advanced a variety of faulty hypotheses to explain scurvy's deadly effects, from "the hurtful qualities of sea air" to "poor circulation of the blood in cold weather." Whatever the cause, its symptoms were dreadful to contemplate:

"The most common symptoms were large spots and ulcers appearing over the whole body, swollen legs, putrid gums and rotting flesh. Physical disintegration was accompanied by depression and lethargy, often mistaken by officers for laziness and greeted with curses and beatings." As noted Captain Michell of the *Gloucester* in his ship's log: "Some lost their Senses, some had their Sinews contracted in such a Manner as to draw their Limbs close up to their Thyhs, and some rotted away."

The effects could be poetically strange. One of Anson's unfortunate invalids afflicted by scurvy had been wounded in the Battle of the Boyne in 1690. He lived just long enough to see his ancient war wounds open up again and his bones break exactly where they'd been broken by sabre cuts in that long-ago conflict. It was as if he'd been killed at the Boyne fifty years before, and not died a putrefying mess in the hold of a warship on the far side of the world. Besides scurvy, the lack of fresh food and a diet of weevil-infested marine biscuits and rancid salt-pork produced other equally deadly effects. Niacin deficiency led to "idiotism, lunacy, convulsions"; thiamin deficiency often resulted in beri-beri; lack of vitamin A caused night blindness. Bad food in general caused weakness and decay. Oddly, only the expedition's cabin boys remained relatively unaffected; young bones apparently retain nutrients the longest. These lads, aged seven to ten years old at the beginning of the voyage, made up an outsized percentage of Anson's remaining able-bodied crewmen by journey's end.

The commodore put *Centurion*'s men ashore on Juan Fernández for an indefinite period to recover their health; the island abounded with goats and wild greens. One of the sailors, so affected by scurvy he couldn't move or eat, was laid out on the grass, a hole dug in which to put his face. Just breathing in the exhalations from the damp earth, according to witnesses, cured him. Over the next eight weeks two more ships from Anson's squadron, *Ana* and *Gloucester*, thought lost, joined him in Cumberland Bay. But Anson ordered *Ana* scuttled—she had been too badly damaged in her passage around the Horn—and her crew and remaining provisions transferred to *Gloucester*.

His squadron, now critically reduced, lingered in the comparative paradise of Juan Fernández until September 1741. Of the 961 men that had sailed in 1740 aboard the three remaining vessels from Spithead, 626 had died, or about two-thirds. Worse fatalities were to come, as Anson at last continued with his mission according to the Admiralty's instructions delivered to him in January the previous year:

> "When you shall arrive on the Spanish coast of the South Sea, you are to do you best to annoy and distress the Spaniards . . ." so they had ordered, "by taking, sinking, burning or otherwise destroying all their ships and vessels that you shall meet with; and in case you shall find it practicable to seize, surprise or take any of the towns or places belonging to Spaniards on the coast, you are to attempt it."

2.

Meanwhile, the shipwrecked crew of the *Wager* underwent their own torments. A notorious mutiny; the hostile elements; death by Indian attack; murder; madness; starvation; suicide. Midshipman Jack Byron's memoir of his adventures, published in 1768, *The Narrative of the Honorable John Byron Containing an Account of the Great Distress*

Suffered by Himself and his Companions, later influenced his grandson the great Romantic poet, George Gordon, Lord Byron. The latter felt a strong affinity for his restless seafaring forebearer, a hard-luck sailor who seemed to encounter horrendous weather wherever he sailed. His long career in the Royal Navy earned him an admiral's pennant and the unenviable sobriquet of "Foul Weather" Jack.

"He had no peace at sea," Lord Byron wrote, "nor I on land." Jack's descriptions of exotic foreign places, dramatic, mountainous scenery, and strange people, the poet also acknowledged, informed his greatest narrative poems—*Childe Harold's Pilgrimage* and *Don Juan*. As did a certain ghastly element in Jack's struggle to stay alive on Wager Island in 1741.

Midshipman Byron watched helplessly as desperate shipmates killed his beloved dog and cooked it in a stew. Despite his grief and horror, the starving midshipman consumed his portion with gusto. Since it was his dog, Byron figured, he had as much a right to the awful meal as anyone. "Exceedingly good eating," wrote one of the dog chefs/assassins in his journal, "we thought no English mutton preferable to it." Three weeks later, starving again, Byron sought out the place where the dog had been slaughtered, hoping to find some discarded bits that might still be edible. He turned up the dog's skin and severed paws which he gnawed at in desperation, tears flowing from his eyes. It was, Byron later wrote, perhaps the lowest moments of his life.

An obscure clause in Admiralty regulations ordained that shipwrecked crews received no pay from the moment their vessel was lost. This legal absurdity translated into an immediate discharge from navy duty for every shipwrecked sailor and now led to much trouble with the crew of the *Wager*: No pay, no service! they declared. A mutiny was quickly underway. *Wager's* destruction on the rocks meant release from the tight bonds of military discipline, just when discipline was most needed. Her crew devolved into a contentious rabble and split into factions, each pledging allegiance to competing authority figures.

Some went with a wily gunner's mate and *Übermensch* named Bulkeley; others with the *Wager*'s now reviled and incompetent acting captain, David Cheap.

Byron followed Cheap and thirteen others north in search of civilization. Eventually winnowed by death to three, their party was captured by Indians and handed over to Spanish authorities who marched them overland to Santiago. Everywhere Byron went on the sixteen-hundred-mile trek, the locals noticed his youthfulness and good looks. Though a chained prisoner part of the way, he received several marriage proposals from village matrons on behalf of their lonely daughters. But Jack Byron turned them all down. His eyes were fixed on his home which he attained after many ordeals and vicissitudes, in December 1745. It had taken him five years to find his way back again.

The last of *Wager*'s surviving crew reached England a year after Byron. Of the ship's original complement of over two hundred, only twenty-nine had survived, the rest left behind in shallow graves or at the bottom of the sea. Many wrote accounts of their ordeal, either to exonerate themselves from charges of mutiny and murder or merely to record the marvelous and tragic things they had seen. Only Byron's *Narrative* has survived the years. A brittle paperback edition from the 1950s can occasionally be found on the dusty bottom shelf in used bookstores, in the section marked "Nautical Interest."

3.

Following a pleasant sojourn on Juan Fernández, the diminished Pacific Squadron, now only *Centurion* and *Gloucester*, rejoined the war against Spain—if indeed a state of war still existed. Anson had not heard any news from England for more than two years; a treaty might have been signed. But in the absence of fresh orders, the squadron must perforce follow the old ones. Accordingly, Anson headed up the coast to Peru, taking six Spanish prizes along the way, including the *Nuestra Señora del Monte Carmelo* and *Nuestra Señora de Aranzazu*, two unarmed merchant ships bearing a quantity of gold bullion. The Spanish captains of these vessels, taken utterly by surprise, had not known English warships had penetrated into the Pacific Ocean.

From dispatches and letters carried by *Aranzazu*, Anson gathered valuable if disappointing intelligence. Not only did the war continue, Don Blas de Lezo had defeated Vernon at Cartagena. This negated one of the Admiralty's objectives of 1740: a rendezvous with Vernon for a combined attack on the Isthmus of Panama. But the main objective of Anson's expedition still obtained, that it should as far as possible "distress and annoy the King of Spain." The commodore now aimed his two remaining ships at the small coastal city of Paita in arid northeastern Peru—not much of a target, but as Anson later wrote in his *Account*, it was "the only enterprize in our power to undertake," that is, with the field guns lost aboard *Wager* and a fraction of his original force surviving. Also, it had been successfully sacked by Drake nearly two hundred years before.

Four ships boats containing sixty men landed at night just above the town on December 28, 1741. Someone in Paita's small fort fired a couple of shots at the invading Englishmen, then the garrison ran. Paita's startled inhabitants, many in pajamas, fled to the surrounding hills, including the governor and his pretty young wife. Anson's men proceeded to occupy the place for the next three days during which they broke into and looted the empty houses. Inevitably, a few Indian women who had stayed behind were raped. Thirty-thousand pounds worth of silver now fell into the commodore's hands, but he forbade the destruction of the churches and the mistreatment of prisoners—a forbearance for which the Paitains remembered him for generations: A British officer, visiting at the end of the eighteenth century found the commodore still talked about with admiration.

ROBERT GAUDI

Still, upon abandoning the place, Anson ordered everything but the churches and the convent burned. The "smoake," as one sailor wrote in his journal, could be seen for miles out to sea.

Paita had been poor—an tiny outpost of the far-flung Spanish empire, wedged between the unforgiving Pacific and the foothills of a dry and inhospitable mountain range. Anson now sought richer quarry: the fabulous Acapulco Galleon that once a year ferried the riches of the Orient from Manila in the Philippines to Mexico. From Acapulco, the treasure went overland to Vera Cruz by wagon and on to Spain. In mid-February 1742, Anson reached Acapulco only to find the Galleon had already sailed—a blessing perhaps, as the ship's 58 guns and 400 crewmembers would have made a tough target. But ever the gambler, Anson conceived a wild plan that just might save his mission. And he now prepared his ships for the difficult Pacific crossing.

After many vicissitudes—more scurvy, storms, a lengthy stay on the South Pacific island of Tinian in the Ladrone Archipelago, the scuttling of the increasingly rotten *Gloucester* (his original squadron of six ships and 1800 men reduced to *Centurion* alone and the 227 men that now comprised her crew) Anson reached the Chinese coast at Macao on November 11, 1742. Here, he refreshed and refitted and careened his remaining warship. He planned to sail *Centurion* back to England via the Cape of Good Hope. But not before he made one last attempt on the riches of Spain: the treasure-laden "prize of all the oceans," outbound from the Philippines to Acapulco, known as the "Manila Galleon" on this leg of her long journey. Anson planned to seize this treasure ship in the Pacific somewhere near her port of origin. Of course, intercepting a single vessel in the midst of such vastness would be like locating a single drop of water in a bottomless ocean.

With powder and shot in short supply, his men sick and heart-weary from years at sea, Anson's decision to find and take the Manila

Galleon was "all the more courageous or foolhardy . . . an act of desperation by a commander who faced professional ruin, a last throw by a gambler who had lost all." Here we have the high-stakes card player of South Carolina, at last showing his hand.

4.

Eight months later, on June 20, 1743, Anson and *Centurion* caught the *Nuestra Señora de Covadonga* in mid-ocean off Espiritu Santo in the Philippine archipelago. It was a lucky strike, aided by a bit of accurate intelligence gleaned from a hard-drinking English double-agent in the service of Spain, met with in a rum shop in Macao. The first shot fired by *Covadonga* at 7:30 A.M. dropped harmlessly in the water. The slow-moving and heavily laden treasure ship then piled on more canvas in an attempt to sail out of the range of *Centurion's* big guns—the intimidating twenty-four pounders protruding from her lower deck. The next shot was fired by *Centurion* at noon. Now, after a long chase, as the two ships closed for the fight, the usually taciturn Anson gave a short, impassioned speech to steady his men's nerves—and perhaps his own.

They had crossed two oceans to arrive at this moment. They had sailed around half the world, they had undergone incredible hardships, endured monstrous storms, lost friends and comrades to dreadful diseases and misadventure on alien shores. This is what they had come for at last, there she was—the Manila Galleon! She contained enough gold to make them all rich; the crew's share of her treasure would keep each man in comfort for the rest of his life. But she also carried something else, something beyond price: glory, which no man on earth was rich enough to buy.

"If a man will not fight for a galleon," as Admiral Wager later put it, "he will fight for nothing."

Anson had spent weeks drilling his skeleton crew of scurvy-racked sailors and young boys in the unconventional tactics necessary to handle his undermanned sixty-gun warship in battle. Flying squads ran up and down the decks flinging open the gunports and firing the guns—not in the usual massed broadsides, but in sporadic bursts that baffled *Covadonga*'s captain. An intense battle ensued in which the Spanish ship absorbed a vicious barrage, including chain shot and round shot and deadly accurate musket fire aimed from *Centurion*'s fighting tops at gaudily attired Spanish officers below. About two hours later, the Spanish gave up. *Covadonga* struck her colors and Anson sent Lt. Saumarez with a boarding party to take possession of the ship.

The expertly trained English gunners had done too good a job: the deck of the *Nuestra Señora de Covadonga* looked like a butcher's yard, "covered with carcasses, entrails and dismembered limbs," wrote the horrified Saumarez. Bodies lay in bloody piles down the hatchways. Among the passengers still alive was the aged governor of the Spanish colony on Guam; he was taken prisoner by the last surviving invalid from the Chelsea Hospital, a captain of marines named Alexander Crowden. By a weird coincidence, Crowden had himself been taken prisoner by this very same Spaniard at the Battle of Almanza in Spain on April 25, 1707, thirty-six years earlier.

With the crippled galleon in tow, Anson sailed again for the Chinese coast. There, he anchored in the Canton River beneath the suspicious eyes of Chinese authorities. A thorough investigation of Anson's prize and the counting of her treasure took weeks. In addition to ironbound chests of gold coins and silver plate, Anson's men found loose coins, jewels, and gold objects hidden everywhere—in secret compartments between decks, behind supposedly solid oak beams, even inside scooped out wheels of cheese. When finally tabulated, the amount amazed everyone:

1,313,843 pieces of eight, 35,682 ounces of silver, one of the richest treasures ever taken by an English ship.

Against the odds and in the face of incredible hardship and after the loss of his squadron and the deaths of most of his men, Anson had somehow fulfilled his mission, striking one of the only successful blows against Spain in the War of Jenkins' Ear.

Anson's attack on *Nuestra Señora de Covadonga* had been a legitimate act of war. But the Chinese authorities in Canton viewed him as little better than a pirate. *Centurion*'s departure was delayed there by the viceroy for months, as Anson anxiously sought the necessary permissions and ship's stores to make his voyage home. After various inscrutable political maneuverings and a few veiled threats on the part of the viceroy, and the intervention of East India Company officials, outfitted at last, *Centurion* was allowed by the Chinese to sail for England.

Six months later, on June 15, 1744, she reached Spithead, running a final gauntlet through a French fleet in the Channel in the fog, France having by now joined the wider war of Austrian Succession against England. Anson had been gone nearly four years and circumnavigated the globe. A mere handful of mariners had achieved that nearly impossible feat in the two hundred years since Magellan. The treasure of the Manila Galleon unloaded on the docks in London in August filled thirty-two wagons. An awestruck populace cheered these cumbersome vehicles as they creaked through the streets to the Tower treasury. Of the 1,600 men who had rounded the Horn into the Pacific in 1741, only 188 had survived the improbable, grueling expedition.

Even more than Vernon, Anson had, with the taking of *Nuestra Señora de Covadonga*, joined the pantheon of English heroes. He later became First Lord of the Admiralty and a great naval reformer, passionately concerned with the welfare of the common English sailor. His share of the prize money from the Manila Galleon made him one of the wealthiest men in England. The *Centurion*, the sturdy vessel in which he had made his voyage at last decayed and was broken up. Her figurehead, a crowned lion rampant, removed in 1745, eventually found its way to a tavern yard at Goodwood, its plinth inscribed with the following bit of doggerel:

Stay traveller a while, and view
One, who has travell'd more than you,
Quite round the globe; thro' each degree
Anson and I have plow'd the sea:
torrid and frigid zones have past,
And safe ashore, arriv'd at last,
In ease and dignity appear:
He—in the House of Lords, I here.

Here indeed years of miserable English weather, wind and rain did their work. The beast finally disintegrated and was taken down, its remains stored in an outhouse. Only one of its legs survives, preserved among other artifacts of Anson's voyage, in Shugborough Hall, now a National Trust Estate in Great Haywood, England.

Lawrence Washington

EPILOGUE

The End of the Story

1.

Just after dawn on the morning of June 4, 1742, Captain Thomas Frankland, commanding the twenty-gun Royal Navy frigate *Rose* of the Jamaica Station, crossing up through the Bahamas, sighted a small flotilla of "four sail two leagues in the wind's eye, two large ships, a snow and a schooner." He gave chase, suspecting pirates or Spanish privateers. A little game ensued in which the pursued vessels raised a series of false flags, beginning with English colors, to which Frankland countered with French. By 11 A.M. he had maneuvered his frigate close enough for a sea fight.

Frankland now fired a warning shot across the bow of the lead ship, whereupon all four vessels hoisted their true flags: the white Spanish naval ensign bearing the arms of Aragon and Castile.

Frankland responded with the Union Jack's bold red, white, and blue. He now engaged the snow; the others were merchant vessels mostly unarmed, probably prizes, while the snow bore "ten guns and carriages for the six pounders and ten swivels . . . with 80 men." Even so, she was no match for *Rose*, a warship with a professional crew and expertly trained gunners.

And yet, to Frankland's surprise, a brisk battle ensued. *Rose* poured hot broadsides into the snow; the Spanish ship returned fire with her six pounders, backed up by volleys of poisoned arrows. Even an amateur sailor could see this was an unequal contest. The English ship could not be beaten by this smaller, under-gunned vessel. But the snow fought on for three more hours. At last, sails in tatters, hull shot through, her crew implored the captain to surrender. He refused, whereupon they mutinied, "hauled down her colors and begged for quarter."

The reason for the Spanish ship's dogged resistance soon became apparent. She had sailed from Havana on February 12, 1742, captained by none other than Juan de León Fandiño:

"He is the man who commanded the *Guarda Costa* out of Havana that took Jenkins when his ear was cut off," Frankland reminds the Secretary of the Admiralty, in a letter of June 12. Also, "he commanded the vessels which attacked Captain Warren off St. Augustine and was commandant of the galleys during [Oglethorpe's] siege of that place."

The *Rose* closed on the Spanish ship and took her crew aboard as prisoners. Frankland got a closer look at her captain. Here he was, the notorious Fandiño captured at last! Lopper-off of Jenkins's ear, partly responsible for all the brouhaha leading to war. Though no physical description of Fandiño survives, one is tempted to imagine him as a thick-set, swarthy fellow with wire-wool black hair, perhaps missing an eye, a long scar from a sabre cut across his jaw, his ears festooned with gold rings. In short, the pirate of legend and N. C. Wyeth paintings.

However, this is probably not the case. Fandiño, now a Spanish officer with commissions from the governor of Cuba and the king of Spain, no doubt dressed and looked the part.

"I have been more particular than ordinary in this narrative, to your Lordships" Frankland concludes his letter to the Admiralty, "to show what a bold, dangerous enemy he has been. He oftentimes has expressed himself he would rather a thousand times have been shot than taken; and indeed naught but such a desperado, with his crew of Indians, Mulattos, and Negroes could have acted as he did."

The *London Gazette* of August 3, 1742 reports that Frankland promptly sent Fandiño to England where he was delivered to the Naval Prison at Portsmouth, charged with the eighteenth-century equivalent of war crimes. But John Charnock's encyclopedic *Biographia Navalis*, a compendium of naval lore (1794–98), reports that Fandiño was "tried immediately for his life" probably on Jamaica.

Historian Edward W. Lawson, writing in the *Florida Historical Quarterly* in 1958, endeavored to get to the bottom of what really happened to Fandiño—and only came up with more questions. Was he tried at Jamaica or Portsmouth? Was he executed in England as a pirate? Or was he granted a trial by naval court martial, "his commission by the King of Spain recognized?" If the latter, was Fandiño consigned to Dartmoor as a prisoner of war until the end of hostilities in 1748? And if so did he survive incarceration in a damp English prison cell or die there from cold and neglect?

A surviving letter points to the latter possibility. Fandiño was a man of the tropics. When stationed off Cape Fear, North Carolina in December 1740, he quickly turned his ship around and returned to St. Augustine. He and his crew he said, had suffered much from the "severe cold" of those northern latitudes.

Still, the record is inconclusive on what happened to the most effective and controversial of all *guarda costa* captains. The waters of history have closed over Fandiño's head; his end remains unknown.

2.

We know more about the fate of Robert Jenkins. His missing ear did not keep him from becoming a respected administrator in the pay of the East India Company, much admired for his industry and honesty. The Honorable Company trusted Jenkins to clean up administrative messes in remote colonial outposts. In March 1741, they sent him out to St. Helena, the desolate South Atlantic island (15.55 South, 5.43 West) where, years later, Napoleon Bonaparte spent his last sad years of exile. A British possession since 1659, St. Helena had become a critical refueling station for Company ships on their way to India.

Rumors of corruption and embezzlement on the part of St. Helena's late governor John Goodwin had recently filtered back to London. Jenkins had been commissioned to investigate and, if necessary, take charge of the island's government and its finances. He landed at Jamestown, the tiny capital, on May 9, 1741, and "immediately proceeded to the castle," where he ordered the island's treasury opened for inspection. What he found confirmed his employers' suspicions. On May 11, after a complete audit, undertaken beneath the muzzle of his pistol, he wrote in alarm to the East India Company board back in London: "Your Honors Estate here is in a worse condition than we expected. The frauds are so errant and so open . . . the total deficiency is £6,284."

Apparently, the late Governor John Goodwin, aided by his coconspirator and current acting governor, Duke Crisp, "a man possessed of no common share of knavery and cunning," had slowly emptied St. Helena's treasury into their own pockets. Only £6.19 remained in the strong box. Crisp, it seemed, had been the mastermind behind the brazen theft.

Jenkins seized Crisp's estate and the resources of other officials involved and remained on St. Helena as acting governor until his replacement arrived aboard the *Harrington* on March 22, 1742.

He left the island on this ship, bound for Bombay, where he died sometime in 1743.

Ian Baker, a local historian, points out the only reminder of Jenkins's stay on St. Helena: an eighteenth-century cottage, on Sandy Bay Road, at some remove from Jamestown, where the earless mariner is supposed to have lived during his clean-up of the island. A black stone built into one of the exterior walls bears the carved inscription: ROB. JENKINS ESQ. DEC. 16TH A.D. 1741.

3.

Walpole's ministry fell on February 11, 1742, brought down by the disaster at Cartagena and the general mismanagement of the war. He had been in power for more than twenty years as England's de facto prime minister, considered the first to assume this role. But he still retained King George II's favor and by royal decree joined the House of Lords as the Earl of Orford. There he served for three more years, still controlling things, most supposed, from behind the curtain, until his death in 1745.

The South Sea Company, whose machinations and vast smuggling operations must bear the bulk of the responsibility for the War of Jenkins' Ear, never recovered its trading privileges under the *Asiento*, which had been abrogated by Spain in 1739. The South Sea Company's interest in this notorious contract was bought out by the Spanish crown for £100,000 in 1750. During the Company's sporadic tenure, interrupted by an endless series of wars with Spain, historians estimate they procured and transported 34,000 African slaves across the Atlantic, losing a "mere" 4,000 of them during the stormy Middle Passage—all the while smuggling an unknown but massive amount of British manufactured goods to the Spanish Colonies.

They survived as a financial concern, dealing in the annuities associated with government debt until their disestablishment in 1853. The last of that debt, incurred during the South Sea Bubble crisis wasn't paid off until the eve of World War I.

4.

James Edward Oglethorpe, founder of Georgia, philanthropist, social reformer, anti-slavery activist, soldier, visionary, left the colony he had founded and the shade of its towering pines on September 28, 1743, never to return. After his departure, the Georgia Trustees lost control of the colony; subsequent royal governors legalized slavery and rum and lawyers who descended in droves on Savannah, their briefcases full of obscurely written documents.

In the end, Oglethorpe seemed to belong to another more heroic age, a figure out of Plutarch's *Lives of the Noble Romans*. He married a wealthy widow the year after his return to England and gradually faded into a long, uneasy twilight—though he led a regiment of English troops, one last time, against the forces of Bonnie Prince Charley in the Jacobite Rising of 1745. Defeat at the Battle of Clifton Moor triggered a court-martial. Oglethorpe had been timid, and some said fled the field—but he had never been a coward. Perhaps old Jacobite affiliations and family loyalties had arisen to cloud his judgement. Though eventually cleared of charges of treason and military incompetence, Oglethrope never again held a military command; evidence exists, however, that he fought incognito at the side of a friend of his youth, Jacobite exile *Generalfeldmarschall* James Keith, for Frederick the Great of Prussia in the Seven Years' War of the 1760s. Keith died at the Battle of Hochkirch, supposedly in Oglethorpe's arms.

By the time Oglethorpe himself died on July 1, 1785, almost no one remembered him or his contributions to civilization, both in England and in the colony he had founded. Newspaper accounts listed his age as over a hundred, confusing him with a brother who had died as an infant.

In his last years, Oglethorpe sought consolation in literature and London and became close friends with the great Samuel Johnson and his biographer, Boswell. The latter had just begun to collect material for a biography of the old general when he died. Oglethorpe's bones, removed in the 1930s from the family vault at All Saints Church near his last estate at Cranham, Greater London, were sought by the president of Oglethorpe University in Atlanta for reburial in a shrine located on campus. Request denied, Oglethorpe's still rests in the central vault at All Saints, largely unvisited.

He remains the "Forgotten Founder."

5.

Admiral Edward Vernon continued to serve in the Royal Navy after his return from the West Indies. But his temper and controversial opinions conspired to end his career under a cloud. He authored two vituperative, anonymous pamphlets advocating naval reform (*A Specimen of Naked Truth from a British Sailor* and *Some Seasonal Advice from an Honest Sailor*) which angered his superiors in the Admiralty. Upon their advice, King George II struck Vernon's name from the list of flag officers; the "Angry Admiral" was dismissed from the service on April 11, 1746. "Admiral Vernon's polemical zeal," concludes his biographer, "and his tactless penchant for pamphleteering no doubt explains why his great services to his country at sea were never recognized by any Government."

But the darkest shadow over Vernon's achievements was cast by the failed Cartagena campaign, one of the greatest military disasters in British history.

"It is the fashion to attribute the failures of the West Indies to Vernon," writes Admiral Richmond in a critique of the revisionists of another era (the 1920s),

> and speak of him in a contemptuous and disparaging manner. His capture of Porto Bello is treated as an operation of no importance, and the failure at Cartagena is put down to his overbearing and arrogant attitude toward his colleague. . . . That Vernon used every method from advice to action to expedite the undertaking admits of no question. Indeed, the fault to be found with him is that he offered too much of the former; but for all that, what he offered was good.

Vernon's stock as a commander has fallen and risen and fallen again over the years since Admiral Richmond's three-volume study *The Navy in the War of 1739–48*. The latest generation of revisionists, beginning with Richard Harding's *Amphibious Warfare in the Eighteenth Century*, published in 1991, once more blames the admiral and not the ineffectual Wentworth for the disaster at Cartagena and the loss of the war. Still, whether you like the man or not, Vernon was essentially right in his simple formula: first, do not engage in a land-based war in the tropics; but if you must, do it quickly before everyone starts to die from diseases for which there are no cure.

But Vernon paid a greater price for his long service to his country than dismissal from the navy. During his frequent absences on England's business in the far parts of the world, his wife and three children died. Upon his own death in 1757 (he outlived his nemesis, Wentworth, by ten years) his estate passed to his nephew, Francis, Lord Orwell.

In 1763, this grateful heir paid for an elaborate monument to his uncle and benefactor, erected in Westminster Abbey in London: the angel of fame crowns a bust of Vernon with a laurel wreath. Beneath this, a long inscription lists his military accomplishments and his famous victory at Porto Bello. Regarding the defeat at Cartagena, in a back-handed, beyond-the-grave slap at Wentworth, the inscription records only that Vernon "conquered as far as naval forces could carry victory."

6.

Another monument to Admiral Vernon's name is perhaps better known: a stately colonial home overlooking the Potomac near Alexandria, Virginia; an open piazza along its eastern facade and a central hallway from front to back catch the breezes from the river on hot summer days.

I visited the house last December as part of a sparse crowd of mask-wearing tourists—it being COVID time—led by a nervous docent who stumbled through her rehearsed monologues as if she thought she'd catch something every time she opened her mouth. We hurried through the "New Room," its Palladian ceilings rising up two stories, and the small dining room with its startling verdigris-green panels and table set as if for an intimate family dinner. The "Old Chamber," once reserved for guests, painted a bright "Prussian" blue (the house's most famous owner clearly favored vibrant colors) led on to the object of my visit: the modest study, its walls simple white plaster, its tall sash windows giving out on the shaded piazza and overlooking an acre of still-green lawn and the river flowing calmly below.

A massive roll-top secretary, of an elegant Philadelphia design, dominates the room. It sits empty of the books and papers and maps—there always had to be maps—that once filled the glassed-in shelves. Other items of interest (a spyglass, a set of London-made pistols, a curious chair with a fan attached worked by foot levers, a strong box made of overlapping iron sheets, a length or two of survey-or's chain) have been placed just so, here and there. Free of dust and human oils, they give the room the air of a stage set in a play about colonial times. But I have come to see the portrait hanging on the eastern wall.

Done in a flat, primitive style and unsigned—though later attributed to the German-American Philadelphia-based painter John Hesselius—it depicts a young colonial gentleman wearing the scarlet coat of a British officer, over a green waistcoat trimmed with gold braid. The black tricorn hat folded neatly beneath his arm also bears a generous border of gold and a cockade later known to have been worn by his famous brother in more successful campaigns during the American Revolution. The gentleman's face is squarish, open, rather plain. A slightly melancholy expression lingers around the eyes, as if he has already seen too much of the world; too many of his friends and comrades die needlessly.

This is the well-known "Military Portrait" of Lawrence Washington, wearing the uniform of Gooch's American Regiment as issued to him in 1740. For decades the portrait was misinterpreted, based on the collarless design of Lawrence's coat—a style popular in England circa 1730. Lawrence graduated from Appleby School in Westmoreland County, England, in 1732. The portrait, long assumed to be the eighteenth-century equivalent of a graduation photograph, purport-edly showed the ambitious young colonial gentleman from Virginia in his best clothes, eager to get a good start in life.

But experts in American colonial military history visiting the house in 1968, offered another, more convincing explanation: Here we have a depiction of the "finest example" of an American offi-cer's uniform from that dreadful conflict, the War of Jenkins' Ear. They marshalled great authority to support this verdict, and their explanation has become official. Though painted about 1750, the portrait shows Lawrence Washington in his uniform of ten years earlier. When the portrait was painted, Lawrence was seriously ill from that worrying cough of his which had developed into tuberculosis. He would soon depart for Barbados in an attempt to recover his health, accompanied by his little brother George. Hesselius, then a traveling artist, was probably instructed to show the dying Lawrence in the prime of life, in the uniform he had worn during his greatest military exploits at the Baradera battery on Tierra Bomba and leading the Americans on the march to La Catalina in Cuba.

George Washington kept this portrait of his beloved older brother with him throughout his long and illustrious life. He carried it on various campaigns during the Revolution, and finally hung it on the wall of his study at Mount Vernon. It hung there on the night our first president died in the bedroom directly upstairs, probably from strep throat, on December 14, 1799, on the eve of a new century, and hangs there still.

Lawrence returned from the botched wars in the West Indies in December 1742 to the estate inherited from his father Augustine at Little Hunting Creek in Northern Virginia. The original modest two-story house built on a bluff overlooking the Potomac on a piece of property then still generally known by its Indian name of Epsewasson, had been rebuilt and added-to several times over the years. Lawrence married the fifteen-year-old daughter of a neighbor in July 1743, and as a wedding present again expanded the place. Another, grander home soon rose on the foundations of the old. This new dwelling, destined to be the country seat of a great American family needed a new name. Lawrence called the place Mt. Vernon, after the fighting admiral under whom he'd served and for whom he always retained the greatest respect.

Vernon had saved Lawrence's life, so the latter believed— through the stringent sanitary practices followed aboard the flagships on which he had been billeted as a marine. The admiral's attention to the welfare of his men, his regular fumigation and vinegar scrubs of lower decks, and the strict rationing of rum had mitigated the diseases which killed so many on the Cartagena campaign. Without them, Lawrence's bones might have been left in the sandy soil of the West Indies or at the bottom of the sea. But as always, history reeks with irony. Lawrence died there anyway, ten years later in 1752, on Barbados, of the tuberculosis no doubt contracted during his military service, his grieving brother George at his side.

I contemplate Lawrence Washington's military portrait in the study at Mount Vernon for as long as the docent will allow—no longer than a minute or two—before she moves us on. Lawrence's original officer's commission from the War of Jenkins' Ear is preserved in the archives at the Washington Library here. It is a blank filled in with his name, one of those signed by King George II and carried in a batch of others by Colonel Blakeney across the Atlantic in 1740. They also maintain, I am told, a fine collection of Admiral Vernon medals, including several variants depicting the false English victory at Cartagena. Both document and coins are off-limits for the moment; the library remains closed to scholars for reasons of COVID until the crisis is over.

An hour later, just before sunset, after touring the outbuildings—kitchen, blacksmith's shop, servants' hall, and smoke house—I find myself on the piazza sitting in one of the Windsor chairs bolted to the old bricks in neat immovable rows. They're exact reproductions of chairs put there in George Washington's day for the comfort of his many admiring visitors.

If time is a river, as the "Dark Philosopher" Heraclitus once observed, you should be able to step back into it at any point—even to the moment where the mistreated soldiers of Gooch's American Regiment threw down their useless scaling ladders and woolpacks, seized up the muskets of dead comrades and began firing back at the Spanish regulars defending Fort San Lazar. Many died pointlessly that day and many more in Wentworth's fetid, fortified encampments before and afterward and in the stinking holds of the transports. Of course, men die pointlessly every day and for less.

But the English learned from the disasters of this maladministered war in the West Indies. They learned preparedness and logistics and the absolute necessity of a unified command structure. They learned to win. Successful naval and military operations enabled them under Clive to dominate India at Plassey in 1757, and under Wolfe to take Quebec and Canada from the French in 1759, and eventually to bestride the world as an imperial colossus for the next hundred and fifty years.

Howard W. V. Temperley one of the first historians of the War of Jenkins' Ear sees in this forgotten conflict the roots of everything that happened later in the century in our half of the world: "from this war issued, in a clear and undeviating succession," he writes, "the series of wars which were waged between England and France during the eighteenth century—wars in which Spain was sometimes a passive spectator, oftener an active enemy."

The last of these was the American Revolution in which both France and Spain joined the fight on the colonists' side, tipping the scales against their mother country and paying back the debt incurred by the miserable treatment of the soldiers of the American Regiment on Jamaica, at Cartagena and Guantánamo, and on Ruatan in 1740–42.

It grows cold on the piazza at Mount Vernon. Pale winter sunlight shines through the parchment-brown leaves of the trees, on the green-grey Potomac and on the Maryland shore across the way. So many years have passed since Lawrence Washington, at twenty-four sick and ruined by bitter experience, sailed up that river, returning home at last.

BIBLIOGRAPHY

BOOKS

Andrews, Charles M. *Colonial Folkways*. New Haven: Yale University Press, 1919.

Anson, W. V. *The Life of Admiral Lord Anson*. London: John Murray & Co., 1912.

Black, Jeremy. *The Origins of War in Early Modern Europe*. London: John Donald Publishers, Ltd., 1987.

Bolton, Herbert E., and Mary Ross. *The Debatable Land*. New York: Russell, 1925.

Browning, Reed. *The War of Austrian Succession*. New York: St. Martin's Press, 1993.

Carlyle, Thomas. *History of Friedreich the Great, Vol. 1*. London: Chapman and Hall, 1895.

Carswell, John. *The South Sea Bubble*. London: The Crescent Press, 1960.

Clowes, William Laird. *The Royal Navy, A History from the Earliest Times to 1900, Vol. 3*. London: Sampson Low & Co., 1898.

Coleman, Kenneth, ed. *History of Georgia*. Athens: University of Georgia Press, 1977.

Cowles, Virginia. *The Great Swindle: The Story of the South Sea Bubble*. New York: Harper & Bros. 1960.

Crane, Verner W. *The Southern Frontier, 1670–1732*. Ann Arbor: University of Michigan Press, 1929.

Crewe, Duncan. *Yellow Jack and the Worm: British Naval Administration in the West Indies*. Liverpool: Liverpool University Press, 1993.

Dale, Richard. *The First Crash: Lessons from the South Sea Bubble*. Princeton, NJ: Princeton University Press, 20004.

Davis, R. Trevor. *Spain in Decline*. New York: Macmillan & Co. LTD, 1965.

Dunkerly, James. *Crusoe and His Consequences*. New York: OR Books, 2019.

Ettinger, Amos Aschback. *James Edward Oglethorpe: Imperial Idealist*. Oxford: Clarendon Press, 1936.

Finucane, Adrian. *The Temptations of Trade: Britain, Spain and thye Struggle for Empire*. Philadelphia: University of Pennsylvania Press, 2016.

Freeman, Douglas Southall. *George Washington*. New York: Scribners, 1948.

Garrison, Webb. *Oglethorpe's Folly: The Birth of Georgia*. Lakemont, GA: Copple House Books, 1982.

Georgia Historical Society. *The Spanish Official Account of the Attack on the Colony of Georgia, in America, and of Its Defeat on St. Simons Island by General James Edward Oglethorpe*. Savannah: Georgia Historical Society, 1913.

Gibson, Charles. *Spain in America*. New York: Harper Torchbooks, Harper and Row, 1966.

Gleeson, Janet. *Millionaire: The Philanderer, Gambler and Duelist Who Invented Modern France*. New York: Simon & Schuster, 1999.

Glynn, William. *The Prize of All the Oceans*. New York: Viking, 1999.

Graham, Gerald S. *Empire of the North Atlantic*. London: University of Oxford Press, 1958.

Grainger, John D. *The British Navy in the Mediterranean*. London: Boydell Press, 2017.

Harding, Richard. A*mphibious Warfare in the Eighteenth Century: The British Expedition to the West Indies, 1740-1742*. Rochester, NY: Boydell Press, 1991.

Hart, Francis Russell. *Admirals of the Caribbean*. Boston: Houghton Mifflin, Co. 1923.

Hartmann, Cyril Hughes. *The Angry Admiral*. London: William Heinemann, LTD, 1953.

Hills, George. *Rock of Contention: A History of Gibraltar*. London: Robert Hale & Co. 1974.

Kelch, Ray A. *Newcastle, A Duke Without Money*. Los Angeles: University of California Press, 1974.

Kennedy, Paul M. *The Rise and Fall of British Naval Mastery*. New York: Scribners, 1976.

Kinkel, Sarah. *Disciplining the Empire, Politics, Governance and the Rise of the British Navy*. Cambridge, MA: Harvard University Press, 2018.

Knowles, Charles. *An Account of the 1741 Expedition to Cartagena*. West Chester, OH: The Nafzinger Collection, 2013.

Kramnick, Isaac. *Bolingbroke and His Circle*. Ithaca, NY: Cornell University Press, 1968.

LeFevre, Peter, and Richard Harding, eds. *Precursors of Nelson*. London: Chatham, 2000.

Lewis, W. H. *The Splendid Century*. New York: William Sloane Associates, 1953.

———. *The Sunset of the Splendid Century*. New York: William Sloane Associates, 1955.

MacKay, Charles, LLD. *Extraordinary Popular Delusions and the Maddness of Crowds*. New York: Page & Co., 1932.

Mason, F. Van Wyck. *Rascal's Heaven*. Garden City, NY: Doubleday & Co., 1964.

McIlvenna, Noeleen. *The Short Life of Free Georgia: Class and Slavery in the Colonial South*. Chapel Hill: University of North Carolina Press, 2015.

McLachlan, Jean O. *Trade and Peace With Old Spain 1667–1750*. Cambridge, UK: Cambridge University Press, 1940.

McNally, Michael. *Fontenoy 1745*. Oxford: Osprey Press, 2014.

Melville, Lewis. *The Life and Writings of Philip, Duke of Wharton*. London: John Eames & Co., 1913.

Montiano, Manuel de. *The Spanish Official Account of the Attack on the Colony of Georgia in America and its Defeat on St. Simon's Island by General James Edward Oglethorpe*. Savannah: Georgia Historical Society, 1913.

O' Brian, Patrick. *Men-of-War*. New York: W. W. Norton & Company, 1995.

Offen, Lee G. *America's First Marines: Gooch's American Regiment, 1740–1742*. Springfield, VA: History Reconsidered LLC., 2011.

Ogg, David. *Europe of the Ancien Regime, 1715–1783*. New York: Harper Torchbooks, 1965.

Pack, S. W. C. ed. *Anson's Voyage Round the World*. London: Penguin, 1947.

Palmer, Colin A. *The British Slave Trade to Spanish America, 1700–1739*. Chicago: University of Illinois Press, 1981.

Pares, Richard. *War and Trade in the West Indies, 1739–1763*. London: Frank Cass & Co. Ltd., 1936.

Parkman, Francis. *France and England in North America, Vol. 1*. New York: Library of America, 1981.

Peckham, Howard A. *The Colonial Wars, 1689–1762*. Chicago: University of Chicago Press, 1964.

Plumb, J. H. *The First Four Georges*. New York: MacMillan & Co., 1957.

———. *Sir Robert Walpole*. London: The Crescent Press, 1956.

———. *England in the 18th Century, 1714–1815*. Middlesex: Penguin, 1950.

Pointis, Jean Bernard Louis Desjean, Baron de. *Monsieur de Pointis' Expedition to Cartagena, Being a Particular Relation of the Taking and Plundering of that City by the French in the Year 1697*. New York: Sabin Americana Print Editions, 2002.

Queseda, Alejandro de. *Spanish Colonial Fortifications in North America, 1565–1822.* Oxford: Osprey, 2010.

Reid Stuart. *King George's Army, 1740–1793, Infantry, Vol. 1.* Oxford: Osprey, 1995.

———. *King George's Army, 1740–1793, Infantry, Vol. 2.* Oxford: Osprey, 1995.

Richmond, H. W. *Rear Admiral: The Navy in the War of 1739–1748, Vol. 1.* Cambridge, UK: Cambridge University Press, 1920.

———. *The Navy in the War of 1739–1748, Vol. 2.* Cambridge, UK: Cambridge University Press, 1920.

———. *The Navy in the War of 1739–1749, Vol. 3.* Cambridge, UK: Cambridge University Press, 1920.

Sedgewick, Romney, ed. *Lord Hervey's Memoirs.* London: William Kimber, 1952.

Shankland, Peter. *Byron of the Wager.* New York: Coward, McCann & Geoghegan, Inc., 1975.

Smollett, Tobias. *Roderick Random.* London: J. M. Dent & Sons, Ltd., 1927.

Spalding, Phinzy. *Oglethorpe in America.* Chicago: University of Chicago Press, 1977.

Sperling, John G. *The South Sea Company, An Historical Essay and Bibliographical Finding List.* Cambridge, MA: Harvard University Press, 1962.

Stachiw, Myron O. *Massachusetts Officers and Soldiers, 1723–1743, Drummers War to the War of Jenkins Ear.* Boston: Society of Colonial Wars in the Commonwealth of Massachusetts: The New England Historic Genealogical Society, 1947.

Talty, Stephen. *Empire of Blue Water.* New York: Crown Publishers, 2007.

White, John Manchip. *Marshal of France; The Life and Times of Maurice, Comte de Saxe.* New York: Rand McNally & Co., 1962.

Wilson, Ben. *Empire of the Deep: The Rise and Fall of the British Navy.* London: Weidenfeld & Nicholson, 2013.

———. *France and England in North America, Vol 2.* New York: Library of America, 1981.

Woodfine, Philip. *Britannia's Glories: The Walpole Ministry and the 1739 War With Spain.* Rochester, NY: Boydell Press, 1998.

Wright, J. Leitch, Jr. *Anglo-Spanish Rivalry in North America.* Athens, GA: University of Georgia Press, 1971.

JOURNAL ARTICLES

Aiton, Arthur S. *The Asiento Treaty as Reflected in the Papers of Lord Shelburne.* Hispanic American Historical Review 8, no. 2 (May 1928): 167–177.

Avery, Emmett L. and A. H. Scouten. *The Opposition to Sir Robert Walpole, 1737–1739.* English Historical Review 83, no. 327 (April 1968): 331–336.

Bialuschewski, Arne. *A True Account of the Design and Advantages of the South-Sea Trade: Profits, Propaganda, and the Peace Preliminaries of 1711.* Huntington Library Quarterly 73, no. 2 (June 2010): 273–285.

Brown, Vera Lee. *Contraband Trade: A Factor in the Decline of Spain's Empire in America.* Hispanic American Historical Review 8, no. 2 (May 1928): 178–189.

Brown, Vera Lee. *The South Sea Company and Contraband Trade.* American Historical Review 31, no. 4 (July 1926): 662–678.

Doolen, Andy. *Reading and Writing Terror: The New York Conspiracy Trials of 1741.* American Literary History 16, no. 3 (Autumn 2004): 377–406.

Hannay, R. K. *Gibraltar in 1727.* Scottish Historical Review 16, no. 64 (July 1919): 325–334.

Hildner, Ernest G. Jr. *The Role of the South Sea Company in the Diplomacy Leading to the War of Jenkins' Ear, 1729–1739.* Hispanic American Historical Review 18, no. 3 (August 1938): 322–341.

Hoppit, Julian. *Myths of the South Sea Bubble.* Transactions of the Royal Historical Society 12 (2002): 141–165.

Jackson, Harvey H. *Behind the Lines: Savannah During the War of Jenkins' Ear.* Georgia Historical Quarterly 78, no. 3 (Fall 1994): 471–492.

Lanning, John Tate. *The American Colonies in the Preliminaries of the War of Jenkins' Ear.* Georgia Historical Quarterly 11, no. 2 (June 1927): 129–155.

———. *American Participation in the War of Jenkins' Ear.* Georgia Historical Quarterly 11, no. 3 (September 1927): 191–215.

Laughton, J. K. *Notes and Documents.* English Historical Review 4, Issue 16 (October 1889): 741–749.

Lawson, Edward W. *What Became of the Man Who Cut Off Jenkins' Ear?* The Florida Historical Quarterly 37, no. 1 (July 1958): 33–41.

Leslie, J. H. *The Siege of Gibraltar by the Spaniards, 1727.* Journal for the Society of Army Historical Research 3, no. 13 (July 1924): 111–145.

Martz, Louis L. *Smollett and the Expedition to Carthagena.* PMLA 56, no. 2 (June 1941): 428–446.

McGeary, Thomas. *Farinelli in Madrid: Opera, Politics, and the War of Jenkins' Ear.* Musical Quarterly 82, no. 2 (Summer 1998): 383–421.

Nelson, George H. *Contraband Trade Under the Asiento. American Historical Review* 51, no. 1 (October 1945): 55–67.

Nowell, Charles E. *The Defense of Cartagena. Hispanic American Historical Review* 42, no. 4 (November 1962): 477–501.

Odlyzko, Andrew and Isaac Newton. *Daniel Defoe and the Dynamics of Financial Bubbles. Financial History* (Winter 2018): 18–21.

Robertson, James Alexander. *The English Attack on Cartagena in 1741: And Plans for an Attack on Panama. Hispanic American Historical Review* 2, no. 1 (February 1919): 62–71.

Temperly, Harold W. V. *The Causes of the War of Jenkins' Ear, 1739. Transactions of the Royal Historical Society* 3 (1909): 197–236.

Young, Patricia T., and Jack S. Levy. *Domestic Politics and the Escalation of Commercial Rivalry: Explaining the War of Jenkins' Ear. 1739–1748, European Journal of International Relations* (2010): 209–232.

INDEX

351

The Colony of
GEORGIA
A.D. 1735

Miles
0 ————————— 150

-- map by palacios

MISSISSIPPI R.

CHICKASAWS

TENNESSEE R.

GEOR

CHOCTAWS

Koroa

LINE CLAIMED
BY SPAIN
AFTER 1670

YAZOO R.

Natchez

MISSISSIPPI R.

ALABAMA R.

ALA

Mobile   Pensa

New Orleans

LINE DEMANDE
BY OGLETHORP
1736

GULF

The Savannah Inset

BLUE RIDGE MTS.

Guaxule

Chowan

CHATTOOGA R.

CHAUGA R.

KEOWEE R.

SENECA R.

TUGALOO R.

BEAVERDAM CR.

SAVANNAH R.

FALLING CR.

SALUDA R.

LITTLE CR.

LONG CR.

BROAD R.

CUFFYTOWN CR.

TURKEY CR.

LITTLE R.

Ft. Augusta
1735

THREE RUNS

BRIER CR.

SCOTIA CR.

Ft. Moore

BEAVER DAM

OGEECHEE R.

SAVANNAH R.

COOSAWHATCHIE R.

GREAT SWAMP R.

NEW R.

Coosaw

Beaufort

The
SAVANNAH
and its Tributaries
1733

0 Miles 50

SAVANNAH